ArtScroll Series®

Rabbi Nosson Scherman / Rabbi Meir Zlotowitz

General Editors

Preparing Your Child for

Published by

Mesorah Publications, ltd

Rabbi Zecharya Greenwald

SUCCESS

An accomplished educator's approach to bring out the best in every child

FIRST EDITION
First Impression ... September 2005

Published and Distributed by
MESORAH PUBLICATIONS, LTD.
4401 Second Avenue / Brooklyn, N.Y 11232·

Distributed in Europe by
LEHMANNS
Unit E, Viking Business Park
Rolling Mill Road
Jarow, Tyne & Wear, NE32 3DP
England

Distributed in Australia and New Zealand by
GOLDS WORLDS OF JUDAICA
3-13 William Street
Balaclava, Melbourne 3183
Victoria, Australia

Distributed in Israel by
SIFRIATI / A. GITLER — BOOKS
6 Hayarkon Street
Bnei Brak 51127

Distributed in South Africa by
KOLLEL BOOKSHOP
Shop 8A Norwood Hypermarket
Norwood 2196, Johannesburg, South Africa

ARTSCROLL SERIES®
PREPARING YOUR CHILD FOR SUCCESS
© Copyright 2005, by MESORAH PUBLICATIONS, Ltd.
4401 Second Avenue / Brooklyn, N.Y. 11232 / (718) 921-9000 / www.artscroll.com

---

ISBN:
1-4226-0019-X (hard cover)
1-4226-0020-3 (paperback)

Typography by CompuScribe at ArtScroll Studios, Ltd.

Printed in the United States of America by Noble Book Press Corp.
Bound by Sefercraft, Quality Bookbinders, Ltd., Brooklyn N.Y. 11232

בס״ד

שמואל קמנצקי
Rabbi S. Kamenetsky

2018 Upland Way
Philadelphia, Pa 19131

Home: 215-473-2798
Study: 215-473-1212

בס״ד עש״ק פ' וישב תשס״ה

דפדפתי על הספר מהרב ר' זכרי' גרינוואלד שליט״א ומוצא חן בעיני.

כבר נתברר לכל העולם שחיוב לחנך הבנים חכמה גדולה שצריכה לימוד. מלבד שהורים מחויבים לשמש לדוגמא בכל הנהגותיהם, היחס שבין ההורים להילדים עיקר המקשר ומשפיע ובודאי ימצאו הורים רב תועלת על ידי חיבור זה.

בפרט בימים אלו צריכים לחזק הקשר עם הילדים לבטל השפעות אחרים שנקלטו בבתי חינוך בקדשי קדשים ע״י ספרי חול שנבלעים על ידם כל מיני תועבות והשפעות חילוניים.

יזכה כב' להמנות בין מזכי הרבים שצדקתם עומדת לעד.

בית אולפנא רוממה
שע"י עמותת "שב שמעתא" ע"ר 580098846
ראש הכולל הרב ר' משה שפירא שליט"א
טל': 02-5374337 פקס': 02-5374339
רח' תורת חסד 1, ירושלים 94464

בס"ד   ירושלים כב ביראת אלוקה תמלה

RABBI YAAKOV PERLOW
1569 - 47TH STREET
BROOKLYN N.Y. 11219

יעקב פרלוב
קהל עדת יעקב נאוואמינסק
ישיבת נאוואמינסק - קול יהודא
ברוקלין. נ.י.

בס״ד ח׳ נסן תשס״ה

Rabbi Zecharya Greenwald has written a very impressive book on the challenges of parenting, with a deep, yet practical, down-to-earth, Torah perspective. I have not read it fully, but the parts that I did see, and reflect upon, make me feel confident to attest to its importance as a guide and focus in the critical area of raising children.

As his rebbeim testify, Rabbi Greenwald is an outstanding educator, with experience and wisdom, and I'm sure his book will serve a much-needed purpose in contemporary Jewish life.

יעקב פרלוב

Yaakov Perlow

TABLE OF CONTENTS

AUTHOR'S PREFACE

◄ Dedication

This book is dedicated to my *Rebbe*, Harav Shlomo Wolbe, *zt"l*, who opened new vistas in my understanding of the world, the Torah, and myself: Although I never lived up to even the simplest lessons he taught us, it is with awe and veneration that I look to him as my mentor and teacher. He was kind enough to direct me, while showing me warmth and concern, for the past twenty-five years. With the exception of my dear parents, he has been the single most influential persona in my life. With his insight, modesty, warmth, intelligence, honesty, and real relationship with *HaKadosh Baruch Hu*, he transformed thousands of *talmidim* into *bnei aliyah*.

It is almost unfeasible to speak about any subject regarding Torah thought, *mussar,* or education for more than a few minutes without one of his lessons coming to my mind. While I cannot say that every word in this book is exactly what my *Rebbe* would have said, I can confidently say that the spirit of this book is in consonance with the *derech* he taught me.

Unworthy a *talmid* as I was and remain, without his patience and acceptance, this book could not have been written. May any good that comes from the reading of this book and implementation of its ideas be an *aliyah* to his *neshamah*.

◆§ Appreciation — הכרת הטוב

First and foremost, נשים מאוהל תבורך, to my most revered role model, my partner and teacher, the woman who quietly assumes the great responsibility and challenge of being my wife and the mother of our children: May Hashem fulfill all of her *tefillos* and all of her selfless and noble aspirations. Her *chesed, tzenius,* and *mesiras nefesh* for Torah make her a beacon of light to our children and to the many hundreds of students and guests who have passed through our home. May we see together בנים ובני בנים עוסקים בתורה ובמצוות.

To my beloved parents, Rabbi Ronald and Mrs. Miriam Greenwald, who were and remain my first and constant source of inspiration: Before I ever even thought of parenting or the meaning of success, they were putting up with me. With tremendous intelligence, insight, and sensitivity, they knew how to gently direct me. They knew when to try to help me and when to sit back and let me find my own way. Any intuitive sense that I have comes from them. I watched as they dealt with thousands of situations in their home and in summer camps, all of which helped me develop the thought process that continues until today. They are geniuses in *chesed* and giants in action. May Hashem grant them years of *Yiddishe nachas* and joy from all their children, grandchildren, and great-grandchildren, till 120.

To my in-laws, Reb Chaim and Mrs. Esther Azenkott, two people whose selfless devotion to Hashem and His Torah is part of a world that our generation is rarely honored to glimpse: May *HaKadosh Baruch Hu* grant Reb Chaim a *refuah sheleimah.* May they live in good health until 120 and enjoy *Yiddishe nachas* from their children and grandchildren.

Last but most certainly not least, to our dear children who provide us with the greatest joy in life and who, with their honesty, challenge and teach us as we all try to deal with our constantly developing roles. They bear the brunt of the fact that parenting is on-the-job training and understand that we love them dearly and are only trying to do what is right.

המלאך הגואל אותי מכל רע הוא יברך את הנערים ...

May they be a continued source of *nachas* to *HaKadosh Baruch Hu* and may we be deserving to see this *berachah* come to fruition.

◄ঃ Acknowledgments

Extraordinary thanks to my mother, Mrs. Miriam Greenwald, who helped transfer the first half of this book from lectures to book form.

Special thanks to my former secretary, Mrs. Jodi Jacob, for her tireless efforts in typing and editing the second half, as well as helping with the amalgamation of the two halves.

Special thanks to Mrs. Devorah Kiel, who actually edited the entire work. I was warned by a number of authors that the editing process would be difficult and painful. I would like to express a special thanks to Mrs. Kiel for somehow managing to work with me in a harmonious fashion that I thought would not be possible.

Thanks to the following individuals who spent time going over and advising or correcting parts of the book: My dear friend and colleague, Rabbi Avigdor Brazil who spent many hours together with me in fine tuning a few chapters; my sister, Mrs. Yocheved Schwartz, who reviewed the first part of the book and made one comment that was essential to the entire work; my student, Sarah Yehudis Vogel, who made many corrections to the chapter or two that she edited in the early stages of this work; Rabbi Nosson Scherman, who, with sensitivity and grace, helped me fix things that needed to be mended.

To my graphic artist, Mrs. Naomi Margolin of Har Nof, for the original cover of my *chinuch* tape series, and for the inspiration for this book's cover; she has always designed that which I can only imagine.

To Rabbi Meir Zlotowitz, who has always reminded me of my own *chinuch*, how I was raised and the role it played in my writing of this book.

I express my appreciation to those at ArtScroll who invested so much time and effort in presenting this book both accurately and beautifully: Mrs. Judi Dick, who edited; Mrs. Tova Ovitz and Mrs. Mindy Stern, who proofread; and Chaya Perel Teichman, who paginated this book.

To my dearest friend, Yechezkel Chaim a.k.a. Herby Zakarin, and family, who has stood by my side and supported all my endeavors with more than anyone could ask from a friend.

May *HaKadosh Baruch Hu* help them see the fulfillment of all their hopes and aspirations in *ruchnius* and *gasmius*. May they see *nachas* from all their children as they follow in the *Derech Hashem*.

INTRODUCTION

How do we define success for our children? Is success a social value, defined by our social peer group? Is success defined by the fulfillment of *our* aspirations? Is success a relative value based on competition within the child's peer group? Perhaps success is allowing every child to be who he "wants" to be.

If success is to be measured by a social peer group, what are we to do with a child who, for any one of many reasons, is not capable of competing in the social milieu? What are we to do when one or more of our children is not prepared to apply himself to achieve the sometimes difficult standards of success set by the community? Finally, and even more difficult to deal with, what do we do when society has unrealistic definitions of success compared to our child's capabilites? For example, would one be considered a "successful" runner today if he did not compete and win major national competitions? Would one be considered a "successful" yeshivah boy if he did not attend a "top" yeshivah, or a "successful" singer if he did not fill the concert hall?

If success is measured by the fulfillment of our aspirations, how can we be sure that our dreams are realistic for our children? How often do parents want their children to be everything they would have wished for themselves? How often do parents want their children to help *them* achieve greater social standing? "My son, the doctor; my son the *Rosh Yeshivah*." Should *our* aspirations determine our child's success?

If success is to be measured by a child's wishes, how will we deal with those wishes that defy the very values we have tried to instill in him? Have we "succeeded" in raising our children if they live by values we consider bad or immoral? Does the child's happiness define the level of success? What if he is "happy" doing things that are wrong?

With all these issues to consider, we can still narrow the definition of success by some objective standard that allows the child to retain his individuality. I propose that we define success as "realizing potential" — the potential to accomplish those responsibilities that man has in this world. The criteria of success are objective, the outcome, individual. The expectations of each individual must be defined by his or her ability. Ability is characterized by natural gifts and developmental investment. *Everything we do to help develop our children's motivation to realize their potential in serving the Creator by recognizing their own innate capacities, as well as their ability to develop them, is a step toward success.*

Of course this must be accomplished through the child's own good feelings and happiness, but good feelings and happiness are not ideals that can be separated from right and wrong. We know our purpose in life, and our goal is for our children to appreciate and value the fulfillment of that purpose. *So we will define success in chinuch as helping our child become the kind of person who strives on his own to reach his potential.*

Often, reading books and hearing lectures on *chinuch* make people feel inadequate. I have frequently heard parents say, "But we can't do everything correctly all the time." "If so many things are important and so many things are dangerous, how can we possibly be successful?" It is essential for us to remember that we were not raised by angels. Our parents had their limitations, we have our shortcomings, and our children will have theirs. These facts of life are all part of the package. This book is intended to help us think through the processes of *chinuch,* to understand the concepts and guidelines of this craft. We will not belabor you with a plethora of case histories but will try instead to build a base of understanding that each individual can use as a catalyst for self-realization in this process.

When we do provide examples, they are almost all scenarios from personal experience. Many of these examples are *my* way of dealing with issues that are outgrowths of a process *I* went through. You, my dear reader, each and every one of you, has your own individual personality. Some of the stories I tell will be strange to you because you are different from me. If you repeat to your children some of the things I have said to my children, they will look at you in bewilderment. I remember a mother who called me after hearing one of my lectures on communication about ten years ago. She said, "I did exactly as you said, I told my 16-year-old daughter ... My daughter just looked at me with knowing eyes and said, 'Ma, who told you to say that?'"

You, dear reader, will have to react in a way that suits *you.* It is my hope that this book will afford a thought-provoking narrative that will empower others to discover their own creativity in this most challenging expedition of our lives.

It would be folly to assure you that if we did everything correctly, we would be guaranteed "Success in *Chinuch.*" Prerequisite to all our actions and overriding all our mistakes is *siyata diShemaya,* which reigns as the most important factor in *chinuch.* We need to *daven* with tears, to request help and strength from our Father in Heaven, in order to even think of succeeding. My *Rebbe* Harav Wolbe often said that the most crucial act in the furtherance of our children's success is our *tefillos.* May we all request help from *HaKadosh Baruch Hu* that He provide us with the *siyata diShemaya* we need so much as we rise to meet the challenge of transmitting the *Emes,* the truth of our *Mesorah,* properly.

Chapter One
THE BASIC MECHANICS
OF CHINUCH

◀ۛ *Defining Chinuch*

C reating an environment in which our children can be successful depends on our understanding of what *chinuch* really means. Once we have a working definition, we can focus on how to be a *mechanech*.

The first time the word *chinuch* appears in the Torah is in *Parashas Lech Lecha*,[1] "*vayarek es chanichav*, he took [what we assume are] his servants." Rav Wolbe always tells his students that if you want to know the meaning of a word, look at the *Rashi* the first time that word appears in the Torah.

Rashi says that the word *chinuch* signifies introducing a person or vessel to the particular occupation for which he or it is intended. *Chinuch* in relation to our children means easing them, hopefully from the outset, into the occupation of living in such a way that they will be able to go through life independently and properly as adults. Right now we are here with them and we can prepare them. They must be given the appropriate tools to be able to grow into independent individuals who will do that which they were taught, even when they are not in our immediate presence or when we will no longer be with them.

There is a difference between preparing someone for life's challenges, which is *chinuch*, and training him, a task with

---

1. *Bereishis* 14:14.

which we are somewhat more familiar. We can train a lion to roll over and have his belly scratched or to jump through a hoop. I recall seeing, as a child, a man sitting on a lion that was balanced on an elephant. As they were being put through their paces, the ringmaster told us how these three archenemies could be trained to work together. That training, however, did not alter their natures. It hadn't given them any tools for change: Without the trainer's whip or the expectation of his edible reward for sitting on the elephant's back, the lion would still enjoy having the man for dinner, or go to battle with his age-old enemy, the elephant.

There is a well-known story of a king whose advisers claimed that there is no appreciable difference between a human being and an animal. Obviously the rabbinic sage in the court disapproved. To prove their point, the advisers said they would "teach" a cat to be a waiter. On the appointed day, to everyone's delight, the cat, walking on its two hind legs, entered the room carrying a tea tray. The rabbi, wishing to disprove the mockery, took a small box out of his pocket and opened it. A small mouse jumped out and ran across the room. The cat immediately dropped the tray, the cups, and the tea, and went running after the mouse, because a cat is a cat, and a cat is not a waiter.

Training is usually dependent on the anticipation of a certain response, be it punishment or reward. We can train children to act in a certain way, and often that training will become second nature to them. Some aspects of raising children do require training; young children begin many behavioral routines through the training process. However, let's not fool ourselves. Training does not mean that they have internalized the behavior, that they understand it, or that it has become a part of them. The critical question is whether they will continue to behave in that way when their "trainer" is not around.

In *chinuch* we give tools to children that allow them to function without the expectation of positive or negative consequences. Obviously, we can use reward and punishment to teach a child the parameters of acceptable and non-acceptable behavior. It is also clear that parents need to begin the training process long before a child is capable of understanding *chinuch*. Therefore this section is not to be misunderstood as an attempt to skip the important instrument of reward and punishment. In Chapter Two, when we discuss discipline, we will speak about reward and punishment as tools in education.

The purpose of chinuch, however, is to give our children the ability to deal with life situations by themselves, because they will ultimately have to live on their own, make choices, and function with the consequences of those choices. Let us begin by discussing some of the necessary basics of creating that environment.

◄९ *Ahavah — Giving*

Love is the most basic ingredient of being a *mechanech*, an educator in the Torah sense; this is true for parent and teacher alike. If we love our children and they know that we love them, we will have the ability to transmit *chinuch* to them. That seems simple enough.

After having been married for four or five weeks, I happened to be conversing with a very great man, who taught me a very important lesson.

> *"Nu, does she still love you?" he asked.*
>
> *I thought that he was teasing me. "Of course," I answered, smiling.*
>
> *"How do you know?"*
>
> *"What does the Rav mean? I know it … I sense it."*
>
> *"That's not good enough."*
>
> *"But, I can see … "*
>
> *"That's not good enough."*
>
> *"We tell one another our feelings … "*
>
> *"That's not good enough."*

That was the end of the conversation and I was confused, but only for a few minutes, because I recalled an important lesson that my *Rebbe* Rav Wolbe once taught us in a *Chumash* class.

Avraham Avinu received some unusual guests: Three *malachim*, angels, came to visit.[2] They asked, "Where is Sarah your wife?" He replied that she was in the tent.

"Didn't they know where Sarah was?" asks Rashi. Sarah is a *tzeddekes*, a virtuous woman. Where is she supposed to be? She is tending to her obligations in her home. Rashi answers, "*Lechabevah al ba'alah*, to increase Avraham's appreciation for her"; they wanted to point out that Sarah was *tzenuah*, a modest woman.

Let's figure this out. Avraham Avinu was ninety-nine years old, and Sarah was eighty-nine. They had been married for approximately seventy-five years. Isn't it a little late to work on their relationship? Rashi says no, the investment in a relationship is an ongoing one.

Love is not stationary. It exists as long as you work on it. If you think you have it made and you neglect the relationship, it will wither. It is not enough, the Rav was telling me, to assume that if you got married, you love each other. If you are not going to consistently work on it, it is not going to last.

It is no different with children. Of course we love them — everyone loves his children. We would give our lives for them. But it cannot stop there. It is easy to say that we love them, but do they know that they are loved? If we do not show our affection regularly, they cannot be sure that we really mean it. We say, "Oh, I love you!" We sign our postcards, "Love, Tatty," so shouldn't they know we love them? It does not always work that way. We each have unique ways of expressing our feelings, and we cannot assume that our children are getting the message.

A child who does not feel loved is in danger. If he does not think he is receiving it from his parents, he will look for love

2. *Bereishis* 18:2.

elsewhere and usually will find it, often with the wrong kind of friends. These "friends" will give him unconditional love because they do not care what he does. We have to love our children unconditionally because this love is a most essential source of stability in their life. Our children must know that we care about them no matter what. Parents worry about how they can show their children love when the children are acting improperly. They worry that their love will convey approval of misbehavior — as if disapproval alone would stop it.

Experience has shown that the opposite is true; if we want our children to stop doing counterproductive things, we have to show them that we truly love them. This knowledge will be the single most potent reason for them to change for the better. Once a child has given up on his parents' love, he does not have the motivation to improve. When *he* feels that his parents do not really care about him, that "they are just worried about what others will say," when *she* senses that she will not be accepted anyway, because "she is such a bad girl," why should he or she try hard to give up that which makes him or her feel good?

> I know a couple, very good parents, who head a well-organized, fine home. The parents have always disciplined their children reasonably and not to excess. But their son went through a very difficult time in school and ran away from home. He was away for a number of years, leaving his parents in the dark regarding his whereabouts. When I next met him, he was already a young adult. I asked him why he left.
>
> "Listen," he said, "I wasn't loved at home, and I wasn't loved in school, and when things got tough, I had no reason to hang around."
>
> When I told the parents what he said, they were shocked. "How could he think that we didn't love him? Everything we ever did, we did for him. We only had two children. We lived for the kids!"

They could not understand it, yet this young man was not lying. It is such a sad story because these parents loved their children, but did not know how to convey that message. The boy did not realize how much he was loved. When he was having a hard time in school, they thought he was just giving them a hard time. When he was frustrated and even disrespectful, they thought *they* were the ones suffering.

We must remember that it is not enough to assume that because we are good to them, children know we care. We can work until midnight to put the food *that they like* on the table and deny ourselves things so that we can buy something special for them, and so on, but they do not necessarily know why we are doing it, or even that we are doing it at all. We do things for our children, yet when we scold them or punish them we often use words or methods that convey a message other than love and concern. More often than not, the pain they feel erases the many gestures of concern and caring in their minds.

> One of Rav Moshe Feinstein's sons said that he always knew that his father loved him. "Among other things, even when we had guests at the table, my father wanted me to sit next to him. In the winter he would always put my socks on the radiator so that when I woke up in the morning they would be warm, and it would be easy for me to get dressed." He also recalled that when determining a time to learn with him, his father took into consideration his playing time with friends.

Harav Moshe Feinstein was a very busy, important man. It would be reasonable to assume that many of those who came to his home were well respected people, including great rabbis and important, wealthy individuals, yet his son knew that his father was proud to have this young boy sit closest to him at the Shabbos table, no matter who the honored guest was. There was never a question in the mind of this boy, growing up in the house of a father who never wasted a moment, who did not take time for family vacations, and did not sit on the floor with him and give him piggyback rides, that his father loved him. Rav Moshe found his individual way to show his genuine concern and love for this son. And when Rav Moshe woke up before everyone else in his household, he took an extra moment to think about his children. His *ahavah* (a word derived from the root *hav*, giving) was so much a part of him that he looked for something he could do to make his child's morning more pleasant.

These are seemingly small things, and what works for one family is not necessarily the answer for another. Each parent has to find a way to show his or her love so that each of the children knows it exists, to overtly show each child in some special, different way that says, *I care about you. I want what's good for **you**. I enjoy doing things that make you happy.*

Children need to be shown love concretely as well, to be hugged and kissed — not excessively and not all the time, but in a casual, sensitive, caring way. While interviewing young boys for the yeshivah in past years, I've often walked over to a father after twenty minutes with his child and asked, "When was the last time you kissed your son?" "How did you know … ?" was the reply.

I don't have *ruach hakodesh*, but when you come up to a fourteen-year-old, put your arm around his shoulders, and give him a warm hello, and he gets all fidgety and nervous, you know that he is not used to being hugged by people who care about him. There's something wrong, something missing. When this occurred, the father often admitted that it had been many years since he physically expressed his feelings for his son. Too much touching introduces children to sensuality, and not enough expression of closeness can make a child yearn for it. Either of these extremes can bring on the challenging trials of incorrect physical behavior among young boys and girls. They need love doled out properly, and if they do not get it, they will find it in some other way.

◄ᶾ *Being Worthy of Kibud Av Va'em*

As parents, we are very focused on the mitzvah of *kibud av va'em*, honoring one's father and mother. Our children are going to *cheder*, to yeshivah, or day school, where they are taught that they must have respect for their parents. Since they're learning about the mitzvah, can't we assume that they'll act on it? Any realist knows that the awareness of a mitzvah is not sufficient to create the environment that is necessary for its proper performance.

The Rambam teaches us a halachah which, on analysis, proves that it's not enough for our children to know that they have a responsibility. *Asur lehakos es beno hagadol,*[3] a father is not allowed to hit a grown child. The Rambam says that it's a transgression of *Lifnei iver lo sitein michshol,*[4] "Don't put a stumbling block in front of a blind man." You will cause your son to react in a disrespectful manner.

Now, the halachah allows a father to hit his child in order to transmit *chinuch* to him, to put him on the right path, and make sure he does not repeat his incorrect behavior. Assuming that the son is already bar mitzvah, Rav Auerbach said, he knows there's a Torah that he has to obey. The Torah teaches the mitzvah of *kibud av va'em,* so why is the father violating the law of *lifnei iver lo sitein michshol?*[5] Why can't we assume that the son will keep the mitzvah of *kibud av* and will not react disrespectfully? The son certainly has no right to react improperly, yet the Rambam places the responsibility on the parent. What has the father done wrong?

Parents have a responsibility to create an environment in which their sons and daughters can keep this mitzvah. The Rambam clearly states that we must create an atmosphere in which our children can respect us, one which is conducive to their looking up to us. If we don't, it is considered our responsibility if they react in the wrong way.

Rav Wolbe says that in our generation this rule applies to even the youngest children. Hitting a child today can have long-lasting detrimental effects. In a society so rife with rebel-

---

3. *Mishneh Torah, Hilchos Mamrim.*

4. *Vayikra* 19:14.

5. That which the Rambam writes regarding an older child now applies to even younger children because the cause and effect is what makes the difference, not the age (Rav Elazar Papo, edition: 5584, vol.1, p. 175).

lion and freedom, where hitting is strongly frowned upon, raising one's hand becomes a risky means of discipline. It almost seems as if everyone has rights except parents and teachers, as if the "rights" of children seem to supersede our responsibility to teach them. Although in our communities, *baruch Hashem*, the concept of *chinuch* still exists, and we still have the possibility to discipline, we must know that our children will react in the spirit of the times in which we live. While an occasional *potch* under threat of anarchy among the children is acceptable, using hitting as a regular tool of discipline is not wise.[6]

We often speak about our children's responsibilities toward us — let's talk about us. We have to be worthy in their eyes, to be perceived as people who are worthy of respect, and this will depend to a great degree on our own actions. If we set a good example and they can look up to us, we will be able to use our authority in ways that parents who are not aware of these principles most probably cannot.

When you know that someone really cares, and you respect that person, you will accept a lot more from that individual than from someone from whom you feel alienated. A grown man's *rebbe*, who has been accepted as a mentor for life, can do almost anything to further the development of his student. To get a slap from such a *rebbe* can be an exhilarating experience. It means the *rebbe* deeply cares about me and loves me. He feels close enough to chastise me, knowing that I am not going to judge his actions in a negative way.

> *I once brought my young son along on a visit to one of the gedolei hador, a very great man, kind enough to afford me a close relationship. We went to him on Purim when I was under the influence of one of its mitzvos, and had not been to see him for a long time. He pulled me down close to his face, gave me a slap across mine, and*

---

6. There is an extraordinarily "current" discourse regarding corporal punishment in the *Pe'le Yoetz* that states that the nature of *chinuch* has changed and, although the words of *Chazal* are replete with discussions of physical punishment, we can no longer employ those methods because the result will be counterproductive.

*said, "What do you think I am, a Purim Rebbe? What,
you come in just on Purim?"*

I was thrilled, because I knew that he really cared about
me, but the *rebbe* noticed that my son was shocked. He
turned to my son and said, "Don't worry, this is because I love
your father." It was the truth!

This is something that's very hard to explain in a society
where raising your hand to a student is such a terrible thing.
The slap was not a punishment given in anger or hate. He
gave it because we were so close that he knew it wouldn't
hurt me or make me question his authority.

It's much harder for parents to do this. Having spoken
to many hundreds of rebellious and troubled young men
and women, I can tell you unequivocally that the child will
remember the slap dealt in anger for years, while the kiss is
forgotten twenty minutes later. Children need to feel that we
care and that we want what is good for them, and that we are
not just coming down on them because we are angry or have
lost control. When they know we care, it is easier for them
to accede to our demands and to accept things that do not
seem reasonable at the moment. Obviously, before that point
can be reached, we will have to invest a great deal of time
and energy in developing a loving relationship.

◄ξ *Knowing Your Child*

We want to transmit *chinuch,* to motivate our children, and
help them get along. To accomplish this, we have to know
who they are and what traits they have working for and/or
against them. (In the next chapter, "Discipline that Works,"
we will take an example of one trait and work through it step
by step.)

Anyone who has a relationship with more than one child
knows that no two children are the same, and that each
child must be evaluated objectively if we want to move him
from one point to the next. We do this by recognizing that
two separate elements co-exist within each child. The first is

personality, consisting of the character traits with which he was born and which develop with him as he grows and are affected by everything that happens to him. The second element is behavioral patterns, which may be an outgrowth of the personality but are not intrinsic to the child.

Take, for example, a girl who by nature is very serious, concerned about details, and wants to have everything figured out. She needs to understand everything and know where it fits into her present picture of life in order to be comfortable with it. This is a personality trait. An outgrowth of this could be that she becomes easily frustrated in certain situations. When she does, she may react in what seems to us to be an unreasonable manner. This type of reaction can develop into a pattern that is not necessarily a part of her personality. This is something that we can help her to work on and to change.

When we look at our children, we see traits that we like and others that we wish were different. We have to recognize, given the child's personality, what may be changeable in the near future and what we can help him work on himself throughout childhood and adolescence. Hopefully, he will eventually be able to conquer that weak character trait by channeling it properly.

We have stories about our *gedolim* proving just how major a task this can be. Rav Moshe Feinstein once said that for thirty years he had been working on one *middah*, one character trait, and he just could not conquer it. Any of us who has tried to change something that is a part of his or her personality knows how difficult it is.

A. Acceptance

Years ago, I studied under Dr. Alexander Myers, a *frum* psychiatrist from Holland who lived in Yerushalayim. Dr. Myers was the head of the Department of Pediatric Psychiatry at Hadassah Hospital, with a very full roster of private clients as well. When I went into *chinuch*, I spent many hours in his office, working with students of mine as well as observing patients (my referrals) who had allowed me to sit in on their therapy sessions.

In those years, one of my children had the distressing habit of banging his head against the wall and hitting himself when he was upset. Whenever he would become angry or frustrated, he would take it out on himself physically — there were months at a time when he had a black-and-blue bump on his forehead.

I couldn't handle his behavior. I tried everything — hugging, kissing, and threatening. By the time my son was two and a half, I decided to bring him to Dr. Myers. To demonstrate the problem, I gave my keys to the child. He played with them for about thirty seconds, and then I took them away. He flew into a tantrum and began banging his head on the floor and hitting himself.

"Ah, very interesting," said the doctor. He gave us a few suggestions on how to deal with the problem and how to speak to him before and after these incidents. My son slowly grew out of the behavior.

Six months later, another *rebbe* from my yeshivah and I met with Dr. Myers to discuss various issues. Dr. Myers corrected something I had said, and I immediately realized that I had been totally off track. I slammed the palm of my hand against my forehead two or three times and exclaimed, "Oh! Stupid!"

"Aha! Aha!" said Dr. Myers, and he smiled.

"What?" I asked, puzzled.

"Aha!" he repeated. "What did you just do?"

"I don't know ... what did I do?"

"What did you just do with your hand?"

"Oh ... "

"Yes," said the doctor, "that's you!"

It was a very rude awakening regarding my nature. I did not batter myself as a child, but there's obviously something in my personality that makes me hit myself when under certain types of stress. I don't do it often, and my children have rarely, if ever, seen it, but it's there. Thanks to this new awareness, I will share a little-realized secret with you that I learned from my *Rebbe* Rav Wolbe.

Most children's personality challenges are come by honestly. They have two parents; they inherit some good traits from each and other less desirable ones, as well. *The behavioral trait of your child that bothers you most comes from you.* The trait that drives you absolutely mad, the one thing that you really cannot put up with — look in the mirror to find its source. Perhaps knowing this will make it a little easier to understand and bear with your children.

Once we have evaluated our child objectively, we parents have to come to terms with who he is, and determine what behaviors we must help him to modify, one thing at a time, step by step. We will recognize that our child was given this set of *middos* to deal with, and these are the tools he has. If we accept him for who he is and who he can be, we will be better *mechanchim*, educators, and he will be a much better child. When a child feels that he is accepted, even though we definitely have to help him in some way, we have a starting point. We have to be able to think positively, look ahead, and think long term.

My wife and I found out that one of our children had some difficulty with reading, a very basic necessity in our society. As time goes by, an inability to read becomes a tremendous detriment to a child's emotional and social development. This is not a behavioral problem that I could help him modify. This child has an intrinsic difficulty with something that he will have to deal with throughout his life.

There are different ways to react to such a problem. One could say, "*Oy vey,* look at this *tzuris*! What am I going to do? He'll never make it! We'll just have to push him so he'll get as far as he can go and that's all." There are parents who do just that; they totally deny the problem and its source, and just try to work with it on a frustration level: We will push him, and his teachers will push him, to do what he cannot do. Unfortunately, those kids get pushed out of the yeshivah system very quickly.

Parents who want to be more responsible have to go beyond their own evaluation. Their assessment shows that their child is having trouble because he is not doing well in school; he is a little frustrated and he acts out in many ways. The next step is to pinpoint the problem and see what can be done about it. The wise parent will not wait until the problem has escalated. The old proverb, "A stitch in time saves nine," was never more applicable than in such a situation.

> I had a student, an eleventh-grader, who couldn't read past second-grade level. Nobody knew he had a reading problem. It was totally ignored through eight years in elementary school and two years in high school. How is it possible that it was never noticed? Everyone made excuses for him: He's lazy; he didn't try; he doesn't like to read.

There are many "easy" ways out, which make it even harder later on. It is obviously going to be very difficult to transmit *chinuch* to this child because his problems were never evaluated honestly. The parents never asked themselves who their child is. What does he require? In which areas is he capable? In which areas does he need help? How shall we deal with this?

If the child has a reading problem, we're most likely not going to solve it in two weeks. Sometimes an evaluation will show that it's really a very simple impediment, and two weeks' work will correct it, but usually the specialist will tell you, as he told us, that it might take a few years and the disability may never change. The child may learn to compensate, he may learn to deal with the situation, but he will probably never open a book and read it easily, swiftly, comfortably.

> There are people who go through life with this limitation, and they do not allow it to hold them back. I recently read an article written by a sixty-five-year-old professor of literature who is dyslexic. When he was younger, his parents were very supportive, and he decided to try to overcome his problem. They helped him and his educators to deal with it and understood his needs. Possibly

because they didn't give up on him, he didn't give up on himself. They had a long-term plan.

Did reading ever become pleasant for him? Reading was not an easy task for him, but emotionally it was satisfying. Although it's still very difficult for him to read, he derives immense enjoyment from it. He prefers to listen to a book on tape rather than to read it, but he is the author of several scholarly volumes. Through recognizing the problem, working with it, around it, and in spite of it for many years, he became successful in the area in which no one would have dreamed he would succeed.

We are very thankful to Hashem that our son, who was dedicated to overcoming his dyslexia and worked extremely hard for many years, now reads hundreds of pages of Gemara with ease and enjoyment.

B. Long-Term Perception Helps

Screaming, hitting, and reacting on a moment-to-moment basis, without a proper evaluation or a long-term plan, is not *chinuch*. *Chinuch* is not a Band-Aid to solve some immediate issue while you wait for the next blow-up. *Chinuch* is preparing your child for life — a hopefully long road.

I once asked a young teenager how he sees his future. "What are you going to be?"

"Nothing."

"What do you mean nothing?"

"Nothing," he repeated. "I'm worthless, I'm not going to get anywhere."

I was appalled. "Excuse me," I said. "How old are you?"

"Thirteen and a half."

"Thirteen and a half? That means you have another 106 and a half years to live. You've given up?"

He looked at me, his face a total blank, and said, "What?"

"Well," I said, "everyone says 'till 120,' so hopefully you have another 106 and a half years to live. How can you give up? Even if you don't live quite that long, for

four bad years you're going to give up on the next sixty or seventy?"

How can we give up on our children when we see something really troublesome, something about which we are truly worried? They have, with Hashem's help, another sixty, seventy, eighty years to live, hopefully in good health. We have a great amount of work ahead of us to ensure that those years will be productive. We can't possibly deal with it right this minute. We have to develop a long-term plan.

Although we sometimes hesitate to evaluate because we fear that we are going to be faced with some real issues, whether learning problems or personality traits, we cannot give up and we cannot make assumptions.

We know that there are children who, from an early age, will always tell the truth even if they are afraid of being punished. Then there are those who, from the time they are two and a half or three, will always say what they believe they can get away with or what they think we want to hear. We can brush these behaviors aside, or we can recognize that one has a great tool, and the other has a great challenge. The child who always tells the truth has a tool that we can help him work with to enhance his whole life, but it's only a tool, because raw honesty can be a double-edged sword.

With his opposite we have a great challenge, because he has a personality that requires that he feel comfortable in any given situation — or he will do anything to get out of any situation which causes him discomfort. If we make believe that certain traits and behaviors do not exist, we will pay for our obtuseness many times over as the child grows and all the ramifications of his persona grow with him.

If Hashem gave us five children, He gave us five totally different sets of circumstances with which to deal. Now, none of us is born knowing how to treat every kind of problem, so if we have no experience, how are we supposed to know what to do? Well, how would you go about getting information about anything else?

C. Seek Professional Advice

If you think your child is allergic to something, you go to someone who knows how to treat allergies. If your child has asthma you don't say, "Too bad I'm not a doctor, so I can't handle this." You go to an expert and make sure you acquire the information you need to deal with the problem. Nor do you go to the first allergist you happen upon in the Yellow Pages. Why should we act any differently when it comes to *chinuch*? So, whom do we approach with our questions regarding *chinuch*?

For a professional evaluation, you want to find a person you can speak with who has a proven track record and is readily accessible. Often it's a matter of finding a Rav or a successful educator. At times this means obtaining a professional evaluation from a psychologist. Either way, the importance of clarifying your child's difficulties is paramount in raising him properly.

D. Prioritize

Once you know your child feels loved and you have evaluated his qualities and weaknesses, you can now begin to set goals. This means choosing one problem at a time to work on, being aware that this is going to be a long-term project. We know how hard it is to change ourselves.

Just take Friday before Shabbos as a classic example. You all know exactly what I'm talking about. We decide to improve ourselves and make the moments prior to Shabbos more peaceful and organized, so we say, "From now on, three hours (two hours, one, a half-hour, even ten minutes) before Shabbos everything's going to be ready ... " Whether we are adults, parents, teachers, businessmen, nurses, or doctors, it makes no difference: The next Friday, ten minutes before Shabbos — boom! "Where's my shirt, where's the tablecloth, does anyone know where the ... ?"

Nothing has changed. We have to maintain a sense of humor and realize that just as it is so hard for us to change our behavioral patterns, it is not going to be any easier for our child. It takes patience and understanding. We have to know that we are going to take very small steps, and with Hashem's help we are going to build our child and ourselves.

The Rambam writes in *Moreh Nevuchim* (*The Guide to the Perplexed*)[7] that if you want to really work on your *davening*, try to have intense *kavanah*, really think about what you are saying in the first *pasuk* in *Krias Shema*. After you have done this for a few years, the Rambam continues, you can move on to the next *pasuk*.

We are astonished, but the Rambam was realistic. The first verse of the *Shema, kabbalas ol malchus Shamayim*, is actually accepting Hashem as our Master in every single thing that we think and do and experience. That does not happen in one day, and it is not going to happen in a week.

When I was in ninth grade, I devised a *Middos*-Incentive Program. I made a list of all my bad *middos*, of which I had many, and said, "Okay, now I'm going to work on them."

I took out the *Orchos Tzaddikim*, learned through it that week, and made a list of dos and don'ts. Every day I checked off another one. Once the week was over, I said to myself, "Okay, now the next *middah.*" After all, the *mashgiach* said we have to work on our *middos*, so I wanted to do it. Within a short time it became clear to me that my *middos* were still very much the same, and if anything, I was developing a negative *middah* of pride about my progress. What a rude awakening! It doesn't work that way. It really has to take time for us to develop and change our *middos*.

We have to be able to keep realistic goals in mind as we work with our children on their growth. We have to learn to be satisfied with the small steps that we and our children have taken. If we think that everything will happen quickly, just the way we planned, we will soon be frustrated and give up. Recognizing that every single little step up is real, meaningful, and a step in the right direction, we will derive the satisfaction that will give us power and energy to go forward. We will be happy and so will our child when we say, "That's great,

---

7. *Moreh Nevuchim* 3, addendum.

you're really doing very well," and mean it, when all he has done so far is to take a tiny step.

If, having decided that you will react in a certain way when a child accomplishes something, you follow through, and the child stops the negative behavior, does that mean that he is now perfect and he will never do it again? Obviously not. But if you can say, "I'm very proud of you," you give the child strength. He can be happy about himself. This gives him the motivation to try again the next time, and it gives us the ability to continue to support him.

E. Focus on Teamwork

Probably the most important element in creating an environment for successful *chinuch* is parental teamwork. The number one cause of children's behavioral problems is parental dysfunction. Every *mechanech* with whom I have ever spoken has agreed that 90 percent of the children who have behavioral problems have witnessed some level of parental dysfunction or disunity. A good environment for *chinuch* demands that the mother and father work together toward the same goal.

Children cannot witness disunity at home and be expected to react as if it were normal. Just as children learn from our example when we speak respectfully to our spouses, they also learn from us, when we do not speak nicely to one another, that respectful speech is not really necessary. If one parent is disrespectful to the other, the child feels that he likewise does not have to treat that parent with respect.

Children instinctively know how to use disunity as a weapon. If the authority of one or both parents is undermined, children can wedge themselves in between the two, instigate fights, and manipulate the situation to get what they want. It comes as no surprise that where there is no authority in the home, children often manifest behavioral problems. Parents must therefore learn to discuss things together, to work together, to react and seek advice as a team. A parent will often call for an appointment at school to discuss a problem. A wise teacher or principal will advise the parents to come together, because if only one attends the conference, he or she may not be able to repeat the conversation and suggestions accurately. The second parent, not having been privy to the exact words and tones, may thus not be receptive to the conclusions reached at the meeting.

"Well, maybe you didn't ask this question … If you had phrased it another way, the answer would have been different."

Parental unity is probably the most important condition required to help our children grow in desirable ways. I know of far too many prominent people who lost their children as a result of disunity in the home, while other parents who may not have seemed phenomenal *mechanchim* or "successes" in the eyes of the world built a warm and loving home. Since these parents worked together with clearly defined goals, their children, even those who were difficult and went far astray, eventually come back, because they felt they had a home to which to return. They had parents who truly loved and respected all the members of the family, and it always pained these children to know that they were hurting their mother and father.

The child whose parents hurt one another is not bothered when he hurts them. On the contrary, he derives a certain gratification from doing this because he himself is being hurt. The pain that children feel when their parents argue is comparable to hearing an unbearable sound, one that makes you cringe and feel physically uncomfortable, as if your insides are shriveling up and you want to run away. When parents fight, that is exactly how children feel, and they never forgive their parents for making them go through that turmoil.

There are situations where teamwork is not always possible. In some homes, one parent is far less capable than the other, or is incapacitated in some way. When one parent is not functioning properly, can the other compensate for it? I believe the answer is yes. There is rarely a no-win situation, but the parent who is capable of functioning properly will have to work much harder to overcome the obstacles. The most difficult thing to accomplish in such a situation is creating an environment in which the children do not feel friction and anger in the home. The more capable and aware parent may have to create a good environment at the "expense" of his or her comfort or pride. Our goal must be to make our children feel valuable and loved, despite the fact that one parent is dysfunctional or noncompliant.

In summary, we seek to bring up our children:

- in a home of love and mutual respect,
- in an environment of acceptance for who they are,
- by setting goals that are reasonable and responsible,
- through proper evaluation,
- with parental teamwork.

With Hashem's help, we can then go on to build in them responsibility, motivation, good relationships, and true communication.

Chapter Two
DISCIPLINE THAT WORKS

Discipline is a tool in the process of imparting knowledge. The dictionary defines "disciple" as "one who receives instruction from another; a scholar; a learner; especially, a follower who has learned to believe in the truth of the doctrine of his teacher." Unfortunately, we associate *discipline* with *punishment,* and we think of a *disciplinarian* as someone who is very strict.

In this chapter we will discuss discipline from the point of view of what works not just for the moment, but in terms of teaching our children something they can live and work with for the rest of their lives. Discipline usually includes some element of fear, for without it, children tend to do what makes them happy at the moment. What is the place of fear in a home that is trying to build itself on Torah values? The Talmud[1] says that a home that is run on fear is not viable; yet, through a "show"[2] of anger, a child must learn that there are limits and rules.

The Torah says, "*Ish imo v'aviv tira'u,*[3] a person has to fear his parents." But to what type of fear does this refer? One kind of fear is trepidation, where you quake because you know someone or something has the power to harm you. Then

---

1. *Gittin* 6b, 7a.
2. *Rambam, Mishneh Torah, De'os* 2:3.
3. *Vayikra* 19:3.

there is fear that comes from respect or awe. Children should not be *afraid* of their parents, but we do want them to *fear* us as a result of, if not awe, at least respect. The Talmud[4] defines that kind of fear as the acceptance of authority — humility and subservience to superiority.

Fear inspired by negativity on our part will not accomplish this. Many homes feature a little sign reminding us that children grow in the manner in which they are nurtured: If you raise your children with (fill in the blank), they will grow with (the same trait). When we are upset we project anger, and our children assume that they are the objects of that anger and are therefore bad. This is negativity, which is not the message we are trying to teach our children. That is not to say that a parent should never "show" anger, but reactions resulting from anger will not be effective in the long run. Our basic premise for discipline should be based on three things:

1) stating what we want in the correct way;
2) being firm;
3) being consistent.

❧ Giving the Correct Message

I was sitting in a waiting room and heard a mother I know well say to her little girl, "If you do not sit straight you're not going to get the soda." At the risk of being told to mind my own business, I said to her, "Excuse me, but why not say, 'I want to give you the soda, so please sit straight.' Or, 'If you're sitting straight I can give you the soda.'" The difference between the two approaches is so simple. Why do we tend to threaten instead of motivate?

The answer is control. When we say, "If you do not sit straight, I will not give you the soda," we are in control. But that is not motivating or teaching, it is just threatening. If we speak this way all the time, control becomes our

---

4. *Kiddushin* 30.

unspoken message on a regular basis. Day after day, our children want five, ten, twenty things. We are either giving our children breakfast, lunch, supper, preparing them a snack, letting them go out, not letting them go out, or controlling many other things they want to do. By making some activities dependent on their actions, we may end up five or ten times a day doing the very thing we do not want to do: teaching them negativity. We may be telling them, "If you do not ... then you won't ..."; "If you won't ..., then you cannot ..., over and over and over again. If we want our children to do something or to not do something, we have to think of ways to present the instruction properly. This is really not so difficult. When you are about to say something, first stop and think: *Is there a better way to word it?*

Obviously, we cannot change overnight, neither our personalities nor the way we speak, but if we think before we speak even a couple of times a day, eventually we will begin to phrase things differently and we will see results.

The little girl wants the soda. She does not understand what sitting straight has to do with getting it. She is not trying to be bad; she is not sitting straight for one or more of a dozen reasons. Maybe she is excited about getting the soda or perhaps she has been sitting straight for ten minutes already and she is uncomfortable. Someone may be kicking her under the table. She is not slumping or fidgeting purposely to annoy us and not get her drink.

If all we want is for her to sit straight so that the soda will not spill, we can tell her that. "You know what, if you sit straight I can give it to you and you will be able to drink without spilling." This way, we have taught the child a lesson and made it easier for her to accept our demand and sit properly. Does this mean that a child will never act out of stubbornness or a desire to upset us? Of course not. We all know that even when we say things in a positive light, the desired response is not always forthcoming; the chances are much better, however.

◄᠎ Being Firm and Consistent

What happens if we present the message properly at first, but the child does not respond as desired? By the second or third try we become angry, because we have done everything right and have not accomplished anything. But if we remember that what we really want to accomplish is to get the child to sit straight when she is eating or drinking, we will recognize that anger is not going to teach her to do so. We have to be firm, not angry, so we take the soda away from her and say, "I'm sorry, I want to give you the soda but I cannot give it to you now. Maybe soon you will be sitting properly and I'll be able to return it to you," and we put it down. She becomes upset.

"I want to give you the drink and I will, as soon as you are sitting straight."

If this goes on for more than a couple of minutes, and the child still is not sitting straight, do not give in. If you've reached the end of your tether because there are others in the room who need your attention, or you give her the soda because you want the peace and quiet, you have not taught her anything. You did not stand firm long enough.

"I still want to give it to you, but I see that you are not ready for it now. Perhaps in three (five, eight ...) minutes we will see if you are ready." Period. No further discussion.

Although we use specific examples in this book, it must be understood that just as every home is different, so is every child, and so is his/her position in the family, our relationship to him/her, and our instinctive reactions to a given situation. In any particular situation, we cannot say, "I said this, and he did that, so now I have to do thus ... Uh-oh, it is not working! Where are the directions for the next step?" We do not function like programmed robots. You must apply the situation we are speaking about in ways that work for you. Because everybody's personality is different, some of us find certain things relatively easy, while others find them difficult. *Not every method is suitable for everyone.* The examples I present, therefore, are only to bring out certain points and to help you think in terms of alternative ways of thinking and acting.

If you are firm in one instance and not in the next, the message you conveyed the first time is lost. If it is important to you that your children sit down when they eat, then they must stay in their seats whenever they are eating — not one time yes and one time no. Giving mixed messages confuses them. It should not come as a surprise that what we try to teach very often does not get learned because we are not consistent with the things that we consider important.

◄ Punishing

Many people in Western society claim that punishing is off-limits. Discipline can be maintained without punishment, they say. They are certainly ignorant of the wider parameters of punishment. They unrealistically assume that "punishment" means corporal punishment. In actuality, when dealing with a child who loves you, when you look with dismay at him because of the way he is behaving, that *is* punishment to him. If you ignore him for a moment because you do not want to hit him, that is punishing him. Saying, "That really makes me feel bad and I do not like to feel that way," is giving him a clear message, and because he loves you so much he does not want you to feel bad. Therefore this is also a punishment.

"No hitting" is a reasonable premise in *chinuch* today, as we discussed earlier, but that is a far cry from "not punishing." However, punishment must be reasonable in order for a child to benefit from it. This is because we are not trying to use punishment to hurt our children but rather to teach them.

If, in anger at our child for hurting another child, we use violence to "teach him a lesson," we are punishing ourselves at the same time. Not only did we fail to teach him that hurting is not a good thing, but in response he will probably inflict more harm the next time. Alternatively, the child might think,

"I'd better get back at him in a different way so that my parents will not find out about it fast enough to hurt me back."

When do we punish? Rav Yaakov Kamenetsky gave us a brilliant guideline. He said that when a child does something appropriate to his age, and you know that when he gets older he will no longer do it, you should not punish him. If the child is doing something totally inappropriate to his age, you *can* punish him. Many of us who have problems with our weight have heard little children say, "Oh, you mean that fat man ... ?" Parents tend to get upset, thinking that this is chutzpah and a reason to punish the child. It is not; the child is simply unaware of the sensitivities involved. If he is old enough to understand, we can tell him that we do not talk about people's clothes or the way they look, and punishing him for it is a totally uncalled-for response.

> *Many years ago Rav Moshe Feinstein was sitting at the head table in the yeshivah dining room. It was Shavuos and we were all in a very serious mood, having learned the entire night and davened Shacharis early in the morning. The atmosphere in the yeshivah was heavy with the intensity of learning amid the simchah of the day; there was no frivolity on our minds.*
>
> *One of Rav Moshe's grandchildren, about five or six years old at the time, was sitting on Rav Moshe's lap. Suddenly in a loud voice he asked, "Zaide, Zaide, how do you get an elephant out of a tree?"*
>
> *Rav Moshe understood some English, but the Rebbetzin had to explain what the child had asked. Rav Moshe looked at the little one and said, "Nu, how? (Vi azoy?)" And the child answered, "He sits on a leaf and waits for fall."*
>
> *We were all sitting there, absolutely plotzing. Get that kid out of here; shut him up! Rav Moshe just smiled at the boy who, thus encouraged, asked another riddle. I wish I could remember the dvar Torah that was said at the table as well as I remember the two riddles! (How do you put four elephants in a Volkswagen?[5]) Rav Moshe*

---

5. Two in the front and two in the back.

continued to smile calmly at his grandson. He displayed neither frustration nor anger.

Although it was Shavuos and we had just spent the whole night learning, this young child sitting on his grandfather's lap was being age-appropriate and not doing anything out of turn. Neither Rav Moshe, nor his wife, nor the father of the boy felt it necessary to react in any way out of the ordinary. A negative reaction would have been out of place, because this is the way a small child acts. We were too young to realize it at the time, but this was a living example of how *gedolei Yisrael* transmit *chinuch*.

◄ Using Yiddishkeit Against Us

Transmitting Torah and mitzvos is a very important part of our concern when it comes to discipline. Because our children recognize that, it is also the most volatile part of their education. A three-and-a-half-year-old child knows that when he is angry at his Abba and Imma, he can get even by taking off his *yarmulke* and throwing it on the floor. How does he know? Who told him that that is going to upset us? Somehow he can sense what is important to us and use it to thwart us.

Before we go any further, we have to realize that discipline is something we can and must learn to use and become good at performing. If discipline degenerates into just a fight between our children and us, we had better know that they are much stronger than we are! If our approach to discipline is to gird for battle, we have no real power, because in the long run misusing any power we have will only exacerbate the child's problem, which is most certainly not our intention. If we continue to do the wrong things long enough, we will "win" by eventually throwing them out of the house, by which time, *chas v'shalom,* they are more than happy to leave. If discipline becomes a battle, they can beat us ten times a day with what they say or what they do not say. Be it a *berachah,* a *yarmulke, tzitzis, tzenius,* you name it; they have many weapons they can use to hurt us. We have to make sure that we are not turning our discipline into a war to see who's stronger, because we all know who will "win."

I have met many young adults who admitted that they rejected everything their parents stood for because they were retaliating — they wanted to make their parents suffer. Grown children who speak this way are still hurting. Perhaps they were difficult children and their parents did not have any idea how to handle them; perhaps not. I'm not seeking to cast blame. We must try to create an environment in which discipline, setting rules and limits, is executed with wisdom, the benefit of experience, and a sense of responsibility. We must be aware of the importance of discipline in our children's lives to help them grow in the right directions.

The way we make *berachos, daven,* dress, *bentch,* and act toward others teaches our children how to behave. There is a man in the shul where I sometimes *daven* who talks to the fellow sitting next to him during most of the *davening.* But every time his son walks away, he grabs him by the collar, gives him a shake, puts him back in his seat, and says, "*Nu nu nu ...* !" Can this man seriously expect his son to respect *davening?*

Boys usually wear their *tzitzis,* but sometimes they forget and sometimes they do not want to put them on. There are many possible situations and scenarios. If we turn the situation into something so crucial that we are ready to lose our heads over it, the one mitzvah the boy is not going to like is *tzitzis.* Each of us can think of something we do not like or do not want to deal with because our parents put so much emphasis on it that they made us paranoid about it. For some people it is a certain type of clothes, a certain way to wear their hair, what they like or do not like to eat. I know people who cannot eat certain foods because they remind them of food battles they fought as children.

What do we adults want? We want what makes us feel good. What do we like to do? We like to do that which make us comfortable. If we are going to discipline our children to the point where they are miserable about the things we are trying to teach them, they will "listen" now, because they know that otherwise they will be spanked, screamed at, sent to their room, or the like. But there will come a time when we will not be standing over them, when we will not be at the table, and then they are never going to sit at their places.

> *I know a man, a teacher no less, who eats as he walks around the room. On Shabbos he takes his seat out of deference to his wife and children, but during the week he will never sit at the table.*
>
> *We worked together, and after watching him during mealtimes for a while I could not control my curiosity. "Why do you do this?" I asked.*
>
> *"I do not know."*
>
> *"How can you not know? Why don't you sit down at the table like a mentsch to eat?"*
>
> *His reaction was spontaneous: "You sound just like my mother!"*

We should try to think of appropriate responses to situations in advance, and not fall back on our instinctual defensive or controlling impulses. Suppose a child is recalcitrant and says, "You made me get up, you made me get dressed, but I'm not going to shul." He pushed a button and waits for the explosion.

"Okay, goodbye," you say, and you leave.

Wait a minute, he thinks, *you're supposed to be upset that I'm not going to shul. I'm using this against you. Don't you know the rules?* Since he has not accomplished his purpose, he probably will go to shul, but a little bit later. If, when you come home, you get on his case: "Why don't you go to shul?" he will think that you are not being honest with him. It would be wiser to hold back. Leave him alone.

The technique goes even further. Sometimes I will say it before the child does, "I'm sorry Dovid, but you cannot come to shul today."

"What?"

"You cannot come to shul. Shul is a place for children who can keep quiet when they have to. Maybe tomorrow ..."

If going to shul is a big responsibility, big enough to pester him, punish him, and hurt him, he has a tool to use against me. But if going to shul is something that he has to merit because it is so special, then I have something I can utilize to teach him.

What, after all, do I want to teach him about shul? That it is this annoying thing you do whether you want to or not, because you just have to? Or is shul a big *zechus*, a privilege that we Jews can use to better *daven* to Hashem?

Teaching him the first way is easy. If I scream at him when he does not come, nag him when he is late, embarrass him, make him feel pretty low, then I have taught him that coming to shul is an uncomfortable experience. If I want to teach him that it is a *zechus*, I'll compliment him every time he goes and tell him something good about the fact that he went. When we come home I say, "Mommy, do you know how beautifully Dovid *davened* today?" Maybe he only said one prayer nicely, but this will encourage him and is a facet of good discipline.

Telling my son that I do not think he can to come to shul today because he has not been behaving well enough there is more effective discipline than saying, "You're going to come, and you're going to *daven* every word because I'm going to watch you, and you'd better ..."

> There is an old Yiddish story about a man sitting next to his son in shul and nudging him, "Yankel, Yankel, I do not hear you, I do not hear you."
>
> After the fifth time, the child looks up and says, "I'm not talking to you."

What are we teaching our children and how are we doing it? There are obviously differences in the way we give a message to a four-year-old, a teenager, and a young adult. We cannot say to a fifteen-year-old, "Do not come to *davening* today," but we can definitely refrain from nagging him, because it may push him in the opposite direction.

When our children act up in negative ways, sometimes it helps to have a good memory to recall how we ourselves felt and acted at that age and stage. A sense of humor is also a definite asset when our kids do things that bother us.

◄ₔ Choosing Issues

There are times when children do things that are wrong or harmful, when they exercise behavior that makes life miserable for everyone else in the house. We should take the long view and decide that we need to do something constructive instead of reacting impulsively, with no thought to the future. In helping a child overcome a challenge, it is helpful to isolate one thing that bothers us the most and focus on that.

Some children seem to be constantly hitting, some scream and yell every time something does not go their way. Some throw things; others close up, run to their rooms, and draw into a shell that does not let you reach them. That is no less dangerous than screaming, no less a concern. Most children will do one or more things that make us feel we just cannot handle the situation anymore and we have to do something about it.

At the same time, we have to be realistic and know that we are not going to "fix" everything all at once, because that is a sure-fire recipe for not fixing anything. Trying for perfection of everything all at once gets us nowhere, but if we work with one thing at a time, there is hope for progress.

To this end, we should be careful to choose a habit that is not an innate character trait but a behavioral response. Jealousy is a *middah*. If a child is jealous, if he wants that which someone else has, that means he feels an elemental need to have whatever it is. Obviously there are things we can do to relieve some of that pressure and help him to deal with it, but a normal, albeit negative character trait is something that we are not going to solve in one, two, or three months, and probably not even in five years. This involves an extremely long-term project and will take just as long as it takes us to change our own *middos*! We can help our child identify the *middah*, discuss it with him, and help him appreciate his need to deal with it at some point in his life.

When it is a question of the child's reaction or overreaction in different situations in a way that hurts him and others, however, that is a behavioral problem — and something that we can try to work with on a shorter-term basis.

We are going to discuss a hypothetical child who acts out in several ways. He does not always eat in a pleasant way, he fights with his siblings, and he screams and yells. When he is in the house, everything seems upside down. We should try to determine which is the one behavior that is absolutely the most important to stop. For the sake of this example, we will focus on his screaming. Screaming makes it difficult for us to respond to the rest of the family in a relaxed, reasonable fashion, it disturbs our state of mind, and it gives everyone a splitting headache. We decide to play down his eating habits and his penchant for fighting for the next couple of months until we find a way to deal with the screaming. It does not mean that we are going to ignore potential harm to his siblings, but in order to be effective we are going to work on one thing at a time. This means that we will not make an issue of the other behavioral concerns for the time being.

Family dynamics are extraordinarily variable. Mothers may or may not be home all day. Some fathers are tough on their children while others are soft, leaving the hard line to their wives. One or the other parent may be inconsistent in his/her disciplining, and so on. Nonetheless, good parenting is predicated on the need to work together — it must be a team effort. If we decide we want to address the screaming first, it must be a joint decision. If there are responsible, older teens in the home, we should invite them to share in the discussion. Once the problem has been isolated, a united front can be presented to the child.

We speak to the child when he is *not* angry. We ask him, "Do you know what happens when you get upset?" Let *him* tell you that he screams. Then we continue.

"When you scream it makes it very, very hard for everyone to hear what anyone else is saying, or even to understand what you are saying. We are going to try to help you stop screaming."

If the child is three years old, that sort of discussion is not going to go very far, but at six or seven or older, we are making him aware that we feel that there is a problem. Depending on his age, we can ask if he realizes that there is a problem. Very often he will. If the child is old enough to be uncomfortable and embarrassed about his uncontrollable reactions, he is going to be very happy to get help in dealing with the situation. It is astonishing how often a discussion will reveal that when something bothers us, it has been bothering the child no less.

Telling him, "Every time you scream it makes us crazy and we do not want you to do it anymore. So if you scream again, we are going to scream back so you will know what it sounds like," is not going to create any level of awareness. Saying instead, "You know, we notice that you've been screaming a lot when you get upset. Do you know why that is happening?" acknowledges that sometimes he does not know, sometimes he does. At times he will admit to it, other times he will not. The response depends on the age of the child and his level of self-awareness. The question itself can help bring that awareness level up a bit. We say to a child, "We love you and we are going to help you deal with this." As much as we want him to stop the objectionable behavior, he himself may want to stop it.

When the child is old enough, we can agree on some kind of a sign. "We are going to do something that is going to remind you about this discussion. When you scream, I'm going to say, 'Sorry — I do not understand what you're saying.' When I say those words, will you remember that what I mean is: 'Please try to get control'?" Very often, if the child is old enough, he will say yes. If the child is not old enough, then we do not bring him into this discussion, we just proceed in doing it. We agree between us that from now on, every time he starts screaming, he is going to be told in a very clear voice, "I'm sorry, I will not answer you when you are screaming." It does not matter if we have to say it two times, five times, eight times. We have a plan. We know what we are going to do. We say, "I'm sorry, I will not answer you when you are screaming. I cannot understand you when you are screaming."

Does it help? He is having a tantrum and is in the process of losing it. That is okay. Simply say, "When you're screaming like this I cannot have you in the room because no one can hear what anyone else is saying. Please leave the room." Sometimes we have to remove the child physically — not angrily, not hurting him — and say, "As soon as you stop screaming, you can come back into the room, and I will be happy to hear what you have to say."

Usually, when a child is in the midst of a tantrum and screaming, he is not ready for a discussion. But sometimes something may have happened, and this time it is not just an unreasonable response on his part. If we sense or know that there is a valid reason for the screaming, that this time he really is hurt, we have to be able to break our pattern when it is called for. Even though consistency is necessary, every rule has its exception. We cannot be so determined to stick to the rules that we end up hurting him or seeing him hurt. We have to be reasonable. If we see that something happened that was not within the normal pattern, we have to be able to change our planned response.

When a child is older, we can agree on a prearranged signal. "You know, when you start to scream, I'm going to pull my right ear," or perhaps, "When you scream, we are going to turn away from you," not because we want to hurt him, but to remind him that when he is screaming like that, we cannot react in any other way. If we are consistent and firm, our children will learn that they have to find another way to get across the message that they are disturbed about something, and they will.

◄ Appreciating Success

Remember that our definition of success in *chinuch* is the ability to help our child become the kind of person who strives on his own to reach his potential. Success in helping a child to overcome a bad habit is relative. If we think that success means that from now on and for the rest of his life this child is never going to scream, we might never attain it. If we have said, "I cannot understand what you're saying," or pulled our ears, or turned our backs numerous times, and he finally stops screaming because of something positive we did, we can consider that an immediate success. He stopped an undesirable action because of a decision that *he* made as a result of our disciplinary action. We did not hit, we did not punish; we *did* get the message across. That is success!

Once we recognize this, we can say quite calmly when he comes back into the room or quiets down, "You know, I'm really proud of you because you remembered and recognized that we had this discussion and you stopped screaming." It is going to dawn on him that he did it — yes, he really did it! Nothing breeds success like success; if we make him feel good about what he did, the next time he may react after the fourth signal, or the third, and perhaps soon after that the second signal, and two months later he may reach the point where he has actually stopped screaming. He may even have learned that, instead of yelling and screaming when he is upset, he can talk about it.

If *we* scream when we want our daughter to do something, she learns that if you really want to get something done, just scream. It works for Daddy. If she feels frustrated, unheard, misunderstood, or invalidated, she sees screaming as a viable tool to get what she thinks she needs at the time. In that case, of course, we must begin by not screaming ourselves. But even then, if for some reason she still feels that screaming is the only way her parents will stop, look, and listen to what she has to say, we must not give in to the screaming or she will know that it works. That is why we must be firm and consistent.

"I'm sorry, I will not answer you when you are screaming. I want to speak with you; I see something's bothering you. Please, say what it is quietly so that I can respond to you in a respectful manner."

Sooner or later she will learn that screaming is not getting her anywhere. She may keep yelling, "I want the purple cup, I want the purple cup," and you may have to say, "I will not answer you when you are screaming. Can you say that a different way so that I can answer you?" ten times, but eventually she will say, "I want the purple cup, please."

Does this mean she has to get the purple cup just because she asked for it properly? No, there will be times when the next part of the discussion will be: "Yes, I understand that you want the purple cup. I'm sorry, I cannot give you the purple cup right now." This is part of the learning process. Speaking properly does not mean that she is going to get whatever she wants. The purple cup may not be hers; the purple cup belongs to her sister who is using it now.

"Yes, I really would like to give you the purple cup. When your sister finishes using it perhaps she will share it with you."

Do not be surprised if the screaming starts all over again. But our reaction to it must be the same. Remember our goal is to teach her to stop screaming, not to give her everything she wants.

Now, we are fully aware that the difficulty with these solutions is implementing them. When one child is climbing on the table and another is under the table, one is on the potty, and another one is supposed to be getting into pajamas, and someone is hitting his brother in the next room, it is pretty hard to remember rules. When everyone is doing something different, and they each require our attention, it is not easy to stop and remember step number one, two, and three, and we will not always react properly. But if we think about this and work out the process in our mind beforehand, some of us will begin to improve 80 percent of the time. Even if we are successful only 70, 50, or even 20 percent of the time, the rule of thumb is: Everything we do that is an improvement on what we have been doing until now is beneficial for our children.

Of course there are going to be times and situations where no amount of psychology or reasoning is going to work. Even Rav Wolbe, who you will recall says that hitting in our generation (even small children) is tantamount to "placing stumbling blocks before the blind," says that sometimes a Band-Aid is necessary. He gives the example of a mother in a chaotic situation: it's okay for her to administer a light *potch* to get the family back in order. We all know that first aid is not professional surgery, yet it fills an important role in emergency situations.

This is obviously not a license to beat a child. We must follow the procedure we have discussed when we can, as much as we can, and as well as we can, for as many of our children as we can. We are not going to become *malachim*, perfect angels, overnight; we have our own challenges and our own negative *middos* to correct. Very often we are imitating our own parents' reactions and we do not even realize it. We most likely cannot guarantee that we will henceforth discipline our children with total clarity and exceptional self-control, but we can take these steps toward becoming better and more effective parents.

In summary, most forms of harsh discipline do not work. We know that some do not work because we have tried them again and again for years, and they have not yet solved any problems. So we know that something is wrong. Maybe there is a better way. That way is to choose one behavioral mannerism, plan what our responses to it should be, and then make sure that we respond that way as consistently as possible. If we choose too many things to work on at the same time, we will accomplish nothing. But if we choose only one habit or mannerism and work with it, we will find it easier to maintain our programmed reaction even in the midst of chaos. We will be able to stick to it because it makes sense and we will soon make progress.

It is extremely important to recognize the little, immediate successes, because that will not only prepare the way for us to take the next step, it will also give the child the self-confidence to move on to the next step. If this girl who has been screaming sees that when she reacted properly, even if we did not give her what she wanted, we listened, understood, and explained why we could not give it to her, she will be encouraged to react in a more reasonable way the next time.

Once we reach the point where this problem is almost solved — and it will happen — then we are ready to think about the next problem. With much *tefillah* and help from Above, each step we take will bring us closer to successful *chinuch* for our children.

Chapter Three
THE NATURE OF COMMUNICATION

Communicating, connecting with another individual, is the starting point in any relationship. It is also the medium through which we convey information and feelings. There are certain prerequisites for establishing communication, whether with children, spouses, friends, neighbors, politicians, or even country to country. These prerequisites are: recognition, trust, honesty, and respect.

A. Recognition: He Is a Person too

There is a well-known story that I heard from my *Rebbe* Rav Wolbe.

> *In a little shtetl near Warsaw lived a man who was very poor. He had no job, no food, and no hope. At his wit's end he sat saying Tehillim in the shul, when Boris, the circus owner, came over to him.*
>
> *"Yankel, I have a job for you."*
>
> *"What kind of job?"*
>
> *"My biggest attraction is a lion and a bear that go into a cage together and fight," said Boris, "and my bear just died. I need someone to dress up in a bear costume and fight with the lion for about five or ten minutes, for which I'll pay 100 zlotys."*

Yankel had never seen that kind of money. If worse comes to worst, he thought, the lion will eat me alive. The 100 zlotys will go to my wife and she will be able to feed the family. He put on the bear costume, made his final confession, and — terrified, clammy, and sweating — was shoved into the cage.

At the other end of the cage a door opened and a lion entered. Yankel edged forward, the lion came closer, Yankel was scared stiff ... but he had a job to do. He took another step and another. Suddenly he found himself face-to-face with the lion. Frightened beyond words, he cried out, "Shema Yisrael Hashem Elokeinu, Hashem Echad!" Whereupon the lion responded, "Baruch Shem Kevod Malchuso le'olam va'ed."

We regard our children as if we are the bear and they are the lion. We are a little nervous about getting through to them because they are younger, less knowledgeable, and less experienced than we are. Children are not always willing to listen; their emotions run away with them, and they do not know how to voice their needs. How do you establish lines of communication with someone who is going to throw a temper tantrum and run out of the room as soon as he becomes upset? You fear you will be misunderstood. As in the story above, if we say, "*Shema Yisrael Hashem Elokeinu ...,*" and just begin to speak, we will find that we are talking to another real person, an individual who can speak and answer.

Our children have thoughts and feelings; they have things they want to say and things they are afraid to say because they do not know how we are going to react. They are real people, and the first step in communicating with them is to recognize them as such.

◆§ Our Service-Oriented Society

We live in a service-oriented society, in which we have high expectations of others. We go to the bank, and the teller is supposed to look up at us and smile and say, "Yes, how can I help you?" She is supposed to process the checks quickly, count out the cash immediately, and smile as we walk away after three minutes. The grocer is supposed to have what we need on the shelves, and the man who sells fruits and vegetables is supposed to have the right variety of produce in all seasons, of whatever it is that we want, at prices that we can pay. That is why they are there, and if they do not deliver, we get upset, because in a service-oriented society we expect service for our money. If we call Panasonic because their product is not working, we expect the person on the other end to respond immediately and to our satisfaction.

The fact is, however, that "society" is a facade, because the bank teller, the vegetable man, and the grocer are individuals, each with his own life and problems. Sometimes the teller seems to be in another world. She counted our money and made three errors; her mind is obviously not on the transaction. She is thinking about the fact that her husband is in the hospital and she has to arrange for care of her children when they get back from school. We do not want to deal with her as a person, because this is a service-oriented society and we do not care what her problem is.

We are paying and we want to be served. We become so firmly fixed in this mind-set that we begin to expect instant fulfillment of our needs. When the grocer does not have what we need, or the vegetable man has no carrots, we do not even imagine that someone in his family may be sick. We do not consider that maybe he has personal difficulties to contend with, because it does not interest us. We need the carrots *now*, because we need to make the soup for our Shabbos guests, and nothing else matters.

Unfortunately, these expectations permeate our closest relationships. Our husbands are *supposed* to provide us with certain things. Our wives are *expected* to provide us with certain services. And we all know what children are for. They are supposed to listen to us, do what we say, and of course provide us with *nachas*, joy, and pride. We create an image of what the other person is supposed to be like, and we really do not see that person as he is. He is not a person, he is "a provider of ..." Children see parents as providers, and parents see children in the role we have created for them. When we look at our children in that way, we are not seeing them as people, just as we do not see salespeople when we walk into a store. We give our plastic smile, the salesperson gives his plastic smile, and at no point is there real *communication.*

"Hello, how's everything?"

"*Baruch Hashem,* fine, how's everything by you?"

"Oh wonderful, thanks."

Almost nobody really cares how you are feeling, or what is happening in your life. We are not there to communicate; we are there to receive service. Imagine if you would begin telling the storekeeper what is going on in your life.

"Well, this morning my husband was not feeling well, and Dovi did not want to go to school. I really do not know what to do about my washing machine ..."

"Let's get on with the shopping! Do you want to buy anything?"

This attitude, unfortunately, takes over in many other areas of our lives, even when we do want to communicate; but if we are not going to recognize the other person's individuality, it is a hopeless task. As parents, we have to realize that our children are individuals with thoughts and feelings. We have expectations: that they will get up on time and go to school, study well, get good grades, come home exactly on time, have only the right friends, not fight with their siblings, and not be *chutzpadik* to the *rebbe* or to us. However, we must recognize that our children are people who are dealing with difficult situations and are feeling strong emotions. They are working through some things, running away from others, and trying to avoid unpleasant situations. In other words, they are real people, just like us. Therefore step number one is recognition.

B. Trust

True communication is based on dialogue, and dialogue is based on trust. Each side has to trust that the other side is willing to listen. Unless there is this underlying trust in the desire for dialogue, you cannot get two people to talk about what really matters. It is no great feat to speak with people on a superficial level, and we often do so, but we are not truly connecting with them. Parents frequently describe their children to me as "closed, not willing to talk to anyone." In many cases, I have sat with such a child for as little as fifteen minutes and learned all about what is going on in his life.

"Who told you that?" the parents ask later.

"Your son."

"But he is so closed."

Sure he is closed, when he feels that no one will really listen to him. Then he will not say anything. But most people, when they feel that you are genuinely interested in hearing what they have to say, do not stop talking. Even so-called "closed" people will speak to someone they trust, someone whom they believe is interested in what they have to say.

There are three methods of talking, and only one of them is effective: talking *to* someone, talking *at* someone, and talking *with* someone. Talking *to* someone means that you are speaking, but he is not necessarily hearing you. Talking *at* someone means that you are getting something off your chest and it makes no difference to you whether the other person hears it or not, accepts it or not. When we are angry and we yell, or go off on a long-winded reprimand, we are often talking *at* people. This basically means that what I am saying is necessary for me to express, and it almost, but not quite, wouldn't make any difference if there were no one to hear it. Talking *with* someone means that you are conducting a dialogue, a two-way conversation, which implies that both people understand and acknowledge what the other one feels.

One of the *rebbe*s in our yeshivah called me up after having a conversation with a boy who was going through a difficult time. The *rebbe* was very excited.

> *"I just had a great talk with this kid for forty-five minutes. We went through everything, and he really understood the problem."*

"Was it a discussion?" I asked.

"Oh, yes. For forty-five minutes we had a discussion."

"Who did the talking?"

"Well, uh, mostly me."

"How many words did the boy say in the course of the conversation?"

"Well, a few here and there."

"So, how do you know that it went well?"

"What do you mean? You could see it in his eyes. He was with me, I could feel it."

"Okay."

The next day I called the boy over and said, "I heard you had a great conversation yesterday with your rebbe."

"Ah, it was nothing."

"Nothing?" I asked. "But did you understand what he wanted? Did you accept what he had to say?"

"No way!"

"But he said it was a good conversation."

"Yeah, sure," the boy said, looking away. "HE had a lot to say."

Now, this *rebbe* was basically a good *mechanech*, but he, like many of us, was so carried away with what he had to say that he never developed a basis for the conversation he wanted to have. It is only too easy to have a very long, involved "discussion" that is almost completely one-sided.

What happened? The boy was nodding his head and looking at the *rebbe*, of course. Children learn at a very early age to put their heads down in shame when it is the appropriate response, to look at us with big doe eyes when they want to seem innocent, to nod or shake their heads on cue, and to say yes and no at appropriate intervals.

> *A close friend of mine came home to Cincinnati from yeshivah one Pesach. As there were not many people in the Orthodox shul there, he immediately noticed a Russian couple who had just joined the kehillah. My friend knew three words in their language: yes, no, and hello.*

Right after davening he walked up to the couple and said hello in Russian. They were very excited and started speaking to him in rapid-fire Russian. Following their head and eye movements, he nodded and smiled agreeably as they spoke. For ten minutes he followed their conversation with yeses and nos, and they were 1,000 percent convinced that he understood every word. As they were winding down, he smiled and started backing away.

The woman saw that he was ready to go and blurted out in very heavily accented English, "Uh, ah, you, you vill, you vill like her!" He quickly said good-bye and made sure not to encounter them again.

Communication! Children are masters of this trick of pseudo-communication. They know how they are expected to react to certain conversations and "speeches," while inside they are really saying, "Enough already ... when is she going to be finished? ... Good! She is finished now ... Oh wait, I have to say that I'll never do it again." That said, they walk out, and we think we have reached them, but nothing was actually communicated. Dialogue requires trust.

What shall we do, however, when we have to communicate without any certainty that trust exists? (We are not referring here to instances of polite social chatter that does not signify interest on either side.) In a situation where there is not yet trust, we need to build it.

◄՝ *Building Trust*

How shall we build a basis of trust? A letter is a wonderful tool for beginning to communicate, depending of course on the age of the respondent. When we have to talk about something that is important to us, our nerves or our emotions can get in the way. Perhaps past confrontations ended dismally. A warm, frank letter or short note that expresses a desire to work things out honestly, to discuss something in a loving way, can be very effective.

A letter can be meaningful; it can change a person's outlook. A spoken conversation can take off in a hundred different directions after we have said the first sentence. It is easier to keep the written word on track. In a written note, you can say, "I find it difficult at this point to tell you the things I want to say, and therefore I am writing a letter. I want you to know how I feel about you and about certain things with which we have to deal. I would love to discuss this with you, and maybe sometime in the near future we will. I do not want to pressure you, but I want you to know that I am ready to talk to you. I look forward to the opportunity to have a good conversation ..."

Of course the content of the letter depends on the age of the child, the situation, and the subject. A child may read it once and say, "Nah, he does not mean it," but he will read it again and again — ten, twenty, or thirty times. In a conversation, repetition is boring, but a letter conveys the same openness, the same love, each time it is read, and it is a good way to open the dialogue you need to have.

Another excellent method for establishing trust is using a third party, someone with whom your child is comfortable, whom he likes, and whom he perceives as non-threatening.

"You know, I was speaking to your mother [or father]. She really wants to talk with you about something, but she is as nervous to talk about it as you are." Or, "You know, worrying about this situation is not accomplishing anything. Why don't you talk to your parents about it?"

"Are you kidding? Talk to my parents? Do you know what they are going to say if I tell them this?"

"Would you like me to say something first? I could tell them that you want to talk to them about it."

Children basically want to talk to their parents. They are anxious about communicating because they lack trust in the relationship and they are afraid of their parents' reactions. It can be much easier when a third party opens the lines of communication. We have to believe that our children want to speak with us, and we must help them believe that we want to speak with them. If for some reason trust does not exist, we have to work hard to start from scratch to build it up. For many of us it will just be a matter of not destroying that which is already in place.

C. Honesty

Rav Noach Weinberg, a master communicator and *mechanech*, once told me that he can deal with any kind of person except a liar. "With liars, you never know where you are. You do not know whether they really accept what you say or not." And because they are not truthful, when we tell them the truth they may not recognize it. How do our children know that we are honest? They know! We absolutely must be honest about our shortcomings, about what we know and what we do not know. Who among us has not had a teacher who pretended to know everything, but never knew how to say, "I do not know." We respect a person who can say, "I do not know."

> *About ten years ago, I went with three very respected Roshei Yeshivah to speak with Harav Eliezer Menachem Shach about a new concept in education which, though somewhat controversial, seemed to us very important. When we presented the problem and a possible solution, he initially said, "I do not know."*
>
> *"I'm sorry," I said to him, "but the Rosh Yeshivah cannot say 'I do not know.' I can say it. That is why I came here. But the Rosh Yeshivah has to know, because I cannot do anything if he does not agree."*
>
> *"No," he answered. "If you believe that this is the solution to the problem, you can go ahead and do it. But if you are asking me if this is the solution, I do not know."*
>
> *"But if the Rosh Yeshivah does not know, how can I know?"*
>
> *"Ah," said Rav Shach, "you have a problem. I understand that. You need me to say that I know so that you can open this program. But let me tell you my problem with that.*
>
> *"One day I'm going to go up to Shamayim, and Hashem is going to ask me, 'Why did you say all the things that you said?' And I'm going to answer, 'I said*

*what I thought was the truth. This is what I understood,
this is what I believe. So I said what I knew to be correct.'
But if you want me to say something that I do not know
just because you need me to say it, what am I going to
do when I get to Shamayim? What am I going to tell the
Ribbono shel Olam? That I did not know when I said I
know, but I had to say that I knew because somebody
needed me to say so?"*

*He said all this in Yiddish. I'm making it a little more col-
loquial, but it was very clear, and that was the message.*

Although I always had great respect for this *gadol hador*,
this great man, this exchange broadened my entire perspective on honesty. In that moment I recognized that every single
thing that this *gadol* says he knows to be true, because
otherwise he would not have said it. When he went up to
Shamayim, and *HaKadosh Baruch Hu* made a *cheshbon*
with him, he surely did not have to be concerned about
any word he had ever spoken. He never, ever said anything
regarding matters about which he was not 100 percent sure
of himself. The validity of his spoken word was obviously on
a completely different level from that of the ordinary person.
This *gadol* was honest to the point where he could say, "I
know that you need me to say something that can make a
difference to people's lives in *klal Yisrael*. It may actually help
people, but since I honestly do not know that it is the solution, I can say nothing." From this meeting I learned the real
meaning of honesty.

We discussed the new educational concept further, and
eventually the Rav made a decision that the school should
be opened.

Parents and teachers often do not know how to say, "I do
not know," or "I'm sorry," or "I made a mistake." They think
that if they say any of those things they are lowering themselves to the child's level. Adults fear that admitting ignorance
or guilt might create the misconception that children are their
equals, or that the child will think that most of the decisions
made by the adult will be invalid. But that is not the way it
works. The study of human dynamics has shown that the

people who can say, "I'm sorry," are those who are trusted, proving such fears unfounded. Just as we respect them and are willing to hear and trust what they have to say, they will accept our word according to the level of our honesty. If we cannot admit to our own shortcomings, if our children never hear us say, "I'm sorry, I made a mistake," they eventually lose confidence in our judgment.

"Yeah, they are always right, no matter what I say. There is no point in discussing anything with them, because they disagree with me right away and never listen to my side." If a child thinks that way, he sees no reason for conversation, and we have severed the lines of communication.

Our children have to know that we can admit our mistakes. They will not lose respect for us. On the contrary, children respect honesty, and if they find it in us it will be easier for them to develop honesty themselves. We should be able to say, "You know, I really messed up yesterday when I scolded you. I was so tired that instead of answering your question, I just started yelling at you for the way your room looks, and I'm sorry. Let's start over again." The child then looks at you and says, "Is that really my parent?" and of course he is willing, even eager, to reopen the conversation.

But all too often we think that there is no recourse. We messed up again; the subject is closed. We will wait for the next mistake. That is not good. We should be able to stop and say to the child, "Wait, come back here. I'm sorry. I'm a tired human being and I reacted incorrectly. Let's start all over again."

It is a breath of fresh air for a child to hear, "You know, I'm thinking about how hard it is for you to talk about this thing that happened in school. I remember when something like that happened to me, how hard it was for me to talk to my parents, because I was afraid of how they would react."

"You went to school?" or "But when you went to school, you were always a perfect student; didn't you always get straight *alefs*?"

I made it my business to show one of my children who is not an *alef* student my second- and third-grade report cards, which are nothing to write home about. My mother saved all our report cards, and all the *gimmels, beis* minuses, and *dalets* are still there in black and white. I can accept that this is who I was in second and third grade, and I cannot complain if my child is the same.

"You know," I said, "I also did not always do so well in school, and it does not mean anything. If you keep trying and this is as far as you can go, that is just fine. If you are *not* trying, it is a problem." This is a basis for conversation. I have to be willing to show my child that a bad report card is not the end of the world. I can encourage him. If he keeps on trying, his grades could indeed change.

◄ఢ *Apologizing*

If you bump into someone and say, "What is the matter with you?" he will invariably turn around angrily and retort, "What is the matter with *you*?" But if you bump into someone and say, "Oh, I'm sorry, excuse me," the response will be entirely different. People recognize when you are sincere and they respond accordingly. When you are angry and screaming at a person, he becomes angry and screams back. When you are open, apologetic, and sympathetic, you allow him to be the same. That is reciprocity in communication.

It is no different with our children. If we open up a one-way conversation, we will be talking to ourselves. If, however, we begin in a way that indicates that we are being honest and that we are willing to discuss a problem with them, we will be helping them to handle themselves. It is helpful to plan in advance how we are going to deal with a particular situation; this way the proper reactions will become ingrained in us.

> *In a yeshivah where I was the principal, there was a boy who made a habit of breaking rules. He would frequently go into the computer workshop when he should not have been there. At one point something went wrong*

with the network system in the workshop, and we were 99.99 percent sure that he was the culprit. After all, we had warned him about this and tried to make him understand that this was really a line that could not be crossed. So this was the straw that broke the camel's back. All the computer classes had to be canceled until we could get the system replaced or fixed.

We called his parents and said, "Please come and take your son home for a while. If he cannot accept limits and boundaries, we cannot have him in the yeshivah anymore. We are sorry. Please come and pick him up."

The boy was very angry and upset. He insisted that he had not done it, but we did not believe him. The whole yeshivah knew what had transpired because he was running around pleading with everybody, "I did not do it, I did not do it. Who did it? I'm getting thrown out." About ten minutes before his father arrived, another student came into my office and said, "I understand that so and so is being thrown out. It was me, I did it."

When the father arrived, I called everybody into the beis midrash — the students, the rebbes, and the father. Now, this boy was definitely a troublemaker. Even if he had not broken into the computer room or damaged the system that time, he deserved to be sent home for a few days. However, he was being suspended on grounds that were absolutely false. I looked at all the students and said, "My friends, Emes is what we live for and it is what our lives are all about. I made a mistake, and I want to apologize to this young man for what I did because I did not trust him. It is true that the reason I did not believe him this time is that so many times in the past things were not as he presented them. But this time it was my mistake. And since it was my mistake, I can only say to him, 'You are invited to stay on in the yeshivah, and we are sorry we troubled your father to come here.'" I sent the boys back to class and the father on his way, and the crisis was over.

The number of boys who came forth to discuss things openly after that incident was unbelievable. Suddenly there was a reaffirmation of a feeling among the boys *that they did not have to be afraid to open a discussion, because they knew it would be dealt with honestly. Their feeling was: "Maybe they'll trust me. After all, if the rebbe said he made a mistake, I can say that I also made a mistake."*

Of course, a rare boy or two took advantage of the incident: "Oh, by the way, remember that time the *rebbe* said he made a mistake? Well, the *rebbe's* making a mistake again." Each child had to be dealt with on a different level, and the desired response was not always instantaneous. Some students came to talk long after an incident had occurred. In most cases, however, students came forward to discuss something they had done wrong, felt bad about, wanted to correct, or about which they felt I had misjudged them. I believe that these approaches to me were directly connected with the time I publicly admitted my error. This happened years ago, and it became part of yeshivah tradition. Even boys who were not in the school then knew about it, because honesty and frankness and willingness to recognize shortcomings is such an important aspect of communication that it becomes a part of one's reputation. Students know to whom they can go, with whom they can talk, who is not going to automatically take one side without seeing the other. They know they can go to someone who has a proven track record of recognizing his own shortcomings, who they know can say, "I'm sorry, I made a mistake."

D. Respect

The final prerequisite for workable and ongoing communication is respect, what we call in Hebrew *kavod.*

Kavod is such a basic human need that Rav Yechezkel Levenstein used to say that if you find two street cleaners arguing about whose broom is better, do not be surprised. Street cleaners are also people and have to feel that they have value. If this value is going to be judged by whose broom is better, then that is what they are going to argue and bicker about.

Children do it all the time. "My father can lift three buildings and two houses and a car all at once." A child has to feel that he has the respect of others. Children need to be respected for who and what they are, and what they have.

Rav Chatzkel also said that if *techiyas hameisim* would happen in the middle of a funeral, the *niftar* would jump up immediately to see who came and who did not come to his funeral. *Kavod* is an intrinsic need and we ignore it at our peril. If our children feel that we do not respect them, if they feel that we look down on them, that we perceive them as dishonest, non-entities, or otherwise irrelevant, even though they already feel that way about themselves, they cannot communicate with us. They can only talk to someone who recognizes that they have a right to think, feel, and speak independently.

We can demand that when children have something to say, they say it properly, but we must give them the right to express themselves. We must never assume that they have no right to say what they feel or think. When they say something that is disrespectful, we have to think about it and understand why. This does not mean that we have to allow disrespectful speech. But we should try to understand from where this behavior is coming.

> *Rav Wolbe once told me that in Yeshivah X, someone wrote, "Hamashgiach chamor — the mashgiach is a mule," on the board. After much detective work they found out who had written it, and expelled the boy from the yeshivah. "And," Rav Wolbe said, "that proved that the boy was right."*
>
> *Obviously something was troubling the boy deeply, about which he had been wanting and needing to talk. His problem was not being acknowledged; he felt that he was not being given the minimum amount of respect he needed in order to communicate what he felt. He wrote on the board in frustration, avoiding a direct confrontation with the mashgiach and others in charge.*
>
> *For all the energy the mashgiach expended in discreetly finding the culprit, he should have expended the same*

amount of energy in finding out what was bothering this boy and helped him. Was he hurt in some way, ignored, or just desperately seeking attention?

When our children are disrespectful, we should not allow it, but we must recognize that they themselves do not feel respected. A healthy child will rarely feel comfortable speaking improperly to someone he feels respects him. Children have the right to think about things that are important to them and to speak freely about those things, but it is not true that a child has the right to say everything he is thinking.

Some time ago, a boy in school had a key to a room that he should not have had. I went to him and said, "Please give me the school keys that you have." He gave me two less important keys that I hadn't known he had and walked away. The next day I called him over and said, "Okay, now give me the key that I asked for." He began to protest and I said firmly, "No games, just give it to me." He realized that I knew that he really had it, and he turned it over.

An hour later he came over to me and asked, "How did the Rav know that I had it?"

"Excuse me! How did I know that you had it? Shouldn't I be asking you where you got the key?"

He really wanted to know how I found out. How could I have known? He had never used it when I was around. It bothered him enough to ask me about it. But it was a question that was totally out of place.

"I'm sorry, young man. You are not the one who should be asking me this question. If anyone should be asking questions now, it is I."

I did not feel that we could leave it at that. When a situation arises in a family, there is a spouse, an older brother, or a friend to turn to for help. Because this happened in school, I went over to one of the other rebbeim and asked him to speak to the boy about my reaction, and find out whether he understood what was wrong. The rebbe spoke to the student reasonably and ascertained that the boy understood. In fact, he came to me the next day and said, "I want to say I'm sorry for asking. It was out of place."

A process of *chinuch* occurred here. The boy said what was on his mind, but I did not agree that he had the right to say it. At the same time, I also did not disregard the fact that he had strong feelings that he needed to express. But he had to learn that his feelings were out of place. *Who is supposed to be angry now, you or I? You have done something wrong and you are coming to question me?* He is not going to see how incongruous his reaction was by being scolded; it needed to be explained. When it was presented in a way that he could understand, he was able to come forward and say, "I'm sorry, I made a mistake."

◄ᶜ *Listening Carefully*

How do children, or anyone else, know that they are respected? The most important rule for showing respect to someone is listening to him and letting him speak. Do we listen when our children say things? Our child begins to tell us about something that happened in school. We care to a certain extent but we are tired. Do we listen when our child is talking and do we hear him out? Or, when he is halfway through do we interrupt and say, "I'm busy now" or, "Okay, okay, I understand, now go and get into pajamas." Or even ... "What! That is what you did? How many times did I tell you ..."

In coming to us to tell us about something that has happened, our child is sharing an experience. He is communicating, and if we do not respect him enough to hear him out, we cut the lines of communication. If he is talking about it, it is important to him. Perhaps he was finally commended for something, or perhaps he was hurt. Maybe he just wants to share an experience with someone he loves whom he hopes will be interested in hearing about it.

Listening is a marvelous tool in *chinuch*. When a parent tells me it is very hard to have a conversation with his son because he does not talk, then I know I can usually ask that parent how much he listens. Sure, you often come home tired after a long day, and that is precisely the time that one of the kids comes to you and begins to tell you about his day. "Yeah, yeah," you say, and continue whatever it is you have begun to do. "Mm, hmm," and you keep doing something else. At some point the child just walks away in defeat, and you do not even realize that he stopped in the middle of a conversation. He was trying to say something, saw that you were not interested in listening, so he gave up.

This behavior damages our own ability to communicate later when we are ready. We cannot understand why he is not paying any attention when we are trying to talk to him. "Okay, okay, Imma, right, right, okay I just have to go and ..."

"Wait, I'm talking to you."

"Oh yeah, okay, sure ..."

He is only mirroring our behavior.

Everyone needs to be listened to, not only children. If we listen to them, they will learn to listen to us. If you ask, "How are you?" and he says, "Fine," the conversation is over, because he knows as well as you do that the "how are you" is plastic, not real. But if you say, "You know, you do not look so well, is something bothering you?" and the child needs someone to talk to, he will tell you what is wrong. Sometimes he will tell you more than you want to hear, but he senses that at that moment you are ready to listen. People, especially children, really do need someone to hear them.

If you are already a listener, then you know that people will tell you everything. People can recognize someone who is ready to accept, understand, and empathize with others, and they tend to open up to them. If our children think that we are interested in what they have to say, they will speak to us. A child who does not have listening parents will look for this trait in friends with whom he can speak freely about his thoughts and feelings. Very often we do not like these friends, but we cannot control the relationship because they are listeners — they listen without interrupting, arguing, criticizing, or condemning. Your child's best friend may be the person who is last on your list of recommended friends, but his friendship is prized because he listens the best and is the least judgmental.

> *I was pleasantly startled one day when I asked a boy who applied to the yeshivah what he did in his free time.*
> *"Well, I like to play on the computer and read, and I like to talk with my father."*
> *"I would like to meet your father," I replied. I did, and he is indeed a wonderful individual, a very unusual person.*

We accepted the boy into the yeshivah. We knew that we could work with him because of that relationship.

⤚₂ *Asking Questions*

Asking a question means that you have heard what the child has said. Otherwise he does not know if you really listened. The query should not sound as if it is leading to condemnation or judgment. It should just be an open-ended question that shows real interest. You are not simply hearing it, nodding your head, and continuing to peel the carrots.

Listening is an art, and asking questions is a tool. To this day I can hear a *tante* of mine asking me questions: "And what do you do about this? What do you think about that?" And I always told her! We parents have to make ourselves available like my *tante* so that our children really have someone to talk to; it will create a most special bond.

Sometimes this is difficult because we feel obliged to react negatively to anything that is not 100 percent positive. There is an old comedy routine about a child burning down the house. While his father is screaming, "What are you doing?" his grandfather is saying, "Oh, what a good fire — just look how straight he made it." The grandparent obviously does not feel responsibility like a parent does. He can enjoy the *nachas*, the satisfaction. He thinks that the child is wonderful, while the parents are struggling to deal with the child's behavior.

If we are critical, or think we have to be critical of every-thing our children tell us, we lose a great opportunity. Of course, as parents building relationships with our children, we often do have to be judgmental. As responsible parents we sometimes have to react to things they tell us, but there is a right way and a wrong way to criticize, which we will further discuss in a subsequent chapter. We most certainly do not want our obligation to listen to jeopardize our responsibility as parents.

Chapter Four

EFFECTIVE COMMUNICATION

I n the course of our communication with all sorts of individuals, young and old, we become more and more aware of our own communication skills or lack thereof. Most of the time we know how other people are going to react when we criticize them: They are going to be defensive and perhaps counterattack. We know it, yet we criticize anyway.

When something is very important to us, we seem to know intuitively the best way to get the message across. For example, if you want to ask your boss for a raise, you would never just walk into his office and make brusque demands: "Listen, it has been a year and a half since you gave me a raise. I want a raise now, and if you do not give it to me, I'm going to be very upset. Not only is it coming to me, but I think you should have offered it by now and not made me come to you to ask for it."

You know that your chances of getting the raise are not the greatest, so you would probably first ask for an appointment and then say, "I have been working here for a long time and I feel like an integral part of this firm. I hope that you feel comfortable with me as well. As you know, the cost of living has been going up for some time now, and I feel that my salary has not kept pace with it. If you can manage it, now would really be a great time for a raise."

When we confront the boss, we know the best way to speak. But when we deal with family members, we tend to revert to the service-oriented mentality. We have expectations. We want them to produce results without delay. But when we do not think about our approach in advance, we end up paying for it, because the other party neither listens, accepts, nor understands our views. And we know this is going to be the reaction before we even open our mouths! We know that if we give our spouses a lecture, we get nowhere, but if we use our thought processes and tune into their sensitivities, we can get almost anything we want. If we think about what we want to accomplish, we can then decide how to approach the problem. If we do not initiate a thought process and everything just flows from our emotions, obviously our communication is not going to be successful.

◄₹ Understanding

Listening is only half the communication process. We need to understand what the other person is saying. When we listen in order to understand what is being said, our response will be more appropriate. Sometimes children are so excited that they themselves do not understand what they are saying. The child runs in and shouts, "You know what happened?" and out pours a torrent of words. He wants to say so many things at once that he is not even sure what he wants from us at that moment.

If we want to understand what he is saying, we can stop him and say, "Just a second. I heard you say something about a ball. I heard you say something about your friend. I'm sorry, I do not quite understand what you are trying to say." Our goal is to reach the level where our children will speak to us about those things that they are thinking about or that are bothering them. When they do, reiterate what they say. Repeating what a child says assures him that you have heard him and that you understand what is bothering him. Normally we do not even let him finish what he is trying to say before we interrupt and chide, "What? You've been fighting again?" Listen to your child, understand what is bothering him, and rephrase it for him. "Are you trying to tell me that ..." or "Did you say that this boy just came and hit you and the *rebbe* saw and did nothing about it?" Often when we repeat what the child said, we find out that we are responding in error.

"No, that's not what I said."

"Ah, so what did you say?" We listen and repeat again until he tells us that we have it right. Now you can respond.

◄≋ *Empathy*

Understand what the child is telling you; show empathy. Let him see that you care.

"That must really have hurt. That must have bothered you terribly. Somebody just came over and hit you? That's so mean, that's so cruel. I do not know why anybody would do something like that."

"Well, the truth is I kicked him in the shins first!"

If we first accuse, "Well, why were you fighting again?" we know what reaction to expect. "Oh, you always say I'm wrong, I'm never right, I cannot talk to you!"

Try a different tactic. "That must have hurt terribly. Just like that he walked over and hit you? That's mean. I think we should call the *rebbe* and tell him what happened."

"Wait, wait, wait! Before you call the *rebbe*, let me tell you the rest of the story!" We have opened up lines of communication. Now there is a possibility that the conversation will continue.

Building lines of communication is a constant process. That cannot be stressed enough. Nothing is going to "work" every time we speak to every child in every situation, but the more we work on our communication skills, the better we will become at it. Of course we all have instinctive reactions and emotional outbursts to contend with, but we have to try to learn to live with them.

Now, when *we* want to speak to our children and want them to listen to *us*, there are different methods to employ. Some of these are actually very simple and can easily become second nature. We used the example of saying to a child, "If you do not sit down I'm not going to give you the soda" versus, "If you sit down I can give you a soda." The more we think about this and work on it, the more often it will succeed, until eventually it will become part of our nature and basic skills.

I often compare communication between people to institutional food. When I was the principal of a high school with a dormitory, the boys complained to me about the food. My administrator said, "Our food is the best — just look at the weekly menu." I said, "If you really want to know how the school is feeding our children, walk into the lunchroom ten minutes after lunch is over. If all the food is still on the trays, it does not matter how good the menu sounds. If the children eat what is on their plates, the food is good." It is very easy for an administrator to say, "Listen, we are providing very good food, we are spending X amount of money, everything's fine." If the children aren't eating it, the money is wasted.

This likewise applies to communication. We can say everything we think is right and everything we want the other person to hear. If the child does not understand it or accept it, the conversation is pointless. There are times, of course, when we have to repeat something many times before it is understood and accepted, and sometimes we have to say things just because we want the child to know how we feel. But when we want to have a discussion, we cannot assume that just because we said it, it was accepted. We might have expressed our viewpoint, but the child may not necessarily have internalized it. We cannot assume that from now on he will think about the issue from our standpoint.

We therefore have to be able to clarify, not only what they are saying to us, but also what we say to them. Sometimes it may be effective to continue the conversation by having them repeat what they heard us say. It is important not to challenge them or put them on the defensive, but to require the same thing of ourselves as we do of them.

"You know what? Let me just make sure I understand what you meant. What you were saying is A, B, C, D. Is that right?"

"Yes."

"Now, do you know what I was saying? Tell me what you heard."

Obviously we do not want to ask them to repeat what we have said too often in a conversation because that can be a bit condescending, as if we are questioning the child's intelligence. Having occasionally counseled couples on *shalom bayis* issues, I have learned that an effective tool is to ask each side what he or she thinks the other party says is the problem. When we have to put ourselves into the other person's mind-set, we can better understand him. This principle holds true when dealing with children.

If we can have a discussion with our child and then switch sides, the child will begin to understand from where we are coming, and we will get an insight into the workings of his mind. Reversing roles is an effective tool on all levels of communication when there is no initial agreement. You can say, "Let's see if we really understand one another. You take my side of the argument and I'll take yours. Maybe we can work it out that way."

◄≀ The Inefficacy of Screaming

Unfortunately, communication in the home often translates into asserting authority by raising our voices and, yes, screaming. If we could see ourselves in a mirror when we are screaming, we would see how ridiculous we look. Take, for example, the familiar experience of putting kids to bed. After the third "Cover me," the second drink, and the fourth "Mommy, I have to go to the bathroom," we go into their rooms and holler, "I said, 'Go to sleep!'" and they start giggling. We do not understand why they are laughing so we threaten them, and they laugh even harder, which is when we really hit the roof.

"You're laughing? You think this is funny? Well, I'll show you how funny it is!" Instead of frightening them into obedience, which is what we were hoping to accomplish, we make them laugh even harder. The angrier we get, you see, the more ridiculous we look. When we get angry, the children know that they now have taken charge of the situation. Once they get us going, once they make us lose our tempers, they are in control.

Here is another point to consider when you think becoming angry is a solution, and this is universal. I have had adolescents say to me on different occasions and in different countries, "If I can get my parents angry, I have gotten back at them."

"What do you mean you've gotten back at them? What did you do?"

"Well, they try to take control of me and I get them back. That makes me feel good."

What does that mean? The teenagers could not always articulate their reasons, but they meant that "getting back" puts them in control. Once we start screaming, kids can provoke us until we totally lose ourselves. They may stop at that point and it is time to stop the game, but we have not accomplished a thing.

Yelling, therefore, means that we are neither in control of them nor of ourselves, and the situation is totally out of control. We are being reverse role models — and this is a very common reaction. The children are screaming and we want them to stop screaming, so we scream louder. That does not teach anyone how to communicate. When we are upset at our children, whether they did not go to *daven* or did not do their homework or came home later than they were supposed to, we "give it" to them. We lace into them. They stand there and basically wait for us to finish yelling. Some deal with it by crying, some bow their heads and listen in dejected silence, others scream and get angry in turn.

Very rarely will a child look at you and say, "You know what, Ma? You're right. I feel bad. I'm sorry." Why not? We have told them in no uncertain terms that their behavior is totally unacceptable. It is not allowed, we have warned them three times, and therefore they are not permitted to leave their room for the next three days. Why don't they just turn around and apologize? Because when we speak in anger, we arouse anger, hurt, and shame in them without giving them any message beyond the anger.

Yelling or screaming is totally ineffective. It does not work. If it seems as though it is effective because we have scared them into stopping for a moment, we must know that we have not taught them anything. We have not provided them with tools and have given them nothing to help them become better people, nothing to teach them a lesson they can understand and think about and maybe remember the next time.

How should we respond when they're screaming? Anyone who has ever tried this knows it is worth the attempt: When everybody is screaming, you whisper. Think about it. When you walk into a room where everyone is whispering, you cannot bring yourself to speak loudly. We have all experienced that. Conversely, it is natural to scream when everyone else is screaming. To reverse the process, you have to initiate a change in the volume. Try it. When everyone is screaming, try to speak calmly and quietly.

"You know, I really do not understand a word you're saying. I'm sorry. I do not understand. What? I cannot understand. Can you say that a different way?" Over and over, three times, five times, eight times. A child will usually struggle to stop, because he realizes that if he really wants you to hear what he has to say, he has no choice. This is the same principle we recommend for good listening. "I'm sorry, no one can listen to what you are saying. Go out of the room, and when you stop screaming you are welcome to come back. We'll be able to have a conversation and I'll hear what you have to say."

We can each choose the way to do this that best suits our personality. We can do it mildly or firmly. We have to use the tools that we, as individuals, find most effective. Those of us who are very straightforward, easygoing, and open can react in one way, while those who are more closed, who find it difficult to express feelings, will have to find another way. The main thing is to think before you react.

It is ironic, but we often know what children are going to answer before we chastise them. We know they are going to react negatively, yet we criticize them in the wrong way time after time, and we are always surprised that they do not answer us with respect. Raising one's voice, whether to a spouse or a child, is not effective because no one wants to be screamed at. It is annoying at best, hurtful and embarrassing at worst. Screaming is practically never truly effective.

✺ Using Silence as a Tool

There is another excellent tool to use in building the basis for communication. It is called silence. With silence, we can often communicate more than with a thousand words. We can just look at the culprit and not say anything. You might ask, "What good does that do?" But just the *look* communicates to a child that something is wrong. Now he has to deal with it and figure out what he is going to say or do. This story is an extreme case, but it will illustrate the point.

> We had a boy in our school who had repeatedly been told that he was not allowed to leave the school premises without permission. One day, as I was driving toward the school campus, I saw him in the distance. He was off campus in a place he should not have been. At that same moment, he saw me and automatically ducked down so I would not notice him. I drove up to where he was hiding, stopped the car, and gave a short honk on the horn. He looked up, very embarrassed. I rolled down my window but did not say a word. So he came over to the car, looked at me, and waited for me to yell at him. It was not easy, but I just looked at him. I could sense his mind racing.

"What should I say?" he was thinking. "What should I do? What's the rebbe going to say? If he asks me why I'm out, I'll say I forgot. I cannot say I forgot; he told me yesterday not to go out. I'll tell him I forgot anyway, no, I ..."

I sat there for two or three minutes, which was an eternity for both of us — for me to keep quiet so long, and for him to stand there wondering what he could say, what excuse to use. He was waiting to be punished, to be scolded, and nothing happened. He was being given full responsibility for what he did.

I put the car in reverse, pulled away, and drove to the yeshivah. He came jogging after me and went inside. He must have been preparing for an explosion.

For three days this boy was an angel. For three days he waited for some kind of response and I gave none, but he knew that I was upset and that he had to do something about the situation. The next move, I hoped in the right direction, would be his.

Some boys in his position would have begun talking right away. He did not, but it made no difference. A very clear message had been communicated. I could have yelled at him, saying, "I do not understand, how could you be so irresponsible? I told you five times in the past week. I warned you that this would be the last time. You know what's going to happen," and on and on. He would have buried his head, thinking only about when the lecture would be over.

Instead, I transferred the responsibility to him without a word being said. For three days he looked at me in shame. He was thinking about what he had done and didn't quite know how to atone for it.

After three days of allowing him to stew in his own juices, I received him warmly once again. Now that he had learned his lesson well, we never had a recurrence.

◄ᒿ Mixing In

When children fight and we involve ourselves, we are basically taking total responsibility for the situation. If we get angry with one or both of the combatants and punish them, they do not have to do anything. We already took care of it. If we hold back and just ask them both what happened, we are throwing the responsibility back into their court. Now *they* must think, *they* must answer, *they* have to work things out.

When children fight with each other and we get involved, there is no way to get to the truth of the matter because we are automatically wrong in someone's eyes. If we stop the fight, put the two of them in front of us, and ask, "What's this all about?" *they* have to think about it.

"Well, he started it."

"Oh no, he started it."

"I didn't ask who started it. I'm asking what you are doing to each other."

"Well, I'm hitting him."

"You're hitting your brother [your friend]? What happened?"

You have to help them work it out themselves by not giving orders, by not reacting physically. Your tendency is to say, "Enough of this fighting. If you're going to fight, I'll put you each in your room, blah, blah, blah ..." Once you do that, it is all over. They go to their rooms for three minutes, and when they come out, everything is okay. Mommy or Daddy took full responsibility for everything.

If we want children to communicate with us, we have to ask reasonable questions and we have to be specific. "Why are you crying?" or "Why did you hit him?" or "Why did you do it?" are too open-ended. These questions do not help him because he is now in a situation where he has to describe something that he knows you are not going to accept no matter what he says. "Why" is asking for an excuse he does not have. "Why" is faultfinding. There is nothing he can say that you will accept.

"What happened?" is something he can answer: "He hit me" or "I hit him." Letting him describe the incident gives you both sides of the story. Do not tell him why he is wrong. Ask the right questions and let him deal with what he did that was improper. Remember, ask the questions and let him answer.

Do not offer explanations, do not tell him what you think. Ask and listen!

❧ Believing Children

It is most important, albeit difficult, to believe our children no matter what they say. They must know that we trust them. Certain situations, such as those in which a child is doing something drastically wrong on a regular basis, have to be dealt with professionally, or in a specific manner. But generally speaking, we are talking about normal children in everyday situations. *Usually a child is speaking the truth even when we think he is not.*

You separate two fighting children and say to the one who was on top, "I do not understand you. How could you do that? I saw you hit him in the face five times. What kind of naughtiness is this?"

The child starts crying. "It's not true, it's not true, I didn't! It's a lie, it's a lie! You're always blaming me for things that I never did."

"But I saw it happen. I watched you chase him. I saw you jump on him. I saw you turn him over, and I saw you hit him five times in the face."

"No, I didn't, it is not true, it is not true."

"Let's change the subject. What happened?"

"I hit him four times in the face and once in the back!"

He is hurt that we said he hit the other child five times in the face. He is not only trying to get out of trouble — he actually believes that we are exaggerating the situation to make it worse than it is, because he perceives four times in the face and once in the back to be less serious than five times in the face.

In some situations there is no excuse like that.

"Why did you throw that book at your sister?"

"I didn't throw the book at my sister."

"What do you mean? I just saw you do it."

"I didn't."

What should you do? You saw the child throw the book. He says he never did it. You can confront him, call him a liar, and end the conversation, because neither of you will change your tune. Or you can say something like this, and it may sound funny but it is not.

"Okay, I'm sorry, I thought you threw the book. I saw it leave your hand, fly across the room, and land in your sister's face. What really happened?"

"I was throwing it at the couch, and it hit her."

You can prove him wrong: "But a minute ago she was bothering you, and you were threatening her with ..." Or you can let him climb out of the little hole he has dug and let him recognize that you know what he did, without confronting him too directly. You do not need to tell him your opinion of him at that moment. You want him to be aware that you know he is not telling the truth, without calling him a liar. Calling him a liar is like taking the phone line and cutting it. You cannot communicate with a liar. If you do not believe what he has to say, why should he say it? If you do not trust him, there is no reason to speak. We cannot let our children think that we believe they are liars.

What is the alternative? You can say, "You know, I understand that you think that you didn't throw the book at your sister. I would like you to leave the room now. I will feel more comfortable if you are out of the room." You should, with great effort, refrain from saying, "You liar, go upstairs to your bed!" Nor should you say, "I believe you, I accept it, I know you're telling the truth." Leave it open. "I hear you. I can understand it. I will feel more comfortable if you go out of the room."

"But I didn't do anything."

"Okay, but I'll still feel more comfortable if you leave the room. That's it. Please go up to your room."

You did not cut off the lines of communication. He left the room with somewhat more self-respect than if you had called him a liar. The relationship will be intact and you will be able to speak with him again, whereas if you had called him a liar you would never be able to discuss the problem with him at another time. Now, an hour or even a day later, you can bring up the subject. Often, a little while later he will come back on his own and say, "I'm sorry I threw the book." When a child knows that there is trust, that the lines of communication are still open, he can return and accept responsibility for things that he has a done.

It is astonishing how often we assume that children are not telling the truth. Sometimes a child will tell a story about something that happened in school that we just cannot believe. We tell the child that he is making it up and he should not lie or exaggerate. In a case like this, we have many unexpected responsibilities: We have to give him the benefit of the doubt — unless we know otherwise, we should not question what he says. We can ask about the situation in order to get more information, or make a phone call to verify what happened. In doing so we often find out that the story he told is very close to the truth. When we accept our children's feelings, when we believe what they have to say, they know that we trust them and will accept their side of the story. Then they have a reason to tell it to us.

I know that in the yeshivah, I was taken advantage of at least one hundred times a year. Whenever something occurred, I always gave the boy the opportunity to tell us his perception of what happened before judging and punishing. At least a hundred times one year, boys told me what their view of the event was, which I knew was only partially true. Despite knowing that it was really a one-sided perception, I knew that I had to believe them. Why? Because if I believed them on this issue, the next time they needed to say something they would tell me the truth. When something is bothering a boy, or he needs to speak about something that hurts him, or something happened that he is afraid to talk about because he thinks nobody will believe him, he will go to whomever he feels trusts him and who accepts what he says at face value.

It works that way at home, too. If we believe our children, they will feel comfortable and confident talking to us. If they consistently get the feeling that we do not believe what they say, they will not bother to communicate with us. Just think about some past conversations with your children. Haven't they often said, "Oh, you never believe me. You never accept what I say," or "You always take the other side. The teacher's always right, the other kid's always right, I'm always wrong, so why should I talk to you? Why should I tell you what's bothering me? Why should I share with you what happened with my friends?"

Of course we have to know the full truth, and we can sometimes leave the child with a little bit of a doubt as to what our true feelings are, but never clearly show him that you do not believe him.

> Our first-grader would come home from school and tell us about one particular boy who was really wild, who acted out in unacceptable ways. Every day he would come home with new, exciting stories about the boy's misbehavior. At the PTA meeting I spoke with this child's father.
>
> "You know, I do not know what's happening in this class," he said to me, "but my son comes home with the wildest stories about what's going on here."
>
> "Uh-huh ... right," I answered. "My son tells me the same thing." He went into the classroom to meet the teacher a few minutes later and, from the look on his face when he came out, it was clear that he had found out a little bit more about which child was causing the disturbance.
>
> In this case, I had not waited for the PTA meeting. I had initiated a discussion with the teacher beforehand to make sure it was not my son who was the culprit, because when he would come home and tell these stories with such excitement and glee, I did not know what to think. Perhaps he was telling me about himself, using his friend's name. Baruch Hashem it wasn't he! At that time he enjoyed the behavior vicariously, but did not have the nerve to do it himself. Never did I let him think that we did not believe him, because **trust and com-**

munication are more important than getting to the bottom of every story.

◄᎒ Living Up to Expectations

Confronting our children head-on is not as effective as helping them to aspire to live up to our positive picture of them.

> *A father once called me about his eighteen-year-old son. "Listen," he told me, "I know that he is transgressing Shabbos — not in the house, but definitely outside. I want to confront him."*
>
> *"What are you going to accomplish by confronting him?" I asked. "He is not breaking Shabbos in the house because he is embarrassed; he still feels bad about what he is doing. As long as he thinks that you trust him because you think that he is a good boy, you know that this is one thing he'll never do. The shame and regret is there, and there's still room for him to say, 'You know what? I do not want to do it anymore.' But the minute you confront him, and show him that you know exactly what's going on, he has no reason to hide what he is doing. He'll be ashamed for a short time, but it will pass. Once he knows that you know, he won't keep Shabbos in the house either."*
>
> *The father didn't listen to me, unfortunately, and what I was afraid would happen, did. The youth finally gave up everything having to do with mitzvah observance.*

When we show our children that we know everything they are doing wrong and that we know how bad they are, they have no real reason to try to live up to the positive image we have of them.

> *I had a student who is now married. However, when he first came to us he was one of the youngest students we ever accepted, and he often acted immaturely. He would do foolish, childish things in class, and then he would be sent to me.*
>
> *I feigned ignorance. I would say, "What happened?" and he would be embarrassed to tell me, because I*

always told him what a great, worthwhile, wonderful boy he was. "Oy," he would say, "I made some trouble," and would be embarrassed to go into the details.

"Oh, I'm sure it was nothing," I'd say. "It'll pass." For years he really believed that I never accepted the stories that were told about him. His rebbes would sometimes get a little upset, but I reassured them:

"Listen, this is how we are going to play it. You have to send him out of the class because he is disruptive, but I'm telling you that this child's self-image is so poor, he has such a low level of self-esteem, that I'm never going to feed into his misbehavior. I want to know everything, but he is not going to know that I know."

Two or three years later, the young man asked me if I really thought he was so worthwhile when he first came to the yeshivah. He always wondered, "Did the Rebbe really think that I was so special?"

"Yes," I said again. "Yes, I did."

Isn't every boy special? Doesn't every child deserve a chance to believe he is special? He ended up being a very special boy indeed, and a very successful young man.

Four years later, he asked me, "Why did the Rebbe act with me the way he did at those times?" I explained the process to him, stressing that I was not playing games. I really did have respect for him.

"You didn't have respect for yourself. You didn't know how special you were, so somebody had to tell you. When you heard frequently enough that somebody in the world believed this, you were able to start thinking that way about yourself. Once you did, you stopped doing things that you were embarrassed about."

This is not only intense *chinuch*; this is communication. This is what we do every day with our children. We are constantly communicating messages of what we think about them and what they should think about themselves. If a child is called a name, he will say, "Yeah, right. That's what you think I am? Okay, so I am stupid. If I'm stupid, what can you expect from me?" When the child is told that he is stupid, he will act stupid. Why should he act smart?

There was a first- or second-grade rebbe in my child's school whom I used to love to watch. Every once in a while I was able to come to school to see how my son was doing. During davening in the morning, there was a time that the rebbe could leave the class for a moment or two. He would come out and we would talk, but he had one ear tuned in to the class. The moment he heard a lull in the davening because he was not standing there to encourage their enthusiasm, he would pop back into the class.

"Wow," he would enthuse, "that's great, unbelievable, you are davening so nicely and loudly." The children would look at each other and look at him and redouble the volume because he was so positive. Once he communicated to them that they were great, that they were davening beautifully, they had all the reason in the world to do so. If he had walked in and said, "I cannot hear anything, what's going on with you kids, don't you know how to daven?" there would not have been that kind of reaction.

We must always ask ourselves, therefore, what it is we wish to accomplish. Do I want my child to be ashamed to fight with the neighbors, not hit his brother, or pour his milk down his sister's back? I want him to go to sleep on time, take responsibility for his homework. I want to get a message across. If I first think about which method is going to work, then I will not follow my first impulse. If I am going to ask my boss for a raise, I will consider the best way to do it, because communication is not merely saying something — it is making sure that the other party hears and understands. Just putting food on the table without making sure that the hungry person actually ingested a nutritious meal is not sufficient.

I have to think, therefore, about the message I want to get across and the best way to make my point acceptable. I cannot assume that anything I say will do the job. In addition, I must remember that the key to effective communication is being positive.

Chapter Five
BUILDING
RELATIONSHIPS

A n *adam gadol*, a great man, once told me that friendship should be a long-term goal of our relationship with our children. We should seek to develop the relationship so that at some point in time we can share one another's life experiences and continue to grow as friends. It is rare to achieve this type of friendship with children who are very young, because it requires a great amount of reciprocal thought as well as a large investment of time and energy. However, the dividends are worth the effort, because as our child grows into adulthood, there is a great deal that we can give to and share with each other. It is extremely rewarding when we can achieve this.

We assume that our children will continue to need us as they grow older. We would like to be there for them when they do, but for them to show interest in our input, we have to concentrate on forming such a relationship early on. Building this type of relationship must begin before children reach adulthood. If we get off to a late start, we can sometimes compensate and the relationship can still grow, but just as in all relationships, there is usually a great difference between friendships formed in early childhood and those made in later life. The friends of our childhood are usually the most cherished and valued, so we should try to begin developing that type of relationship with our children from the time they are small.

Building a relationship with a child is very similar to building a relationship with an adult. We feel more confident about the latter; when it comes to our children we become a little bit nervous. Remember our story of the lion and the bear? Sometimes we look at our children as if they were lions, a different species. How are we going to build a relationship with this child? We assume that we do not speak the same language or think alike or feel the same way about things. That frightens us and we are hesitant about opening up and trying to get close.

Rav Wolbe teaches that if you open your mouth and say, "*Shema Yisrael Hashem Elokeinu, Hashem Echad,*" you find out that under that lion's suit is a human being who can respond, *Baruch Shem Kevod* ... You will find someone who also has feelings, sensitivities, and thoughts, needs and desires and fears — in short, another human being. Your child is a human being with whom you can share a great deal. Once we recognize this fact, we have something on which to build.

Why are we so afraid of getting close to our children? The reason is that our children engender within us a tremendous amount of emotion, and we are concerned with how they will perceive us. *How much of my inner self can I reveal? How close can the two of us become? I do not want my child to know everything about me.* We can and must use *seichel,* common sense, in this area. Being open is essential, yet when we build close relationships with adults we understand the need to keep certain things to ourselves. This does not mean that trust and love and understanding cannot exist; it just means that there are certain things that are either intensely private or simply not prudent to reveal. We must learn to use the same reasoning with our children.

It is a mistake to think that in a close relationship everything has to be said, regardless of the consequences. This is a serious error. There are obviously going to be more things that we will keep to ourselves in our relationship with our children than with our closest adult friends. After all, children cannot be expected to deal with adult problems, dilemmas, and conflicts. However, the general principles of developing friendships with adults and with children are similar.

In building a relationship with an adult, you have to give of yourself and give the other person a chance to reciprocate. You have to let the friendship develop at its own pace. Often, when we jump into something too quickly, we regret it afterward. Building a relationship is something that takes a great amount of time and effort.

◀৳ Building Trust

There is a mishnah in Avos[1] that states: "*Kenei lecha chaver,* buy yourself a friend," which means one must invest in the acquisition of a friend. Rabbeinu Yonah explains the three basic components of friendship:

1) Having someone with whom and from whom we can learn,
2) Having someone with whom we can grow and who cares enough to make sure that we do not do things that are detrimental for us, and
3) Having someone with whom to share secrets and private thoughts, with the full confidence and trust that they will not be spoken of with others.

All three components are based on trust, but let us focus first on the third one.

A. Trust Through Sharing

Sharing private thoughts is one way to show friendship. It can be very meaningful to a child for you to say, "I want to tell you something. I'm going to go there, do this, consider that …, but please, don't tell anybody." In sharing a secret, we show trust in him. When you give a child trust, he wants to live up to your expectations, to be worthy of that trust. Sharing a secret brings us closer to our confidant. We very

---

1. *Avos* 1:6.

often tell our children what we want and expect of them. Let us be a little bit more personal in terms of revealing who *we* are or sharing an experience *we* have had. You can tell him about something that happened to you when you were a child, how you dealt or did not deal with a situation similar to the one he has just experienced. You can reveal to him what difficulties you had. A child sees this as sharing something personal with him.

Sharing is something that takes place in all healthy relationships. I have the honor, *baruch Hashem*, of having a mother-in-law who has never been seen eating something all by herself. I have never seen her finish something that she made, even if she prepared it for herself. If there is someone else, even a child, in the room, she insists on sharing her food. "Come, you have to have some too. Join me, eat, enjoy." This is something that builds relationships, and it is beautiful.

I remember once when my wife was expecting, she craved a peach. Peaches had just come into season and were very expensive. We were living on a tight budget and ordinarily I would not have bought any, but if your wife has a craving for something, you have to get it for her. So I bought one large peach and gave it to her. Our little ones were in the room, and she started cutting the peach into slices. "Imma," I said, "you realize they don't know what a peach is. One peach costs twelve shekels ..." But this was her natural reaction. If you have something, you share it with your children. That does something toward building the relationship that few other things can do.

When *I* get hold of one expensive peach, I make sure to finish it before I get home so that no one else sees it. But then my children find the pit in the car, and they know they missed out. Usually this happens with a box of Pringles, not with a peach, but it's the same idea. If we have something we like and we share it, we are showing love. When they see that we want for others that which we want for ourselves, it builds a relationship. One of the nicest compliments you can pay to a friend is to say that he will give you the shirt off his back.

Sharing forges a very special bond, and it is within our power to share and to create this special relationship.

B. Trust Through Delegating Responsibility

When we speak of delegating responsibility to ensure a more solid relationship with our children, we do not mean making them responsible for the things we want them to do. "Okay, since you're so responsible, you can do the dishes for the next three weeks." That kind of responsibility is not what they want and it does not mean anything to them. But there are things in every household that require someone to be responsible for them. They can be small, but important.

I will give several examples, but every household is so different, that some things can seem totally foolish in one house and extremely important in another:

"We know that we can depend on you every Friday to find out what time Shabbos comes in and let everybody know. It seems like a very little thing, but if we are reminded of it an hour or so before candle-lighting time, it would be a big help." This is something a child could feel good about.

"For Shabbos, I'm buying something really special for all the children, and I want *you* to give it out to the other children because I know you'll do it fairly." This develops a sense of responsibility even though it is a small thing.

Send an older child to buy something with a younger child. You can trust children; they are smart and can figure things out. When a child is old enough to be trusted with that kind of responsibility he will be aware of your trust. We usually trust people who trust us, and children are no different. They will rely on those who rely on them and discuss things with those who discuss things with them.

◆ઙ Learning How to React

The second element in building a lasting friendship, according to Rabbeinu Yonah,[2] is learning how to react. When

2. Ibid.

our boss does something we do not like, we think five times before we respond. When our friend does something that does not please us, we think twice. When our spouse does something we disapprove of, we most often do not think at all before we react, and when our child does something objectionable, we do not even let him finish doing it before we jump on him. Thinking before we react to something that has been said or done is a basic and crucial part of building a good relationship.

We know that to get along with other people, we sometimes have to swallow things that are uncomfortable. We have to be able to listen, to hear, and sometimes to *not* respond. If we want to develop a relationship with our children, we have to learn to keep quiet sometimes, even if we see and hear things that we do not like (within reason). If children know that everything they say and do will be criticized, they will be sure to say and do less in our presence. If a child is always worried about what Mommy and Tatty are thinking, what they are going to say about every move he makes, he will just become more secretive and share less and less of his life with them.

We want our relationship with our children to come as a natural consequence of growth. We want them to develop healthily and share with us the things they are experiencing. We would like to live through their experiences with them, but if we cut them off five times when they are telling us about one, they're obviously going to stop talking. If we do not let them finish a sentence, if we criticize everything they say, they will not say anything.

In our dealings with adults we somehow are more sensitive to these things, and we assume responsibility for the reactions set off by our actions. With our children, however, either we think that we have the right to react in any way we wish, or we do not even think about how we are reacting because we are so emotionally involved. We sometimes assume that since they have to listen to us anyway, our reaction does not matter. But if we want to build a relationship with our children, then we really have to think about our reactions. Stop and think for a minute about the reasons behind what they are doing or saying. Think about it *before* you react.

> *A teenager walked into his house one day and asked his mother, "What would you do if, just if ... just if, mind you ... if one of your kids would go off the derech and leave yeshivah? What would you ... ?"*
>
> *This intelligent, aware mother had the presence of mind to think for a few seconds before she answered. Deeply concerned that her child was hinting at his own state of mind, she answered, "I would probably make a very in-depth, serious evaluation of what I did wrong."*
>
> *Her son was astonished. "What?"*
>
> *"Yes," she said slowly, "if that would happen, I would assume that I'd done something wrong, and I would try to evaluate what it was and try to fix it."*
>
> *The conversation that ensued was a good discussion regarding a friend who was having problems. This mother's concern was reasonable. She thought, "One second, what's going on? If he's asking this question, maybe he's in trouble. Maybe he's frustrated. Maybe something's bothering him." At the same time she realized that coming down hard on him would accomplish nothing.*

As it turned out, this boy was sharing something. Some parents would have voiced a gut reaction: "Well, I'd throw him out of the house." This is exactly the wrong thing to say. We react in all kinds of ways — intellectually, emotionally, hormonally, and as a result we deal with situations in many different ways. *But if we think before we speak, we have a much greater chance of building and maintaining good relationships.*

We have to be somewhat flexible. Often, as our children grow older, their demands become more challenging. When faced with new situations, we are not always sure how much we should give in and where we should draw the line. At such a point, we have to ask people whom we trust, people who have more experience. We know, however, that if a child is really determined, he is going to get his way. Being flexible is much more effective than waiting until the situation reaches an impasse in which both sides have taken their final stand and neither can back down anymore and still save face. Before a parent threatens a child with an ultimatum, he has to consider what he is going to do when the child does what he wants anyway.

We are living in an era when not only are things different from the way they were when we were growing up, but every five years things are no longer the same as they were five years earlier. Harav Moshe Shapiro, a *gadol baTorah*, told me that in our time, three months is a *dor*, a new generation. Imagine! A generation gap can be created in only three months. Lest you think that such a statement is an exaggeration, consider what is happening in the world today. Processes that once took months and years to evolve are now carried out in hours. In three hours, the news of the world changes. Whatever happened this week is inconsequential by next week. Today's headlines are tomorrow's fish wrappings.

It follows, then, that in today's world we need to be able to react somewhat differently from the way our parents reacted. We as children accepted ideas and discipline that our youngsters are not willing to accept. That does not mean that we have to capitulate and give in to them on everything. As parents, we have the right and the responsibility to assert authority. We must be very clear about the limits we set and express them in clear terms. At the same time, we have to be careful not to make decisions before we know what we are talking about, before we have thought about them. We have to know exactly where our boundaries are in order to allow ourselves the little bit of flexibility that we need, because if everything is an ultimatum and there is no place for movement, we are in danger of fostering the very rebellious attitudes that are so prevalent in our society. Rav Wolbe has said that in this generation a child at a year and a half is already breathing in the atmosphere of rebellion, the atmosphere of "don't tell me what to do."

I was not the best-behaved or most studious pupil when I was in school, but I never would have said certain things that students say today. It can be mind-boggling to hear children criticizing their teachers today. We used to say, "Oh, that stupid teacher, I hate him." Children have been saying that for at least one hundred years. But today a child will say, "The teacher has no right to tell me to be quiet. If he wants me to be quiet, he has to know how to ask. That's not the way a teacher should talk."

There used to be a humorous little sign that said, "Please be quiet while I interrupt." That attitude today is so prevalent that it is no longer funny. We must learn to be a little more flexible when we deal with our children, somewhat more careful of how we present things, because presentation is very important in getting them to do what we want them to do.

It is not a question of being right. When you are driving up to an intersection and you have the right of way, and there's an eighteen-wheeler coming from the other direction at seventy miles an hour and the driver is ignoring his yield sign, you stop even though you are in the right! Being right does not always mean being smart. We have to be smart and anticipate realistically what we can get our children to do. When we see that we are not going to be successful, we have to decide beforehand how we are going to handle the situation so that we do not end up doing things that are going to harm and ultimately destroy the relationship.

◄ঽ The Right Way to Give

In relationships with adults, we are aware of when someone is trying to make us happy and do what is in our best interest, and we feel a responsibility to do the same for them. Conversely, when we feel that we are being taken advantage of, that people are unloading their responsibilities on us with no understanding of our needs, we feel resentful. It is difficult for us to help those individuals. It is extremely important, therefore, to give to others in a way that makes both sides happy. It is good to give *tzedakah*, but as we know, the best way to give it is so that the recipient does not feel that he is at the receiving end.

> In the yeshivah, we very often raised a small sum of money to buy a needy student a suit, a pair of shoes, a sweater for Yom Tov. We tried to fill the most urgent needs. There was one boy whose mother was seriously handicapped. His father was a driver for an unsuccessful bus company and earned a meager salary. This boy never let anyone buy anything for him.
>
> "No, I'm not poor. I don't need anything."
>
> "Yes, but you have holes in your shoes."
>
> "I know, but in a couple of weeks I'm buying new shoes, I just ..." and he found an excuse not to take.
>
> He went on to a yeshivah gedolah, and since his parents were not able to do very much for him, he decided that he needed to do something to earn money. He had learned some basic skills, but decided that he wanted to be a shochet. He began to skip sessions at the yeshivah and worked odd hours in a bakery in Yerushalayim, sometimes into the wee hours of the morning, saving money so that he could study shechitah.
>
> When I found out that he was skipping classes, I went to visit him and he told me, "Don't worry, everything's fine, everything's perfect. I missed a few shiurim, but now everything's going to be okay."
>
> I couldn't get anything else out of him, so I approached a very close friend of his and found out about the shechitah course.
>
> Two weeks later I went back to him. "Oh, by the way," I said, "I have a friend who knows that in our yeshivah we teach different trades. He just gave me a sum of money to help support that project to help kids who want to learn a specific thing."
>
> He looked at me skeptically. "Really, what is this, tzedakah?"
>
> "No," I protested. "The money's been donated already. If it isn't used soon, I don't know what's going to happen to it. Didn't you once say that you wanted to study a vocation?"

"Yes, well, there's this course for shechitah and it costs $1,800."

"Well, I have $600, and I want you to take it toward that course."

He was taken aback. "No, no, no!"

"You don't understand," I insisted. "If you don't take it, I'm going to have to give it back. This money is allocated. It's got to be used!"

He was afraid to tell me that he was going to have to miss yeshivah to take this course. Still, when he saw that somebody wanted what was best for him, he finally took the money. He was able to take it because he felt that I loved and cared about him. A short while later, when he had second thoughts about the course — regarding whether he was studying with the right person and whether the price was reasonable — he had someone to come to. He came to me, and we discussed all these issues.

The truth is that when I gave him the money, it was not just for the course. I gave it to him because his shoes still had holes in them, he had not bought a suit in a year and a half, and his hat looked like it had gone through a war. He needed money and he would not take it until he could maintain his dignity and self-respect.

As parents, we need to remember this when we want to give. While it is true that we have to make certain reckonings, and obviously we cannot give a child everything he wants whenever he wants it, we need to share and give in ways that let a child know that we are thinking about him. Not because of what he did to earn it, and not because he asked us for it six times, but once in a while we should just drop a gift into his hand simply because *we want to give it to him*. We certainly do not want our gift to be inspired by any of the following scenarios:

- He requests something, you fight about it, and you finally capitulate.
- Your daughter said something not nice to her little sister, you say she is not entitled the gift, but then you realize

that there is no connection, so you give it to her anyway.

- She is crying because the teacher said she has to bring money to class so that she can go on the trip, so you gave her the money along with five conditions.

That is the way we often give "gifts," but how happy can a child be with gifts that do not serve to build the relationship we want to build, or show the love we want to show? We should rather give our child a gift:

- as a reward for something he did to help out at home;
- because we love him and want to show it, without considering whether he "deserves" it or not;
- as a bonus in his allowance;
- because he did something nice two weeks ago that we remember and appreciate.

And this brings us again to the idea of thinking ahead and deciding not only what we want to do but how we want to do it.

A. Who Is Responsible?

Who should be responsible for making the relationship work? This is an interesting question. Is it the adult who has taken on the responsibility of having a child and raising him, or is the child responsible? Who should be the catalyst that makes the relationship work?

We cannot expect a child to be the moving force in a relationship until he is much older, almost adult. We have to expect more from ourselves than we expect from him. We are the ones to initiate building the relationship and we are going to be the ones to turn things around if it is started off on the wrong track. We tend to get our dander up when things go wrong in an adult relationship, and we say, "Well, he's going to have to invest a lot of effort if he wants to rebuild this relationship." We cannot take this attitude with children. We are the ones who have the responsibility, and only we can initiate change.

One of the most painful experiences I have had as an educator has been to explain to a child or adolescent that one or both of his parents were incapable of providing for his emotional, physical, and psychological needs. The sad solution was that the child had to take responsibility for the situation at home. He had to be the one to learn how to act so that his parents would react in a more normal fashion. It is painful and difficult, but when a sixteen- or seventeen-year-old lives in a dysfunctional home, and the parents are not willing to assume any responsibility, we educators often have no choice but to speak openly with that child.

There are ways for us to coach a normal parent, however. Instead of saying, "Will you take out the garbage," say, "Oh, *zieskeit* (sweetie), can you do me a favor and please take out the garbage." Is this so much harder to do? It involves just moving a few words around. Or you can say, "You were so great today. Can you finish it off by taking out the garbage?" What is the problem? Are you afraid the child is going to say, "I'm tired too, I can't take it out"? If you respond, "I said you have to!" you have botched it. Or if you say, "Okay, I'll take it out," you are taking the responsibility when you want him to be responsible.

This is where we have to be flexible, perhaps swallowing our words and saying, "Oh, you're tired too? Okay, you can do it in the morning." Compliments work too, by the way. We like compliments too, don't we? When we feel good about something, we are more inclined to do what is asked of us. In any case, it's up to us to build that relationship. We cannot wait until the child is old enough to recognize that the relationship has gone sour and only then start thinking about how to make it better. He will have given up long before then.

B. Self-Respect

What sensitivities do we need in order to make a healthy relationship happen? Certain things are intrinsic to dealing with all people, and with children in particular. Among them is instilling self-respect. Thinking about how we can build up a child's self-respect, that feeling of who I am and what I am worth, and concern about damaging the child's self-respect are obviously going to be part of the very strong sensitivities that we need to develop.

Stubbornness usually has its source in a feeling of inadequacy. When we feel inadequate in a situation we become stubborn, because when we are not sure of ourselves, we have to take a very strong stand. When we are confident and strong, we can handle doubt and the feeling of not being sure. Since children by nature are always questioning things and feeling insecure, they become stubborn and dig in. How do we work with a stubborn person? Certainly not by being stubborn in return! We have to be sensitive to the issues that will place him in a situation in which he feels he has to be stubborn.

> *I once went to a store with my eleven-year-old son who needed a pair of slacks. We had different ideas about it, and I had a feeling I would be fighting a losing battle, because boys this age already know what they want. It was not the price I objected to. The pair that he picked out had, in my opinion, a very garish and ugly emblem on the pocket. We looked around in the store but could not find anything better. We had reached an impasse.*
>
> *"I don't know," I said. "These are the only ones in your size, and they're not nice."*
>
> *"That's not so," he replied. "They're beautiful."*
>
> *"Well," I said, "let's go ask the owner if there are any others."*
>
> *"Listen," I said to the store owner, "this is the only pants in his size in the store. My son's a little embarrassed because they're a little garish. Is there another pair of pants that ..."*
>
> *"They're not garish," the man replied, offended. "Everyone buys these pants."*
>
> *"Well," I protested, "he's almost bar mitzvah, and he's starting to think about the way he looks. He might be a little embarrassed about the emblem."*
>
> *My son is looking at me in astonishment, probably thinking, "What, me? Embarrassed? I'm not embarrassed. I like those pants."*
>
> *"Well," I said, "they're not terrible. If they are the only ones you have, he could wear them, but I was just*

wondering if you have anything else." Meanwhile, my son's looking at me and worrying about what I'm going to say next.

There was no other pair of pants, so I called my son over to the side. "What are you going to do?" I asked. "Are you going to wear these?"

"Well, I guess if there's no other pair, I'll wear them."

"Okay, then we'll have to buy them." And I bought the pants.

On the way home, he said, "Ta, do you think you could take the emblem off?" I sat up until two in the morning removing it.

Had I taken a stand over these pants, there was no way I would have succeeded, because we were not talking about committing a sin, about doing something evil. We are not even talking about doing something that was out of place in his particular school. There were other boys who wore those pants. It was I who was uncomfortable about them. Does that mean that he cannot wear them? No, but if I want him to agree with me, is fighting the way to accomplish it? Obviously it is not. By giving him more respect than he deserved and by telling him that I knew how sensitive he was about growing up, that he wanted to look more respectable, it made him wonder if he was comfortable with those pants.

Talk to your child. Give him respect. Be sensitive to what he is probably thinking, and then play the game. We are older, more experienced. We know which buttons to push. With this child that is what worked. With another child, something else might work. Once again, I would like to emphasize that no one else can play *my* game. I cannot give you a general script with words that will work in every household every time. The conversation will vary because every relationship is as distinct and individual as every parent. There are many ways to be attuned to another person's feelings.

C. Fear of Rejection

Children fear rejection. We have to be very sensitive to this feeling and not turn that fear into a reality. Children can feel rejected very easily, especially by their parents, whom they love and need so much. We have to be careful not to say anything that might make them feel that they are unimportant. When we get angry, we may often say things that make our children feel as if they are disposable, that they are only here to provide us with the *nachas*, the parental joys that we expect, and if they do not, then we can more or less do without them.

It is very hard to build a relationship with someone who we feel is rejecting us. Parents, in times of distress, sometimes say things like: I'll throw you out of this house; who needs you; get out of here; leave me alone; I don't want you; I don't love you; I hate you. The parents do not really mean it, but *words like these cause deep wounds that are not always visible.* Sometimes there is enough love in the house to mask them, but once spoken, words like these are never forgotten. The less we say hurtful things and the more careful we are about what we say in general, the better chances we have of building a healthy relationship.

When children, especially adolescents, are doubtful about something, that is when they project the greatest degree of confidence. They know everything and are 1,000 percent sure about it. There is nothing we can tell them or teach them. Our experience and intelligence do not count. They know it all. Once I saw an apt little sign that read, "Ask your teenager while he still knows everything." We have to be very careful how we speak and work with children. If they see that we are not afraid to say, "I don't know," they will be less afraid to say it as well. If an adolescent is being rebellious and confident about how right he is and we say, "You know, maybe you're right," he immediately begins to doubt his decision. But as soon as we say: "You don't know what you're talking about; I have more experience than you; listen, I went through this fifty times — everyone goes through this," you have lost the battle. He is not hearing a word you say.

Just say, "You know, I never thought about it that way. You might be right." Watch how he will come back with, "Yeah?

I don't think so. I was just playing with the thought, I didn't mean it."

Let us be smart. We know that we have the tools and the experience, but arguing with children is not going to help when they doubt themselves. If we want them to work something through and help them resolve a situation, we first have to realize that the more confident they seem, the more doubt actually exists. Do you still really want to argue the point? Good luck!

We must try to discuss the issue with them. When our child makes a statement that we disagree with, we can remark, "Oh really? I didn't know that," and then ask a few questions. When we ask for details, he realizes that he does not know anything about the subject. We did not put him down; all we did was to ask questions for clarification. We were not judging or complaining, we were just asking in order to understand. On the other hand, if we show up his lack of knowledge and confront him with it, he will come back with, "What do you mean I don't know what I just said? I know everything there is to know about it," followed by, "You know what? I don't want to talk about it."

We can only build a good relationship by staying out of the line of direct confrontational fire from our teenage children. Ask a question about the topic, be interested, allow your doubts to surface in a general way, indicate that you are not so sure he is wrong, that there is room for discussion. This approach contains all the elements we have been talking about in building a relationship: giving, talking, sharing, and being sensitive. We are going to be doing everything right. Well, almost. We cannot let ourselves become discouraged, because even if we get it right just 20 to 30 percent of the time, we are still making a big improvement!

D. Reciprocity

We expect our children to reciprocate, to begin making an effort to build their relationship with us, but reciprocity is something we can never demand. It does not work when we say, "I do everything for you, but you don't do anything for me; don't you see how hard I'm trying?" By being patient, giving, and staying attuned to your child, you will help him develop the will to reciprocate. Most children, as they grow older, realize how much their parents are doing on their behalf and they want to help them in return. It is refreshing to hear a child say, "My mother works so hard, how can I make her feel a little bit better? How can I make her day a little bit easier?"

Some children are more sensitive than others, of course, and they see the overall picture at a relatively young age. Others are more egocentric and have greater needs. The first type comes home and says, "Hi, Imma, do you need any help, is there anything I can do for you before I go outside?" You know you have been doing something right, because he is saying that he feels loved and cared for. A sibling in the same house walks in and says, "Ma, you didn't do my laundry yet? So when are you going to do it? I've been waiting two days already for that sweater!" *When the child acts in a more demanding manner it means that his needs are greater.* We have already established whose responsibility it is to build the relationship; this child needs more understanding from you and needs more attention in order to feel cared about and loved.

With some children, when we give them something five times and deny it to them once, they seem to forget the five times we gave them what they wanted. This is a much more difficult situation to deal with, but we must deal with it because each of our children is different. When we do not give that extra dose of reassurance when it is needed, it seems as if we did not do anything at all for that child. For the first child, we did what we deemed was right. We were being fair and honest, and it worked. It does not work with the second or third or fifth child, not because something is wrong with us or with him. He just needs so much more. We have to strive to provide for the unique emotional needs of each of the children with whom we are blessed.

When a child's emotional makeup sometimes makes it difficult for him to reciprocate, we are going to be disappointed if we expect it of him. We know that there are adults, spouses, parents, friends, and teachers with whom we have one-sided relationships. Not everyone knows how to draw on his emotions and share them, or how to give of himself. The only way that we can teach reciprocity is by expressing and developing a good, close relationship. We have to give this type of child the time he needs to grow and reach the point where he will reciprocate. If we fulfill our responsibilities, at some point in time the child will learn to give back. He will modify his behavior in order to keep a balance in a relationship that we have made important to him. If we express, ask, and consistently invest, we will see a change. The child will respond.

◄־ Showing Gratitude

It is a genuine human need to repay good. Rav Chaim Shmulevitz[3] says that very often we find that when we do people a favor, they pay us back with a slap in the face. Anyone who does things for people realizes that occasionally he may get a knife in the back, so to speak. If you do good and do not expect a pat on the back, you will be pleasantly surprised when it happens and you will not be disappointed when you do not receive even the barest thank you. Why is this?

Rav Chaim goes on to say that *hakaras hatov*, recognizing the good that someone does for you, is such a basic human necessity, such an ingrained, natural reaction, that when a person cannot fulfill that responsibility, he will subconsciously look for a reason to justify getting out of it. If I feel that I deeply owe an individual something and I do not feel that I have it within me to repay him, I will look for something he does wrong and blow it up out of proportion so as to be free of my debt. Now I no longer owe him anything. It can happen with regard to *chinuch* or any other area of life. We see it as a facet of human nature. You do something for someone.

3. *Sichos Mussar.*

You invest time, effort, and sometimes money to help him, and the person does not really have a way to pay you back. Because he does not want to be beholden to you, he will eventually develop a thesis, a theory of how bad you were to him, instead of acknowledging the good.

Children, unlike the adults for whom we do things, are in a constant mode of taking from us. If we show appreciation when they try to reciprocate in small ways, that eases the way for them to pay us back, to return the good we have done for them. They will do it whenever they can, because reciprocity is a real need. Being thankful to our children when they do something to help us gives them the feeling that they can reciprocate. Our show of gratitude gives them an opportunity to express their own inner thankfulness.

> The Chasam Sofer was the rabbi in his city. As often happens, there was a strong group of dissenters who fought his every move. On one occasion, he was faced with a particular group of people who were seriously trying to harm him. Their behavior caused him great distress. He said to his students, "I don't understand this. I never did them such favors that they should be running after me like this. What do they want from my life?"

People who try to help others are not always able to fulfill all expectations and demands and such individuals might experience this phenomenon. After the first few times that it happens, they can better understand that it is human nature. When we do not acknowledge the good things our children do by telling them how good they made us feel, the children feel like they are taking but cannot repay. In such a situation they remember the one thing we did wrong and not the five things we did right.

People of stature who work on their *middos* know that they have a debt of gratitude and live with it constantly. I once knew an unusual parent whose oldest son had gone through a very difficult time in the eighth grade. The boy came to our yeshivah afterward and, *baruch Hashem,* became an exceptional *ben Torah* and is now doing very well. It was always such a pleasure to speak to this boy's father, because he made us feel so appreciated. Even five years after his son finished school, the father's gratitude was as great as if his son had just graduated. This father was an exceptional human being.

Most people are uncomfortable once they have already expressed their thanks. They do not know what to say or do next. Some think they are obligated to buy or give something, and then they feel guilty when they do not follow through.

> *Rav Yitzchak Hutner was once offered a ride.*
> *"I accept, but I want to pay you."*
> *"Please! You don't have to pay me."*
> *"Yes, I must pay you. It costs money."*
> *"So you'll owe me [a favor]."*
> *"No," said the Rav. "That's far too expensive!"*

The concept goes even further. There is a Gemara[4] that says that at one point Moshe Rabbeinu called the Jews *kefu'ei tovah*, ingrates, meaning that they were acting in a manner which showed that they did not recognize the good. What, asks the Gemara, did they do wrong? The Gemara answers that at the time that Hashem said, *"Mi yitein v'hayah levavam zeh*, Who will insure that *klal Yisrael*, the Jewish people, will always remain on the level they were on at the time of *kabbalas haTorah?" klal Yisrael* should have said, *"Atah titein.* You, *Ribbono shel Olam*, You will help insure that we will retain that level." But they did not. They did not make that request. Even failing to ask for something is *kafui tov*, ingratitude. *Tosafos* explains that they did not ask because they didn't want to be beholden.

Sometimes, as we learn in the above Gemara, we do not want to be given something in order not to owe. That too is *kefius tovah*. I'm not talking about the wise adage,[5] *"sonei matanos yichyeh*, he who hates gifts will live." One should not seek favors from people. But when someone needs

---

4. *Avodah Zarah* 5b.
5. *Mishlei* 15:27.

something and he is reluctant to receive it because he does not want to be beholden, that is actually one aspect of the *middah* of ingratitude, because the feeling of owing someone bothers and pains him. It has to be satisfied either with repayment, with a constant burden of owing, or, as we said, finding a reason not to owe anymore.

If you are starting to rebuild a relationship now, whether your child is age three, fifteen, or twenty-two, you have to take the attitude: It is now or never. The sooner you begin, the better chance you will have of building a real relationship. Relationships can last forever. Unfortunately, the reverse is also true: If we look back and see that we did things to destroy the relationship and there is no way of correcting it, it is very sad. But let us not give up. We can begin immediately to try to forge those bonds that will allow our children to respond to us in positive ways.

Children bear grudges that can last a lifetime. If they are now fifteen years old or older, and they did not get the understanding they needed when they were three, ten, and eleven, we will suddenly find ourselves at a loss. We are strangers in their lives — outsiders! If we are smart, we can start to rebuild, to look for ways to mend the breaks and do what we can, even now. But the relationship in the future will never be the way it could have been had we been doing things properly from the beginning.

When this child becomes old enough to marry, our lack of a relationship will become even more painful. He will have so many new experiences, problems, and unexpected situations to deal with which we will not be able to share with him. We will see the child suffering, but because we did not invest enough in a relationship in his youth, we will not be able to share in shouldering his burdens now. He does not want to be given the benefit of our experience, we cannot explain what we think because he is not interested in hearing what we have to say, and there is simply no foundation for a sharing relationship between us.

If we have done the "right" things with a child but had difficulties with him during his teenage years, there is a possibility that the relationship we built earlier is still viable. Perhaps we realized that we could not demand reciprocity, but if we invested initially, we have not lost the relationship. We let those difficult years go by while we stood on the sidelines, but as he becomes more aware of his needs, he does not forget our availability and our love. Many of these children come back to us. It is extremely important, therefore, that we somehow find a way to let our children know that we love them and want what is in their best interest.

The crux of the matter is that we are now, albeit belatedly, attempting to build a relationship with our child. If an adult is important to us, we are very careful not to say certain things that might prejudice our friendship. Should we not take similar care with a child with whom we want to preserve our closeness? We should not, and may not, fear telling our child, "No, this you cannot do," but we should be understanding and careful when we must deny them what they want.

We cannot always explain why we are saying no. There are circumstances when we need to say no about something that the child deems important. On these occasions we can say, "I know this hurts you; I know that you're upset because I'm not letting you do this, and I hope that some day you will understand. I'm not saying that you don't understand because you're not smart, or because you're not old enough. Right now, in this situation, you cannot understand where I'm coming from, but the answer has to be no, and I'm sorry if it's hurting you." You can be clear and set limits, but be confident in what you are saying because you are demonstrating sensitivity toward your child at the same time.

We can do everything we have to do, we can fulfill our responsibilities (which are sometimes overwhelming) in constructive ways, but — and I cannot repeat this too often — we can never do everything right. No one does everything perfectly. We are ahead of the game if we manage 10, 20, 30 percent better. If we look for perfection from our children, we will be disappointed, and if we demand perfection in ourselves, we will be defeated before we start.

The tools we have been discussing have to become a part of our psyche, part of the way we think. Then we can use them more often. Gradually, *b'ezras Hashem*, we will make fewer mistakes and less frequently say things that we do not want to say. When we do say something wrong, we can try to correct it. No one becomes an angel overnight. No one does everything right with all their children, especially when they have a large family, economic conditions are difficult, and the stresses of life as we live it in this generation are constant. There are no quick tricks. We are going to think and talk about the ideas presented here, and try to implement each one as it is needed. But no one can promise you that if you say A, your child will say B.

I once saw a book that gave explicit instructions on having conversations with your children. I, personally, was very uncomfortable with having the dialogue all laid out.

"Uh, oh, he didn't answer me the way he was supposed to. What do I do now? Is it too late at night to call the author?"

We have to take into account our own personalities, our child's personality, and all the tools Hashem gave us to face the challenges of building relationships within our precious families.

Chapter Six

TEACHING
RESPONSIBILITY

As parents, we are the ones responsible for dealing with family problems as they develop, but we want to teach our children how to assume responsibility so that they can grow up to be responsible adults. Although we want them to take responsibility during their growing years, as it makes life easier for everyone in the household, our main intention is to help them function properly when they are grown. We enjoy the fruits of our educational efforts when we see our young children take on jobs like caring for their younger siblings and helping with household chores, but our most important goal is to help them become responsible individuals. How can we accomplish this?

A person cannot assume responsibility without certain conditions being present:

- He must be capable of taking on that particular responsibility.
- He must be capable of evaluating what is needed.
- He must have the authority to see it through.

Before we can give over responsibility, therefore, we really have to understand both what we can expect from our child and what is our goal. Is the child capable of fulfilling our request? Does he have the level of judgment necessary to deal with the situation into which we are about place him? Does he have the authority to deal with it?

We often ask one child to watch over other children. This is a major responsibility. Will the others listen to him when we leave the house, or will they say, "Just leave me alone"? Is he capable of dealing with problems that may arise? Do we think ahead and figure out what situations may crop up and whether he has the tools to deal with them? If so, we are responsible parents who are delegating responsibility in a fair and sensible way. If not, we are irresponsible. By burdening a child with a responsibility for which he is not ready, and therefore cannot possibly fulfill, we are not teaching him to be a responsible person.

Generally speaking, when our children do something wrong, we assume the responsibility. And when we want them to do something right, we take responsibility for that as well. We criticize our children for not living up to our expectations, but we never truly consider them responsible for what they do.

Picture this all-too-common scenario: Your child comes home with a note from school. He was not behaving and you are requested to come to speak with the principal. Why? Who is responsible for the misbehavior, the child or you? By sending that note, the school is telling him that you are responsible. By acquiescing and going to speak with the principal, you are telling the child that you are indeed responsible. You are the one who will have the inconvenience of setting aside whatever it is you were going to do to go to the school to work out your child's problems. By giving in to this, and assuring the teacher that from now on your child will behave, you are not teaching your child responsibility. You are bearing the burden for things that he did and also for the things that he is supposed to do.

What we really need to do is give our children the responsibility for their own actions. When something like the above occurs, we have to speak with the child first.

"The *rebbe* wants to speak to me? What can I tell him? What should I say?" Even a child of eight should be able to answer this question.

"Am I going to tell him that you are going to behave from now on? I'm not in the classroom. I don't know what went wrong; I don't know what it is that you should be doing, so I don't know what to say. You have to tell me what to say."

We have to try to help the child assume responsibility, but what do we usually do? We say, "Oh, you misbehaved again? You are not doing your work and your *rebbe* said you are acting fresh? Now what am I going to do with you?" Then we go talk to the *rebbe*, who will tell us the whole story, and we try to figure out what to do. In this scenario you and the *rebbe* have taken responsibility for the child's behavior, and the child is left out of the picture.

This happens at home as well. We get involved in the children's fights, we take sides, we deal with it, we work it out. We make the compromise that will lead to peace. However, when we leave them out of the decision-making process, we are not helping them to become responsible people.

Picture the following event. You receive a call from an elderly neighbor informing you, in most indignant terms, that your son and his friends broke her window while playing ball. You apologize, assuring her that you will look into the matter, and you call the boy home. Depending on the nature of your child, he will breeze in either defiantly or nonchalantly, or he will enter with reluctance and apprehension. In any case, he knows what to expect.

There are two ways to deal with this. One: You take over. Depending on your nature, you can either stay in control or lose your temper, but you let the child know in no uncertain terms what you think about such carelessness, irresponsibility, and disregard for property. You can go on to ground him for a few days, during which time he may not play ball. You can insist that he use his allowance or birthday money to help pay to replace the window and remind him how often he has been warned not to play in that place or with those boys, and so on. There is no limit to the recriminations and threats that a creative parent can heap on a child's head. Incidentally, the child is probably looking anyplace other than into your eyes as he impatiently or resignedly waits for the end of your tirade.

"You know that you are not allowed to play ball close to any houses ... you know that you are not allowed to use a hardball ... and how many times do I have to tell you that the neighbors rest in the afternoon and you are not allowed to disturb them ... Now you are going to have to ..." Was anything you said absorbed, accepted, or internalized? By dictating the terms of the situation and its repercussions, you have taken the responsibility on yourself. Why? Did *you* throw the ball? Is it *your* fault that it went through the window? Obviously it is not. Then why do you become so upset and so involved in the unraveling situation?

The second approach is to ask, as calmly as possible, "What happened?"

"Well, ummm ...," he will say. He knows that you know, but you have to get him to tell the story.

"Well, we were playing, and ..."

"What were you playing? Oh yes? Where were you playing? Really? How did it happen? Was there any way that it could have been avoided? What should we do about it now? Our elderly neighbor must feel terrible. She must have been frightened. How is she going to pay for the window? Do you have any suggestions?"

Now the burden is on him. "Uh, well ..."

"We need some answers here, because we have to work this out."

Wait for him to answer. Don't offer the answers. Leave the problem with him for as long as you think reasonable. Tell your son he has to come back in twenty minutes, an hour, or two hours, with an answer. For at least twenty minutes he is going to have to think about it. He is not going back to his room to play. For twenty minutes it will be his responsibility to evaluate what has happened and how he is going to try to remedy the situation.

That is teaching responsibility.

≈ Levels of Responsibility

Being a role model is an extremely important part of teaching responsibility. If we assume responsibility for the things that we do wrong, for problems that we create, then it will be a little easier to teach our children to do the same.

I faced a difficult situation some years ago with a parent whose computer was connected to the Internet. The parents were convinced that they had control of the situation, but I saw that their son was beginning to lose interest and concentration in his learning and in his other activities in yeshivah. I called him into the office and discussed with him, among other things, the fact that he had access to the Internet.

"Yes" he said, "but I only use the Torah net, and I'm very careful. Chas v'shalom, I would never go to any bad sites."

"I really hope you are being honest with me," I answered, "because I would hate to know that you are hiding something, and it is probably hard to keep really straight on something like this."

"No, no, no, my parents are very careful and so am I."

Another couple of days passed, and he went home for Shabbos. When he came back he was absolutely incapable of concentrating on his learning.

The next day, while he was in yeshivah, I went to his house with his parents' permission. It is difficult for an amateur to totally erase his footprints from computer files, and I opened up certain files that were more than enough to tell me that the young man was hurting himself in his spiritual growth and in his ability to learn Torah on a serious level. Who was responsible? Where did the blame lie?

His parents were ready to punish him in a myriad of ways. "Excuse me, my dear, wonderful parents," I said. "You brought the tumah, the impurity, onto his desk. You gave him access to everything. You trusted him, which is a very nice thing to do, but that level of self-control is beyond what most fifteen-year-olds are capable of.

It is being unrealistic, if not irresponsible. You must take the blame."

I called in the boy to discuss the situation, as it was something that had to be dealt with immediately. He told me that for the first two weeks he had just been looking around on the Internet, and it was only in his last session that he found objectionable sites.

"Although I'm blaming you because you weren't honest with us," I said, "I'm not sure if I know too many fifteen-year-olds who are capable of controlling themselves in such a situation. So this does not make you a rasha, an evil person, but you have to make a very big decision now. Either you ask your parents to remove the modem from your computer, or you have to find another yeshivah. Because once you have gone so far into where you don't belong, you are going to have to make a sacrifice. It is your decision. I'm not telling you what you have to do or how to do it. You work it out with your parents. Whether your parents allow you to have it or don't allow you to have it, under whatever conditions, has nothing to do with us. My condition is either the yeshivah or a modem, not both."

We teach computer classes at the yeshivah and this boy was very, very good. If he had a modem, he'd get to any site no matter what limits were set, so he had to face the problem head-on.

"You see," I told him, "this is now a level of responsibility that you have to try to take on yourself. You have to make the decision."

Baruch Hashem, he made the right decision, and it really was his decision.

There are two levels of responsibility in cases like this. On the first level, the parents are really responsible for what happened, not the child. The Gemara[1] says that if somebody takes a child, cleans him, dresses him nicely, feeds him, puts a pouch of money around his neck, and then puts him on the doorstep of a house of disreputable women, "Ma ya'aseh haben v'lo yechta, What should the child do and not sin?" A

---

1. *Berachos* 32a.

child who has been given the opportunity to fall, will fall. Who is responsible? Isn't it the parents who have placed him in this situation? That is level one.

The second level of responsibility is his. "Yes, I understand how it was that you did these things that you should not have done. I consider you a good boy and I'm not throwing you out or punishing you, but you have to make a decision, your own decision." I gave him a real responsibility. He might tell his parents that he is faced with this decision, but if so, he is going to have to let them know what I said, along with the condition I had attatched.

He might have decided to look for another yeshivah, hoping his parents would not find out about his activities. I didn't know what he would do. I took a chance by leaving it up to him to make the decision. The easiest thing to do, of course, would be to make the decision for him, to call his parents and say, "Take out the modem." But that would only remove the challenge for the moment; it would not solve anything, because the boy would not have taken responsibility for his actions.

The parents could say, "You know, we made a mistake. We weren't aware of what kind of a trial we were giving you and how difficult it would be. We didn't even know what the possibilities were. We thought that certain restrictions would be sufficient." That would be smart.

Our responsibility in the yeshivah, however, was to prevent this free-for-all atmosphere and information highway from entering our school, while at the same time help this boy overcome his fall. We all fall, we all make mistakes, and it is not the end of our lives, or at least it should not be. There is a place for *teshuvah*, for rectification. The child has to assume responsibility by making a decision as to what he really wants to do; the parents have to assume responsibility for what they did and help him deal with it; and the yeshivah cannot turn away and refuse to have anything more to do with him. Teaching our children responsibility means accepting the onus for our part in any situation and empowering the child to acknowledge his part.

◄℞ *Responsibility and Davening*

Another area in which parents often deny their children responsibility is getting up on time in the morning. We want our boys to get up for *davening*; we want our girls to get up to go to school. Older children have to wake up in time to meet their schedules, to accomplish all they have to do. The scenario usually goes like this: "Yankel, you know you have not been getting up lately. That is bad. You are not being responsible. You are not getting to class on time. You are missing the *minyan*," and so on.

"Uh-huh."

"Well, from now on, you are going to get up on time, okay?"

"Mm-hmm, all right."

"Do you understand me? From now on I want you to wake up on time even though you are on vacation. Now, what time do you have to get up for *davening*? 8:15? Okay, tomorrow, at 8:15 you are going to wake up, right?"

"Okay."

"Are you going to wake up?"

"I'll try."

"What do you mean you will try? Are you going to wake up, or are you not going to wake up?"

"I'll do my best."

At 6 o'clock, you are already up waiting to see what is going to happen. At 7 o'clock you are on pins and needles. At 8:15 you must find out if he has gotten up. You tiptoe into his room and he is snoring away. At 8:20 your stomach starts to churn. At 8:30 you are angry. At a quarter to 9 you are seething. What is going on here? He was supposed to wake up at 8:15. At 9 o'clock, you lose it completely. You walk in and start shaking him, "You were supposed to wake up at

8:15. What happened? Why didn't you wake up? Don't you know that you missed *davening*?"

"(Yawn) Forgot. I'll say *Krias Shema* and go back to sleep."

"But you were going to wake up ..."

At 10 o'clock, when he gets out of bed, you ask what happened.

"I was tired."

"Okay, you were tired, but you said you were going to wake up at 8:15."

"Yeah (yawn), I wanted to wake up but I couldn't." Did *he* say that he was going to wake up at that hour or did you tell him that was when he was going to wake up? You were the one who assumed the responsibility in that episode. Your son was not interested, didn't make any promises, didn't even think he could do it. Maybe he thought about it for a moment or two, but he had nothing to do with this decision; it was yours. The proof that you were responsible is that you were standing tensely at the door at 8:20.

Think about it. Once a child is capable of assuming resposibility (refer to Introduction) whose problem is it that he didn't *daven* with a *minyan* — his or yours? Whose problem is it that he didn't get to school on time — his or yours? Once we teach our children that this sort of thing is *our* problem, it stays that way, and we cannot really solve the problem because we cannot assume someone else's responsibility.

Assuming responsibility for everything is a difficult habit to change. It is harder to change than to stay the same, because it is time-consuming and inconvenient. But it works. Changing this habit means giving your child the responsibility for waking himself up in the morning or getting to school on time. Let's see how it works.

You call him in and begin this way. "You are probably not happy with the fact that you are missing *davening* in the mornings."

He has a choice. He can say yes or no. It is his choice. If he says, "No, I'm okay with it," you can reply, "Okay, you are a big boy. You are bar mitzvah. If you miss *davening*, that is your problem. If you don't *daven* with a *minyan,* that is also your problem. Do you feel good about that?"

"Yes."

"Well, I'm sorry to hear that. I feel bad that you feel good about it. I probably did something wrong. Maybe I'm not a good example. Maybe I didn't teach you the importance of *davening.* Maybe I just didn't do enough to make you feel how good it is and how special it is to *daven.* I take responsibility for my part, but I cannot take responsibility for yours. Since you are bar mitzvah, I hope you will find a way to appreciate *davening.*"

Then you might offer to study the meaning and the *halachos* of *davening* with him, or try to find ways of injecting positive messages about *davening* into the family environment. Most kids who answer that way have some pretty negative feelings about *davening.* Perhaps when he was younger he was pressured or embarrassed into *davening.* Possibly when he was tired it became a negative and hurtful experience. But once he feels this way, you have to deal with it.

Of course you can fight with him every morning, pull off the covers, douse him with water, scream, and yell. You can do that for years, but it is not going to solve the problem. On the other hand, with a little more consideration and thought on your part, he can realize that on a regular basis you are unhappy for his sake, that you feel bad because he is missing something. You sincerely believe this is something that he is lacking, and you are willing to help him if he is in agreement.

If, on the other hand, he admits that he does feel bad about missing *davening,* but it is hard for him, you can ask him why it is so hard to wake up in the morning.

"I'm tired."

"What makes you tired?"

"I go to sleep too late."

"Do you want to solve the problem?"

"Yes."

"Well, can you figure out what you should do?"

"I should probably go to sleep earlier."

"Do you think that would solve it?"

"Probably, most of the time."

"Okay, so how do you want to do it?"

Do all you can to help him through the process, but remember that it is his move.

Does this mean that from now on he is going to go to sleep at 10 or 10:30 so that he gets the sleep he needs? No, of course not, but he is at least beginning to think about a means of achieving his goal. He is probably starting to consider the ramifications of what it means to go to sleep after midnight every night. If he is convinced that you truly believe it is *his* problem, he will be compelled to start dealing with it.

"Would you like me to wake you up in the morning?"

"Yes."

"What time?"

"7:15."

"You want me to wake you up at 7:15? How many times should I wake you? I can do it two or three times. I'm not comfortable with more than that."

"No, once is enough."

"Are you sure?"

"Yes."

You go in the next morning at 7:15 and wake him up. "Remember," you say, "you said I should wake you only once."

"Okay, I'm coming, I'm coming."

You walk out, and he goes back to sleep.

Whose problem is it? His. When he wakes up later, he is going to look for your response. If you start in, "Well, see I told you, you know ..." you are taking responsibility. If you just go about your business, he is going to be uncomfortable.

"Oh, well, I thought I could be up on time, but you didn't wake me."

"I did, but maybe I should try harder next time. Should I pour water over your head? How much should I do?" Let him decide, give him the responsibility. As long as it is his problem, he will eventually find a solution. When it is his problem you can help him. You are on the same team.

What are the ramifications of tardiness? Will they throw the child out of school? The school and the parents have to work together so that the child will realize that it is a very serious situation. I don't think that children are aware of how important it is. Someone, the teacher, the principal, the parent, has to say, "You have come to school late every day. We want you to know that if it happens again X number of times, then such-and-such will be the consequence. If you come late, you are not going to be allowed into class."

We tend to think that a child is happy when he is thrown out of class because he can play around and have a good time, but children don't feel good about themselves when they are not where they belong. There are, of course, children who have been sent out of class so often without the reasons for their misbehavior having been properly addressed that they come to believe they don't belong in school! On some level they become comfortable with the situation, but this is not the case with the average child.

Your daughter comes home and says, "Well, it is not fair! The teacher said that I'm not going to be allowed into class if I come late again."

"What can I do?" you ask.

"Call the teacher?"

"Why should I call the teacher? What am I going to tell her? Is she wrong?"

"Yeah, it's not fair. There are other kids who come late."

"I don't know, maybe she feels there is a difference. Is there?"

"Well (grudgingly), other kids come late once in a while. I come late every day."

Our problem is that we are afraid of the ramifications. We are embarrassed, we are afraid of what will happen, what the school administration will think. But to reply as we have just shown you, the child realizes that she is the one with a problem.

"What can I tell the teacher? That *I* won't come late? How can I tell her that *you* won't come late? Do I know what you will do? I always think you are a good and responsible girl who wants to get up and out on time, but how can I give my word for your actions? Perhaps you are the one who should speak to the teacher."

Let the child deal with who he or she is. We usually don't do this. We start when they are three years old, and then when they are ten, fifteen, and eighteen, we don't understand why they are not responsible children and why they are not able to assume responsibility for what they do. Why are they always blaming the whole world for their problems? Why are they always using excuses to explain that it is not their fault that they are where they are?

Does this mean that when we do it the right way it is going to work all the time? No; but we have a much better chance of succeeding when we give them the responsibility.

◄ *Responsibility to the Irresponsible*

Assigning responsibility to a child who is not responsible seems to be a dangerous thing to do, because we are telling him that we trust him. Of course, we don't give responsibility beyond a child's capability. We would not let a five-year-old decide which school to attend. However, within the reasonable parameters of a child's ability we want to tell him, "Yes, you can take care of this situation." He, however, is not sure that he can. Building trust means giving responsibility even when we do not think he will be able to fulfill it all the way.

In every negotiation, both sides must take trust-building measures. If you mistrust someone, you cannot give him responsibility. If you want him to be responsible in a given situation, he must have the authority and the capability of fulfilling his part of the contract. It is the same with children. When they want our trust, we should try to give them responsibility in certain areas, even when they don't deserve it 100 percent. Their desire to prove to us that they are trustworthy will push their efforts up a notch. Knowing that we trust them automatically lifts them one step closer to deserving it. If we tell them that we trust them to make the right decision, they will decide correctly most of the time.

Let's say a child wants to go somewhere, and you know it is not the best thing for him. You tell him he cannot go because he will do things he should not be doing. You can explain as much as you want that this will cause him to do things that are beneath him, but by saying no, you have taken over the responsibility for his actions. He will react with bitterness and anger because he wanted to go and you didn't trust him.

There is an alternative.

"What do you think is going to happen if you go? Is it going to be good for you, or can it harm you in some way?" It is not so easy for him to lie and say, "Well, it is going to be great for me." He will probably say he is not sure.

"Do you think that if you go, you are going to be able to control yourself? If you are sure that you are not going to lose yourself in that atmosphere and everything's going to be okay, I'll let you go. But if not, then I think you should not go. I'll leave it up to you."

More often than not, you will be pleasantly surprised to hear him say, "I'm not going."

Of course the amount of trust you can grant the child depends on his age and character. It must be understood that a child has to be capable of the task given him. Obviously, a seven-year-old cannot accept the responsibility to judge whether or not something is harmful to his spiritual development.

◄ε Choosing Friends

Many years of experience have taught hundreds of *mechanchim* that a foolproof way to strengthen a friendship is to try to break it up. My *Rebbe* Rav Wolbe says that it is not wise to try to split up friendships. You need to help the child understand his preferences, or at least make it difficult technically for him to spend time with the other child without telling you about it. There is a third option as well. In the yeshivah we had two very difficult boys who were "good friends." All attempts to temper their relationship were counterproductive. We finally decided to put them together completely and totally. We put them in the same room, at the same table, next to each other in the *beis midrash,* and made them *chavrusas.* It only took five or six weeks till they decided that they didn't like each other.

What should we do if we don't approve of our child's friends? In the rare instances that we are absolutely sure that we will be able to completely control the situation, we can try to nip in the bud any unsuitable relationships. But if your child is with children you disapprove of all week long, at school or elsewhere, you are not really in control. If you stop him from seeing them with force and anger, you will only be pushing him closer to them.

This is not to say that you should just give up and say, "Okay, if you want to go, go." If we have reached the point where we have the communication we spoke about earlier, we know we are talking about things that are important to them, they know that we respect and trust them, and they want to live up to that trust.

Obviously we cannot start from zero and just say, "Okay, do whatever you want, I trust you." That is what my student's family did with the Internet problem. But when a child has grown up believing that he is trusted, he does not want to lose that regard. He wants to be worthy of having responsibility. We, on our part, have to be willing to sacrifice some of our expectations, because he is not going to do everything right.

✌ Doing Chores

We want our children to help at home. Some jobs kids enjoy and some they don't. This of course differs from child to child. We usually go to great lengths to get them to do the things they don't like, but that is not teaching responsibility. Since responsibility means knowing that "this is my job and I have to do it," it is much easier if the job is a pleasant one. At first, try to give them tasks that they like so they will feel good about doing them. Gradually they will understand that they are trusted and have a secure place in the family. Introducing them later to jobs that are slightly less pleasant and less fun will assure you of a better chance of getting those jobs done.

Sometimes we can be our own worst enemies!

"Sara'le, please do the dishes."

"Oh, I just did such-and-such."

"Sara'le, you really have to do the dishes, I need help."

"Okay, I'll do the dishes."

Then you stand there like a policewoman. "No, not like that! You are getting soap all over the place. Come on, you are getting everything wet, it is not ..."

Is she going to want to do the dishes again? No.

Do you want her to? No.

"She is too young," you say. "I'd rather do them myself because I have to clean up after her anyway."

But if you teach her to do the dishes in a nice way and let her do them wrong, clean up after her, and, as she gets a little better at it, compliment her, she and you will be pleased with her growing skill.

"Wow, you splashed almost no water on the floor. I'm happy to see that you didn't use too much soap. Very good." With such encouragement, it may take her ten times to learn to do the dishes properly. That is an investment of about three hours. The return is a hundredfold. Without that investment, without letting her grow into that responsibility, for the next ten years, four times a week, half an hour a day, you will have to do the dishes by yourself — because you didn't have the patience to teach her.

Yes, it is easier to do it yourself to avoid repairing the mess afterward, but only for the first dozen or so times. After that you will have another helper for the next ten years, because you made her feel good about doing it, and because when she finished the job, you gave her a big hug and kiss and said, "You know, you saved me today. I was so tired that I couldn't stand up any longer. Thank you so much." You will both feel good.

We "sacrifice" when we teach responsibility by letting the child make decisions. You let your son build the *succah*, and it turns out a little bit crooked. You compliment him and, when he is asleep, you take a bunch of nails and screws and you fix it. If you stand there telling him, "Well that is crooked, and look at this, didn't you see it, and why didn't you watch this," and so on, he is certainly not going to want to do it next year.

It takes tremendous resilience for a child to want to take responsibility when he is criticized at every step. You must find ways to get him to feel good about what he is doing. Rav Wolbe says we are not supposed to give out chores in order to make our lives easier, but to help our children recognize that they have a responsibility in the home. This has to be our aim. If children begin to feel that they are an important part of the family by making their own decision about what they want to do to help, we have a much better chance of helping them develop a feeling of responsibility to the home.

◆ Accepting Blame

Sometimes children find it difficult to accept responsibility for something they have done wrong. We can brand them and blame them and cut our lines of communication, or we can deal with the situation intelligently. The technique is the same one we use to establish effective communication. If we call our children liars, we cannot expect them to show responsibility. When we blame them, they have to deny culpability. When we ask them what happened and they know that we saw what happened, it is harder for them to deny it.

Even when they are in total denial, we cannot cut off our trust completely, leaving nothing for them to hold on to.

When we say, "That is not so. You did it, I saw you and I know why you did it," we are not only calling them liars, but we are taking responsibility for what happened. Then we send them out of the room as a punishment and they walk out feeling bitter and angry.

If we say, "I know you didn't do it on purpose, but I will feel more comfortable if you leave the room," there is a better chance that the child will think it over and say, "Dad, I'm sorry." We have given him the respect and trust to take responsibility. We have not called him a liar, and we have not embarrassed him by forcing him to admit he did something wrong.

Your son is supposed to study for a test. You know that he left school at 4 o'clock and stayed at a friend's house until 5. At 5 o'clock he came home and said, "I'm hungry," went to the refrigerator, and messed around in the kitchen until 5:30. Then he went upstairs and played with the computer until 6 o'clock.

"Chaim, did you study?"

"Yeah."

Did you study? when you know he didn't, is not a good question.

"Chaim, you probably would like to study, because you just got home a little while ago and you have been very busy and you have a test tomorrow."

It is too easy for him to push off responsibility. It is better to help him accept it. If we ask an open-ended question and he can get away with a yes or no, it is not responsible on our part. If we say, "I know you want to study, you are probably better off doing it now," then even if he had wanted to push it off, we are making him deal with it now.

He will be thinking, *Mom knows I didn't study and that I have a test tomorrow. Do I want to study, or do I not want to study? Do I want to lie and say that I did study? What should I do?*

If we ask if he studied and he says yes, we have to take the offensive. "Oh, really? When?" We are almost forcing him into the next lie, and he will always find an answer. If we want to help him accept responsibility, then we have to give him distinct boundaries. "You left school at 4, you were at Shloimie's until 5, then you were in the kitchen. You have not had a minute to study. You are probably worried about the test tomorrow."

"Oh, sure I am, really, yeah, that is right. Of course I'm worried about the test tomorrow." Or he will say he is not worried about the test tomorrow.

"But you haven't studied and you don't want to do poorly, do you?"

Of course a child can say, "I don't care if I do poorly," and of course there is always a way to get out of responsibility. If this is the pattern you have established, your children will have become totally disinterested in accepting any kind of responsibility. So, if you can be more thoughtful about helping them accept responsibility when they are younger, they will learn to accept it routinely. You must help them by asking the right questions. The difference between saying, "Did you study?" and "I'm sure you'd like to study and I know you have not had time" is the difference between priming the child to tell a lie and allowing him to deal with the problem.

"Yes, I really do have to get around to studying for the test."

Basically, it comes down to helping children think things through. We have to present options in such a way that *they* will have to make the decisions. Sometimes this means allowing them to fall and make mistakes so that they can become more responsible for what they do. We know that if we want to do something right, we can learn from our mistakes. Immigrants to a new country who are not afraid of being laughed at for their linguistic errors and accept correction are the ones who learn the language fastest. And those who are afraid to make mistakes, because they don't like being corrected or don't want to look foolish, don't learn the language as quickly. Every new undertaking is like that. The first time we don't do it so well, the second time is a little better, and the third time sees us on the way to success.

Hopefully with these tools — thinking through what we wish to teach our children and how we present it — we will be able to help our children become more responsible human beings.

Chapter Seven
MOTIVATING OUR CHILDREN

The catalyst of all goals and aspirations is the *neshamah*, the soul. The soul is the power source within a person that aims for the stars, that wants to become all it can be. The *neshamah* wants to rise as high as a person can possibly go, to become an angel with total fulfillment and purity. Inasmuch as our *neshamos* are limited by our physical beings, however, our goals and aspirations are going to be based on what we believe we can do. If we knew what we are really capable of attaining, we would have much higher aspirations and much greater goals, but generally we don't want something that we believe is totally beyond our grasp. As much as we would like to have it, it is not a goal; a goal is something we believe is within our reach.

This is the basic mechanism of motivation: There is something I want, and I know it is achievable. If I want it but don't really believe that I can attain it, I will not be motivated to work toward it. If we want to motivate our children, therefore, we have to understand the place of this mechanism within the framework of their education. To help our child set goals, we have to know what he wants. Today he wants this, yesterday it was something entirely different, and tomorrow it will be something else. Sometimes we don't even have yesterday, today, and tomorrow. We have ten minutes ago, now, and fifteen minutes from now. Setting a goal at that level is very difficult.

Rav Wolbe once said something deceptively simple. It is really one of the deepest things I've ever heard. He said, "If you want to know what you really want, on the deepest level, not just wanting to want but really what is most important to you, look at what you are doing."

This is so anticlimactic. We want to hear about our inner *ratzon*, our will; we want to hear about our aspirations for greatness and for goodness. But what we really want is what we *do* — because we cannot escape what we actually do. Among our options we may want one thing more than others, like the boy who constantly says, *"I wanted to help in the house, but I couldn't."*

"You mean you wanted to go out to play."

"No, I wanted to help."

"Then why did you go out to play?"

"Because I was bored."

"Okay, that's fair. You were bored, so you wanted to play."

"I didn't want to play."

He can say that he wanted to help from now until tomorrow, but in choosing between helping and playing, which one did he want more? The one that he did!

Israeli Prime Minister Sharon is a very heavy fellow who is known for his extremely impulsive behavior and outspoken ways. When he was the commander of all the armed forces in Israel, a young journalist once questioned him.

"Mr. Sharon, you're very well known for your tremendous will power. Why is it that you're not successful in dieting?"

"Well," he retorted without a second's delay, "I guess I just really want to eat."

This was not only a sharp answer, but a very straight and honest one as well. We do what we want to do. When our children talk about things they want to do, therefore, we have to look at their actions, because wherever they are, is, to a certain extent, where they want to be.

We often want to change this. In all honesty, when we say that we want to help them set goals, we really want them to have *our* goals. Since what they want is what they are doing, if they *really* wanted to change their behavior, they would.

Of course when they want something, they will turn our lives upside down and inside out until they get it. But when it comes to the important things, where are they? Where they want to be. We want them to be somewhere else. Before we assume that we can help motivate them to change, we must make sure that the goal becomes something that they want. Helping them to realize that their goals are similar to ours is the real challenge of motivating children. The first rule is: Sell! Every educator and every parent has to be a salesman.

◀ᴢ Selling Your Goals

What is selling all about? It is about getting the other person to believe that he needs, absolutely needs, the Jacuzzi, because if he does not have it, his back is going to hurt and he is going to be uncomfortable. He will be deprived. Everyone else has one. It is exactly what he needs for that half hour of relaxation (which he is never going to have anyway) at the end of a very difficult day.

A salesman has to get people to want the item he is trying to sell. If we want someone to buy a pitcher, we have to explain why this pitcher is going to make him the class act in town, and that if he does not have it, he is missing something. When we want someone else to accept our perception of something, we have to be willing and able to think of how to make it a worthwhile goal for him.

Obviously we are not talking about such peripheral things, and we are not talking about advertising so that we can profit. We are talking about the things that matter and helping someone recognize his own, real needs. It is just not enough for us to tell them that it is important to us.

"Well it's important to you, that's nice. To me it's not. I'm not going to buy your pitcher; I'm not going to buy your

Jacuzzi; and my goal is not to get better in school. I'm doing fine. I'm having a great time. You mean you want me to work harder? No way!"

If we want to transfer our values, aspirations, and goals to our children so that they internalize them, we must become master salespeople. How can we get our children to share our goals? We can begin by sharing an interest in the things they want. We are very good at telling our children what they should want, what they should be, what their goals ought to be, but meanwhile we are denigrating things that *are* important to them.

"So you need a bicycle? That's important to you? But what about your life?"

"What do you mean? That *is* my life."

That is not our perception of his life, but at that moment it is his. We cannot label what he wants as frivolous and then expect him to adopt our values. It does not work that way. If we want our children to share our goals, they have to feel that we respect theirs. Sometimes a child wants something very badly, and he knows it may not be acceptable to us. We have to try to get him to believe that what we want is just another aspect of his own desire.

> One boy in our school, a very bright young man, finished school at sixteen and decided that he wanted to join the army. In Israel, as in most countries, induction is at eighteen, so what he really was saying was, "I don't want to go on to yeshivah gedolah, to post high-school studies."
>
> The usual way to handle this is to call the boy in for a "talk."
>
> "Well, what are you going to do with your life? Are you going to throw it down the drain? The army is no place for you!"
>
> In Israel the discussion is about the army; in America it's about choosing a profession. In every society there are going to be conflicts between the children's goals and their schools' goals.
>
> I had no reason to take a stand on the army issue for this boy because he was sixteen years old and could not

sign up for another two years. In Israel, with its present social polarization, he figured that his choices were limited — he would have to either go to yeshivah or go into the army. If he wanted to go into the army, there would be no reason to continue in yeshivah, and no reason to do anything else either, because who is going to hire a sixteen-year-old? He would obviously end up just hanging around, and probably set a pattern for becoming a very unsuccessful person in general.

After Purim, we discussed the following year's plans with each boy in his class. We worked with each boy individually, ascertaining what he planned to do, which school he would apply to, which program he would join; and each student knew where he was going.

I didn't say a word to this young man. I didn't even call him in. He was very strong-willed, and wielded tremendous power in his group. Had I argued with him at that point, six other boys would have joined him. All along he kept saying, "I'm not going to yeshivah, I'm not going to yeshivah, I'm not going to yeshivah," but nobody was fighting with him. When every other boy had known for a month what he was going to do, this boy was definitely wondering. Each time I passed by, he would look at me out of the corner of his eye, and I would just smile.

Two days before the end of the term, I called him in. "You know, this conversation is just between us," I said, "but I think you're suited to be an army man." Shocked, he squinted at me. Had I winked when I said that? Was I serious?

"Listen, you want to go and you should. I think it will be very good for you."

"What? Do you mean it? Really?"

"Yes. Do you think that everyone has to go to yeshivah? You'd make a good soldier because you have the motivation to do well."

All his defenses were down. I wanted what he wanted for himself.

"You know, you still have two years until you can join. Now I think that if you're going into the army, you

should go in on a higher level, and you'll be a much better soldier. Who knows how they'll look at someone who
comes from an unstructured framework? You should be
the person who gives the Daf Yomi shiur, the daily Talmud
class. Let them look at you as a successful human being.
You're bright and talented, you have charisma, and
you're a leader. You're not just a nothing. You're a special
fellow. I think that perhaps you should think of going to
some kind of program for the next two years where you'll
work hard, and then go into the army."

This boy is a bright, beautiful person. Everybody likes
him. He has the makings of a very great rabbi to lead the
next generation. My highest aspirations for him were not
involved with the army at this point in his life, because
he could become a Rosh Yeshivah, the head of a great
learning center. He didn't dream of such things. He was
totally removed from any such thoughts. Discussing this
with him at that point would have been counterproductive, so we spoke about his ambitions.

"But we have to make two conditions," I said. "One
is that you don't talk to anyone about this discussion,
because I don't want anyone brainwashing you against
going into the army. This is between us. In two years I'm
going to come to you and say, my friend, the time is up.
This is my guarantee to you. I promise that I will come to
you and say, 'That's it! It is now two years!'"

Although he was brilliant, he had never put too much
effort into learning, so he could not go to a top yeshivah.
We sent him to a new school with a Rosh Yeshivah who
was a very charismatic, empathetic person. I checked
up on him every once in a while, and he was really
learning.

Around Pesach he phoned me at 12:15 one night. "I'm
sorry I'm calling so late, but I learned till 12, and someone else was on the phone until 12:15, and I'm sorry it's
so late, but during the day I have no time to call because
I'm learning ..."

"Really, don't worry, it's okay. What can I do for you?"

"You know, Rebbe, I was thinking that maybe for next year, I should go to a better, a more advanced kind of program."

I sent him to another yeshivah for a Shabbos to see how he liked it. The Rosh Yeshivah met him and said, "I want a boy like this."

"Would you take him as a learning partner?" I asked.

"Yes."

"Okay, he'll come to you."

"What do you mean, he'll come? Don't you have to ask him?"

"No, he's my student and he asked me for advice. So I know he's going to join you."

He did go, and he learned with the Rosh Yeshivah. I visited him a number of times and at the end of the second year I said, "Okay, your two years are up."

He looked at me, thought for a second, and he smiled. He winked at me and went back to the study hall. Two years before, he wanted to do one thing, and at this point he wanted to do something else. His options were still open for the future.

Now, ten years later, he is one of the top men in one of the most advanced kollels in Israel. He is going to pass Torah on to the next generation, and he is going to do a good job of it.

I am relating this story, obviously, to illustrate a point. If I had denigrated his goals and tried to replace them with mine, I would have had no chance of success. As soon as he recognized that I honestly believed that there was validity to his desires and I just wanted him to be better at what he would be doing, I was able to guide him. I didn't fool or trick him but helped him to open his mind to other alternatives before he made his decision. If he were to call me today and say he wants to go into the army, I would not argue with him. It is his decision. He has the right to decide how he is going to spend his life, but it should be an informed choice.

In the marketplace, employers generally know how to motivate employees. The employee says half a sentence, barely touching on something that is more or less what the employer desires, and it is transformed into a goal.

> *"What a good idea that is."* The employer grabs it and runs with it.
>
> *"Did I say that? Right! I guess I did,"* the employee says. The boss gave him respect and now he can listen to what the boss has to say. He probably had a half-formed idea relative to some aspect of a company initiative. The boss wants him to take over in that area or move along in a certain direction, so he shares in the *"employee's idea."*
>
> If the boss says, *"Listen, what you've been doing is a waste of time; what I'd like you to do is this,"* he will not encourage a desire on the employee's part to shift his focus.
>
> *"You've been doing a great job, and I've noticed recently that you've started to take an interest in A,B,C. Would you be willing to take over a little more of that?"*
>
> *"Oh, yes, that's just what I'd like to do! Thank you for this opportunity."*

We can apply this technique to motivating our children by using their abilities in something they do well to help shape their future goals. If they are convinced that they can do something, hopefully they will be inclined to do it.

◄ Success Breeds Success

> We had a sweet, good student from the United States in our yeshivah in Israel. When he arrived, he said, "Rebbe, I don't know how to learn Gemara. I can't learn Gemara." His brothers, he knew, were geniuses. He was a nice boy but not brilliant, and he was convinced that he didn't have the capability to learn well.
>
> "Why do you say you can't?" I asked.
>
> "Rebbe, if everyone would tell you for ten years that you can't learn, you'd also believe that you can't."
>
> "Okay," I said, "let's see."

The mashgiach made a deal with him that for the next few weeks he would not be allowed to say the words, "I can't." "That's excised from your lexicon. You can say, 'It's hard,' but you can't say, 'I can't.'"

The mashgiach then began learning a few lines with the boy every day until he learned an entire blatt of Gemara be'al peh (a whole page by heart). He called the boy's father in the United States. "Listen," said the mashgiach, "we have a present for you for Yom Kippur!"

"Yes, what is it?"

"Your son is going to say over a blatt Gemara by heart, an entire blatt of Gemara!"

"What?" said the astounded father who was a talmid chacham, a scholar, and a distinguished educator.

"Just listen ..." The boy took the telephone and proceeded to recite the entire blatt.

I can't begin to convey the emotions of both father and son. When the boy finished speaking to his parents, he came to me in euphoria.

"I did it! I did it! I can do it!"

Four weeks earlier we had told him, "If you put your mind to it, you'll make it." He had said, "No I won't, I'm wasting my time."

We gave him, in small doses, the ability to be successful. Now he wants to do it again. I walked in on their learning session. He looked up with a smile.

"I'm working on the next one."

And now he is a young man who has achieved far more than any of us ever dreamed.

If you can do one, you can do ten; if you can do ten, you can do a hundred; if you can do a hundred, you can do a thousand. On the other hand, if a child does not want to do something, it doesn't help if we talk ourselves blue in the face. He will just drag his feet, he will just drag himself. Okay, he will do us a favor, but he has no motivation. We have to sell him on the idea somehow, help him to believe that he can follow through. We can force him to try, but it will probably have a short-term result that usually does not last. Sometimes we can push a child to taste something, just to whet his appetite, and then he finds out it is not so bad. But this cannot be done on a regular basis or in every case.

It is not like convincing a child to go into a pool. If the water is a little cold, you can push him into the water, and after a few minutes it does not feel cold anymore. But in a situation that has important or life-threatening ramifications, it is dangerous to do that. We have to use the tools we have been talking about, because pushing will not change a person's goals and aspirations.

If a child does not believe in himself, we have to let him know that we believe in him. We know ourselves that if someone we respect and love has confidence in us, it boosts our own self-confidence. At the least, it weakens our thoughts of worthlessness or doubts about our abilities. There is no end to the stories we can tell about children who didn't believe that they could accomplish something but with constant positive reinforcement, did.

"You are great, you are really good, you are phenomenal!"

This is especially true when the child believes he is nothing, that he is low and bad, because that is what he has been told a thousand times as he grew up. If he is told the opposite often enough, he begins to believe it. When a person has self-confidence and believes in himself, he will want to reach a goal. When he wants to reach a goal, he will.

◄⅔ Working with the Child's Goals

Are there dangers in this approach? Yes there are, because when you go along with the things that adolescents want, it can end up with them taking over completely. There are certainly risks involved when you work along with a child's goals when his goals are not those you would like to see him attain. But we must consider the alternatives. If we cannot interest the child in what we feel is desirable, then we have to work with his goals, clarifying the things that he wants, and using them to help him achieve what is truly good for him.

Our Sages[1] tell us, *"Mitoch shelo lishmah, ba lishmah* — a person can eventually reach a desirable level even if his initial impetus comes from ulterior motives." The Rambam ordains[2] that *we must teach children using ulterior motives.* If you want your child to learn, if you want to teach him to be successful, he says, give him candy or something he likes. Let the things he likes be associated with the things we want for him. When we say to our child, "If you learn well, I'll give you a dollar ... If you're successful, I'll buy you a bicycle," we are using his goals to achieve things that are good for him. Instead of saying, "I don't care what you want, I want you to learn," we should ask, "What do you want?" The child does not want to become a champion bicycle rider; he wants a bike just because he likes to ride one. We are plugging into something he is motivated to acquire, and we are using it to urge him to do something we want him to do. This is exactly the same as telling an older boy who wants to study in Israel for a year that he will have to reach a certain level in his studies and then you will send him.

We prefer that our children do things because they are the right, good, or noble things to do, and because they want to please us. Since the truth is that they want to do what appeals to them but need our help to focus on what is good and desirable, our use of ulterior motives is not only *not* bad, but necessary, normal, and healthy.

Of course, not everything has to be connected to a "candy"; there are things that must be done just because they are a normal part of everyday living. Obviously, as a child matures, our ulterior motives must take on a different perspective.

"I'm sure you want to be respected."

"You are a special person. You want other people to understand and perceive how special you are."

Once the motivation is in place, it must be constantly reinforced. Children know when they are doing well and we

1. *Pesachim* 50.
2. Introduction to *Perek Chelek, Sanhedrin.*

cannot fool them. We have to recognize the good in them and use it.

> We had a boy in the yeshivah who was bullying some other students.
> "You know, you're such a sweet guy," I said to him, "everyone must love you."
> "What?"
> "Yeah, look how many kids like you." Except for the weaker boys whom he was bullying, many boys did like him and I named eight of them.
> "Do you know why they like you? Because you're nice to them. The more people you're nice to, the more popular you will be."
> It was not necessary to remind him of the undesirable way he was treating a few boys. Was he going to be nice to everyone from that moment on? No, but a process was started.

Sometimes parents cannot seem to find anything good about their child. If, Heaven forbid, you feel that way, ask a friend of his what he thinks of him. Ask someone else who knows him, because others can see how good your child is. Everyone has good points, and if you cannot find them, you ought to turn to others for help. Never say, "Oh sure, when he's in *your* house he's great. When he's at home, *oy vey*, then the trouble starts." If he is good in someone else's house, he has some good qualities. Let's not turn that against him.

If he can be good elsewhere, why can't he be good at home? If he can be so sweet to somebody else, why can't he be sweet to me? If he can be so respectful to somebody else, why can't he be respectful to his rebbe? And so the complaints go.

Your child feels your negativity and will have no reason to behave better with you. Why is he so good in someone else's house? The first time it was probably because he was shy, but after that he knew the people praised his behavior. Perhaps the second time he was also ashamed to misbehave, but by the third time, he didn't want to disappoint these people who think he is great, so he continued to behave well in their home. In his own home, however, where you are already disappointed in him and he knows you gave up on him a long time ago, he has no motivation to change. Now it is up to you to find some good in him and work with it.

I often see a home where such a pattern has developed. For a few months, no matter how well the child does in school, they cannot believe me when I give them a good report. "What are you really telling me? What are you hiding?"

I have called parents to tell them about an earlier or later dismissal than usual, and the parents' immediate reaction is, "Oh no, what did he do now? If you're calling, I'm already worried."

That is an untenable pattern. If parents are intelligent, I will tell them that they have to start believing in their son. "You can't suddenly tell him, 'You're great,' because he knows you don't mean it, but you can tell him that the *Rosh Yeshivah* called and said he is doing well. 'We were surprised at first, but now we're so happy because it has happened three times.'" *What?* The boy thinks, *My mother thinks I'm doing well. She believes the Rosh Yeshivah?* Now when he is home, his behavior improves because he does not want to destroy that belief.

◄₰ Handling Conflicting Goals

As children develop, more of their goals often don't seem to tally with ours. We should not be disappointed by this. Most children have a good relationship with their parents. Although there are areas of conflict, they basically want to be good and do things to please their parents. They want to be successful within the system. Sometimes a child wants a certain article of clothing or a certain style of haircut that we disapprove of, and this frightens us. *Oh no, he wants to be different, he doesn't want to grow up in the right way.*

If you build this conflict into a crisis, the child doesn't feel respected. He thinks he has no place in our society and this can very well turn into a self-fulfilling prophecy. We very often create alienation. By thinking of his short-term desires as life goals that differ from ours, we will have a crisis on our hands. We need to be a little bit more understanding.

"We understand. Even though you want to do such-and-such, we know you're not saying, 'I don't want to be like you.'" Let the child know that even though he is fighting you a little, you don't view it as fighting you all the way. You have to let him know that there are so many things he is doing right, things that do fit into the patterns in which you have raised him, that you don't have to worry about smaller things to the point where it becomes a conflict.

Although it is normal for us to have fears, acting on them is not productive. Our children have to know that we believe in them, that we know that they are going to be successful, that they are great kids, and that we know that they want to be good. We ourselves want to be good, but from time to time we do all sorts of things we should not — in the way we raise our children, in the way we communicate with our spouses, in our occasional lapses in careful speech, and in the way we deal with friends. It does not mean that we are bad people and that we don't want to be good. We are quick to make excuses for ourselves because we "understand" our own mistakes. Our children are just like us. They are basically good, though on occasion they may lapse.

The bottom line is this: If we give our children the motivation to be successful, they eventually will develop into young adults with self-confidence. The more they accomplish, the more they will believe in things at which they can succeed. By giving them that confidence, we hope to celebrate their successes together with them.

Chapter Eight
UNDERSTANDING
ADOLESCENCE

We are going to try to understand the basic elements of adolescence from the somewhat unusual perspective of — the adolescent. Our goal is to see how we can help our adolescent children develop a self-awareness that will make it easier for them to deal with their adolescence and consequently make it easier for us to deal with them.

◂ℰ The Teenager's Point of View

The whole process of dealing with adolescent children has a great deal to do with their self-awareness. Therefore, we really have to understand more clearly what is going on in their minds so that we can help them to understand themselves and us. Comprehension of our teenagers' frame of mind has practical implications for building the relationship between us.

This point can be illustrated best by sharing a lesson taught by Rabbi Yisrael Salanter. He would say that when a child plays with his paper boat in the bathtub and it sinks, he is distraught. He says that the feeling is similar to that of a man whose merchant ship sinks on the high seas. To the child, his little boat represents his dreams and his aspirations. He worked on that boat the whole day until he finished it, and he was hoping to play with it during the entire bath time. Instead, it sank. Now everything is lost; for him the whole world is lost.

Rabbi Salanter's story does not give us a tool to deal with children, but it does illustrate an understanding of what is going on in a child's mind. Once we have achieved that understanding, it helps us to deal with his feelings. The story does not tell us what to do, but it indicates that through a better understanding of our child's point of view we can understand how we have to react. It would be cruel to say to the child, "Oh, it's just a paper boat. What did you expect? Forget it; it's nothing." To him it is something. To him it is important. This example is basic to understanding someone else's perspective. We have to try to understand what the child is feeling and think about what he is going through if we want to deal with him effectively.

◄₴ The Adult's Point of View

As adults we relate to things differently from children, not only because we are older, but because we have experienced and learned so many things along the way that have changed our opinions and molded our understanding. We have responsibilities that resonate beyond what is happening at the moment, and therefore our perception of the world is somewhat different from that of a thirteen-, fourteen-, fifteen-, or sixteen-year-old boy or girl. The young man or woman stands at a different place in life, and therefore his or her perceptions, emotions, and reactions are different from ours.

Most adults fail to recognize that the state of adolescence is an important, distinct, and necessary stage in a person's development. We wish our children past it before they have had a chance to begin it, and there is a good reason for that. We well know that having children in their teens generates conflicting feelings and enormous challenge, but it is not a stage we can skip or ignore. This stage is crucial to one's growth.

For the next few chapters we will continue to address this extremely broad topic in an attempt to facilitate our understanding of the adolescent mind. We want to learn how to react better to their perception of things and help them understand themselves.

◄⅔ The Values and Purposes of Adolescence

In broaching this subject, the first question I ask myself is why there has to be a period of adolescence. Maybe we should not even acknowledge such a thing. Where do we see any discussion about adolescence in the Torah? The Torah seems to teach only that a girl at the age of twelve and a boy at the age of thirteen become fully responsible for everything she and he does. One thing we do know is that they are not yet fully responsible to the point where we can say, "This is your obligation; you must do such-and-such." They are fully responsible to the point where a *beis din*, if there were one such as we had in the time of the *Beis HaMikdash* — a full court system — could pass a death sentence on a young person as a result of his or her actions. In the eyes of halachah, a teenager is just as accountable for his actions as an adult.

This means that the Torah considers teenagers to be responsible, aware, capable of making decisions, and able to choose the right thing. This seems to be a tall order when we look at our twelve- and thirteen-year-olds. We know that they are required to perform all the mitzvos. For example, if a child makes a *neder*, an oath, he has to keep that *neder* as if he were a person of thirty-five. There is no difference. The transaction of a thirteen-year-old is completely valid, according to halachah. If a thirteen-year-old boy is just playing, and he says to a girl, "*Harei at mekudeshes* ... — Behold, you are consecrated ..." that is *kiddushin*, a marriage vow, and it would require a *get*, a halachic divorce, to undo, which means that, as far as the Torah is concerned, these children really are adults. If they actually are considered adults, then where does adolescence come in? Who has time for adolescence?

I found one source that explains the difference between a thirteen-year-old and a twenty-year-old. Unlike the full-court system, Hashem does not mete out the harsh penalty of Heavenly punishment, *din bi'dei Shamayim*, until a person is twenty years old. Now, in order to define the reason for this period of grace, we first have to understand that this indicates a difference between a thirteen-year-old and a twenty-year-old. Exactly how does that translate into our perception of adolescents?

We'll try to understand with the help of the *Ohr HaChaim Hakadosh*. This *Ohr HaChaim* is taken from the commentary on the weekly portion of *Ki Sisa*, where the counting of the tribes is implemented through the *machatzis hashekel*, the collection of the half-*shekel*. The verse states that every individual has to give *terumas Hashem*, Hashem's portion; all adults from the age of twenty and up have to give the same amount — rich and poor alike. This requirement starts from age twenty. The *Ohr HaChaim* explains that at the age of twenty, and only at the age of twenty, the intellectual maturation process is completed. A person reaches his full intellectual capacity only at the age of twenty, and therefore he can be counted only from that age.

In looking more deeply into the foundation of this mitzvah, we discover a very important reason why a person is not punished until he reaches this age: He has heretofore not reached intellectual completion. He is not yet equipped with enough intellectual prowess and power to wage the war of breaking the evil inclination and overcoming his natural instincts and desires. Before the age of twenty, how can one completely understand and know his own desires, his own will? Is a teenager able to determine whether his actions are really going to make him happy? When he reaches twenty, however, he becomes mentally competent to wage war against the *yetzer hara*, the evil inclination, to understand things intellectually and overcome obstacles, and to define and choose the right way of life.

The *Ohr HaChaim Hakadosh* speaks of five basic elements marking the difference between a thirteen-year-old and a twenty-year-old. Before we ascertain what he means by that, we need to take a look at what "maturity" means. Only after defining the term can we discuss how the teenager matures into adulthood.

The *Ohr HaChaim* (*Shemos* 30:13, end) states:

ואומרו כל העובר וגו' מבן עשרים שנה

כאן הודיע סוד מה שלא חייבה התורה לאדם אלא עד שהוא בן עשרים (שבת פט:), שהוא לטעם עד שיגיע לגדר זה שתהיה נפשו שלימה מהשגת המושכל מההדרגות הרוחניים האלהיים, אשר נפש ישראל משם הוא ולזמן הנזכר תשיג, והוא סוד אומרו (תהלים ב ,ז) ה' אמר אלי בני אתה אני היום ילדתיך, ועיין בדברי הזוהר, (משפטים צ"ח) ויש טעם נכבד למה לא יענש אדם עד גבול זה, (1) כי הוא לצד שעדיין לא שלמה דעתו בהכרת המושכל (2) ובהשכלת הידיעה (3) ובתגבורת המספיק להערכת מלחמה, לשבור כח המסית ולנצח תאות הטבעיות, (4) ולהשכיל ברצון הנפש, ולהבחין את אשר ידבר בלבו אם לאושר, ובהיותו בן עשרים הנה הוא שלם בדעתו להחזיק מגן וצנה בתגבורת השכל וההבחנה (5) והבחירה בדרך החיים, והבן:

"There is an important explanation as to why a man is not punished [by the Heavenly court] until this point [age twenty, and that is] for the reason that he is not yet completely established in the following:

(1) the recognition of concepts, which we will call 'Recognition';

(2) the understanding of knowledge, which we will call 'Understanding';

(3) [the development of] sufficient strength to wage war to break the powers of the seducer [the evil inclination] and the conquering of [his] natural desires, which we will call 'Judgment';

(4) the determination of whether that which his heart tells him is for his benefit, which we will call 'Decision Making';

(5) [the ability to] choose the road of life ... which we will call 'Ability to Implement.'

"And when he reaches twenty, behold the maturation of his intelligence is complete [and he is able] to wield the shield and breastplate, with the strengthening of understanding, defining, and choosing the path of life ..."

In summary: When a young person becomes bar or bas mitzvah, he or she becomes a mature adult, with the faculties of knowledge, understanding, judgment, and decision-making — hence the full responsibility that is bestowed upon him/her by the Torah. However, there is still a maturation process of all those faculties that needs to take place from now till the age of twenty. It is our responsibility to help develop those existing tools during this interim period.

◄◊ Maturity Means Responsibility

What exactly is maturity? Is a teenager mature at thirteen or is he not? Is he responsible for his acts or is he not? The answer is yes, he is responsible at the age of thirteen, but at the age of thirteen he is responsible only *bi'dei adam*, as far as man is concerned. This condition is based on the fact that for the implementation of punishment in a human court, the demands of proof and warning and all the other elements required make it too difficult to carry out. This would make punishment through a human court very rare. That is why Hashem says that boys of thirteen and girls of twelve are responsible.

However, because *HaKadosh Baruch Hu's din,* His justice, and His measurement of man are infinite, immediate, and exact, it makes no difference whether there are witnesses or not — whether the person was warned or not — if he has committed a crime. Whatever he does, wherever he does it, Hashem is there and Hashem knows all about it. Hashem says, as it were, "I'm going to hold off implementing My *din,* My penalty, until the person's maturity is fully developed," because only then is he fully responsible on the level that *HaKadosh Baruch Hu* demands.

Unfortunately, knowing this is not sufficient for a parent to rely on, because our twelve- and thirteen-year-olds need a lot more help from us than just understanding the concepts. Still, we have to understand these fundamental elements of maturity and responsibility, because they are the elements that make a difference. So here we are with our adolescent children, and in accordance with the techniques of *chinuch* we are advocating, we are going to deal with who they are *now*. We will not deal with who they might have been or what we could have and should have done while they were younger, but with *what we have to do now.* We will get back to the *Ohr HaChaim* shortly, but first let us understand what our children are experiencing during this "stage" of maturation.

◄׳ *A Person in Transit*

I would like to describe the persona that we call an adolescent. My perception, based on thousands of hours of conversation and dealings with young people, is that the adolescent is a "person in transit." If you have ever traveled from one country to another with a transit stop in the middle, you know that you feel somewhat disoriented. You are there and you are not there. You left where you were, and you are not yet where you are going. You are hoping everything is going to work out, but you are not quite sure exactly what your status is. You are going to have to catch a connecting flight. You want to make a phone call, but you realize that you do not have any local currency. You would like to ask some questions about where you can find a kosher restaurant because the airline neglected to order your special kosher meal. You do not speak the language in the country where you are changing planes. You are slightly at a loss while you are in transit. You are not on your own turf. You are not where you feel comfortable and secure.

An adolescent is a person in transit. He has left childhood and he is expected to act like an adult. He is on his way, but he is not quite there yet. He feels at a loss. In the airport scenario, when we adults feel at a loss, we do not admit it. We do not want to be mugged or taken for a ride; we do not want to spend four times the true price in the duty-free shop, so we just do not go in. We avoid certain situations so that it will not be obvious to others that we are tourists in transit and they should not take advantage of us. Well, young people have their own protective ways of making sure that nobody takes advantage of the fact that they are in transit, but of course that is where they are.

Do not be fooled by the confident front your adolescent child displays. Do not be deceived into thinking that his confidence is coming from a secure place. His show of confidence is coming from an extreme and serious need to be perceived as confident at a most trying time in his life, when he is feeling least confident. The Hebrew word *yeled*, boy, is derived from a person's status as a *nolad*, one who has been born. The *nolad* is in a passive state. He or she is called *yeled* or *yaldah* till the age of twelve or thirteen. *Yaldus*, childhood, happens to a person without his willing it. The child is passively absorbing all forms of information during this period of his life. Then, at the ages of twelve and thirteen, he becomes a *bachur* and she a *bachurah*. The root of the word *bachur* means choice or choosing. At the ages of twelve for girls and thirteen for boys children become capable of all the things mentioned by the *Ohr HaChaim*. They are now in the active stage of making choices, which, of course, is why they have now become responsible. Something has changed in their very essence.

Children begin their lives as passive, accepting individuals; with adolescence they become active, decision-making individuals. Today, adolescence comes earlier and children mature sooner and are more aware of the world around them than ever before. Today we know that children can be extremely challenging even before the age of thirteen.

◄ᾰ Physical Changes

Adolescence is a physically trying and demanding time. How many things are going on in this child's mind and body? Before he or she can even face the mental changes, there are hormonal changes occurring that may cause moodiness and irritability. Growth spurts happen unevenly and affect the child's feelings about himself. These kids may have to deal with acne, which is an insult to their self-perception. If you can remember going through this when you were young, you will remember thinking, "Everyone will be looking at me, and what am I going to look like?"

They are extremely anxious about their height, because all around them their contemporaries are growing. Some who are shorter than they think they should be will react with hurt and disappointment, while some will compensate by making their presence felt at all times. Others are very tall, and both they and we regard them as older than they actually are. Often they feel big enough to do whatever they want and that overconfidence is dangerous. Sometimes, because of their size, we demand more of them than they are capable of producing. Meanwhile, they are not at all confident with their newfound size and they will totally shirk all responsibility given them.

"My son is short, but he doesn't seem to mind."

He does mind. And if he is tall, he minds. He has to deal with the fact that everyone thinks he is ten when he is fifteen or vice versa.

I can remember in our yeshivah, the *rebbeim* were able to put an arm around a thirteen-year-old's shoulder — he fitted in exactly — and it was a great way to show affection, encouragement, and warmth. Two or three years later, the kids were as tall as we were, or taller. We look at a boy and we say, "Wow, you've gotten so big," or "You're getting so tall," or something to that effect. He is not hearing what we are saying. He is looking at his friends and he is observing the boys who are taller than he and growing more quickly. Then he looks at the boys who are shorter than he and he worries,

"What's going to be with me?" He does not know how he is going to develop and he is concerned about what he will look like one day in the future. Boys and girls are sensitive to every single aspect of the maturation process that we take for granted. They notice the change in the shapes of their bodies, in their appearance, and most of all how their contemporaries see them. They wonder, "What am I going to look like and where do I belong?" That, of course, is because our physical being is so much a part of who we are, and we identify with our physical bodies to a great extent.

Sometimes we do not even realize that the child is going through enormous anxiety because he thinks he is not maturing fast enough. He is afraid that maybe he is not going to mature — or maybe there is something wrong with him if he is not developing at exactly the same pace as some of his friends. That alone is enough to cause anxiety in a young person. That alone is a heavy load for him. It is something to be aware of and to speak to him about. Young people should be made aware of the changes that are going on in their bodies, and fathers should teach their sons what is happening to their bodies, how it is going to affect them, and some of the new things that are going to happen of which they have to be aware.

Adolescence is an even more trying time for girls. They face more physical changes than boys, and if they are not forewarned about certain aspects of their development — if these things are not discussed, if they are not aware of what is going to happen and how to cope — it can be a very scary experience for them. We must prepare our daughters for the upcoming changes in their hormonal cycle. They have to understand what is happening to them.

When a child understands the process of growth and knows that it takes time, and that some people develop more quickly than others, a great part of their anxiety is neutralized. But these things need to be openly discussed.

Although this is not the platform for an in-depth discussion regarding this sensitive subject, let me just say that it *must* be dealt with. A father has to speak to his sons about these changes and a mother must speak to her daughters, because most children know the "facts of life" beyond anything we can imagine, though we do not know from where they get their information. Part of what they know or think they know is information we do not want them to have. Nevertheless, we want to provide them with a mature, adult, respectable way to view themselves. They must not associate their feelings, emotions, and desires with *shmutz*, literally dirt, automatically looking at themselves as "bad." They have to know that they are normal and they need to be helped to find ways to cope with their new, strange feelings. We want them to be aware that these instincts are there for a good reason and that they may be utilized in the future with holiness and purity. We can help them understand that the instincts we have been given are there for us to use as givers, not as tools for fulfillment of our own desires.

> *I remember a young boy who studied in a school where I was on the staff. He was a lovable boy. He was a little bit chubby and a bit baby-faced, though he was already in tenth grade. Now boys in tenth grade want to get hold of their father's shaver ..."Come on, I need it, I have four hairs, don't you see?" What is he saying? "Someone notice — I have four hairs, I need the shaver."*
>
> *Children want to show that they are growing up. This boy was having an extremely difficult time. We could not figure out what was bothering him. His parents were asking, "Why does he feel so belittled? Why is he acting out so much? What's going on?"*
>
> *I had a number of discussions with him, and at one point he just broke down. He said to me, "I know that I'm not the same as everybody else and that something's wrong with me. I'm a baby and I'm not going to grow up, and that's it." He felt immature because of his nature and because of the way his body was developing. He felt at a loss to the point that he was sure he was not ever going to mature, that he would never be accepted by his peers. He was in fact really frightened. He assumed that he was going to stay a little boy.*

> With a brief discussion and a little bit of biology instruction, a little bit of humor, and a little bit of sensitivity, we were able to convince him that this was something he did not have to worry about and that he would start to see a change within a certain amount of time, which of course he did.
>
> This boy developed into a fine young man. But those twelve months, that entire year, in which he saw his friends developing faster than he, placed him in a situation that he could not handle. He did not know how to cope. He thought that he was inadequate and that he was not going to make it.

My point in telling this story is that it is difficult for us to climb into a mind-set like that. We have been away from it for a long time; we do not remember. Maybe we never went through it, because everyone, after all, is different. The fact that everyone is different is enough to make a boy or girl feel insecure, competitive, and inadequate. I can tell you, as someone who has watched young boys for many, many years, that there are boys who are so self-conscious of being on the short side that they are constantly comparing themselves with their peers, and they actually choose a place to stand in shul that will minimize the difference. Should he stand next to his father or not? After all, his father is tall and he is short. Or perhaps he will avoid standing near the neighbors because the neighbor's child, who is the same age, is taller.

I have noticed this in the yeshivah repeatedly. When the boys would line up to take their seats, sometimes there's a short fellow who intentionally wants to sit near the big boys for protection, while there are usually some shorter boys who want to stay only with other short children who do not make them feel inadequate. This is an extremely personal matter and very subtle. We have to notice it because we are parents, and if we do notice that there is such an issue, it is something to bring out into the open and discuss, allowing the person to discuss his feelings. That self-awareness makes it easier to help him and removes tension and anxiety.

In one of the yeshivos I had the privilege of establishing, there was one thirteen-and-a-half-year-old pupil who came from a family in which all the men developed early and were physically mature at a young age. He was underdeveloped, small, and a very unhappy child. He even once said to one of his teachers, "I'm so physically immature!" His behavior at school was so normal that we never suspected how worried he was, but the remark made an impression on his rebbe and we brought it up at a parents' meeting. His father, a strapping man of six feet, four inches, was astonished that his child even mentioned the subject.

It seems that at home his behavior was extremely erratic and seemingly chutzpadik. He would not go to shul. He would repeatedly fight with his older brothers who were all over six feet tall and he would never walk with his father anywhere. The next time he came home, his father told him that when he himself was about fifteen, he suddenly went through a very drastic change. All of a sudden his beard began to grow, his voice grew deeper, and so on.

Knowing that his father had been physically immature until the age of fifteen lifted a mountain from this boy's shoulders. He did not know if the changes would happen to him at fifteen or sixteen or fourteen and a half, but he now had confidence that he would eventually become "manly." He asked his father a number of questions, and after that conversation the boy was a changed person.

✌ Intellectual Changes

Now let's return to the *Ohr HaChaim Hakadosh,* who points to five areas of intellectual maturation. They are:

Recognition of different concepts
Understanding of concepts
Judging or weighing concepts one against another
Decision-making or choosing one concept over another
Implementation or following through on the decisions made.

All these are separate but intrinsic parts of *bechirah*, the ability to choose. You can consider any one of them separately. One can realize that there are issues, but not be capable of understanding. One can understand a concept but not necessarily be able to weigh it vis-à-vis its many components. One can weigh the various components of a concept, but not necessarily come to the right decision. One can come to the right decision and still not have the power to implement that decision. If you read the *Ohr HaChaim Hakadosh* carefully, you see that he is saying that these are the five areas in which a person has to mature.

On the one hand, the adolescent is capable; he can make decisions, he can judge, and he feels comfortable doing so. But on the other hand, Imma and Abba have always said to him, "When you're older, you will understand." This always used to make sense to him, but it does not seem to any longer. Our old faithful line, "When you grow up, you'll understand," does not work now. It does not work for a few reasons. First of all, it is not necessarily true. One of my sons was smart enough to answer this cliché, "One second! Our neighbor is older than you and he disagrees with you." In other words, "When I grow up, I may very well not agree with you at all!"

Surely there are people your age who think differently from you. This makes the words "when you grow up you'll understand" not only condescending, but quite possibly wrong. Who says that age has anything to do with understanding? I have met people who are older than I who are greatly lacking in intelligence. I know people who are grown up but never "grew up." Age really does not have too much to do with understanding. Some children are smarter than their parents. They catch on faster, they just know things, they are "with it." Some children are intuitive, quick, intelligent, and understand some things even better than some adults. This type of child can sense that he has a high level of understanding and we cannot just tell him, "You don't understand." We have to think about it; we have to figure out what we should say instead.

We are ahead of our children in certain ways, and we should figure out precisely how. But we have to be able to share that with them. We have to be able to explain to them why we are ahead of the game, if we are. If there is an area in which you see that your child is sharper, smarter, or shrewder than you, go ahead and give him some free rein. Let him express himself in those areas. Let him do well in those areas. There are children who, for example, just instinctively know what to do with an electric drill. There are even children who know better than you what to do in some situations. Listen and take the time to hear them out. Discuss it. They can say some pretty smart things. They are not dumb. They are old enough and smart enough that *HaKadosh Baruch Hu* has decreed that they are responsible for every decision they make from the age of thirteen on. That means they do possess judgment. That means that they can understand concepts.

Adolescent children can make decisions. If they could not make decisions, the halachah would not hold them responsible for their decisions. But we hold the rope from both ends, as it were. We want them to be responsible, because they are adults now; we also want them to completely and totally accept everything we tell them. That is hardly realistic nowadays. We may have to learn how to have conversations with our teenager. We may have to learn how to discuss things with our children and not just tell them what to do.

Now I am in no way condoning the permissive school of thought that says that children should do whatever they want and you have no right to tell them what to do. We have the right to tell our children what to do, and there are times when we have to enforce our authority, using various and sometimes even unlikable methods. But this does not happen often. For the most part, we should use discussion and *chinuch* as the major means of helping our children become independent and capable of independent thinking.

The maturation process that the *Ohr HaChaim* describes is that of a person who understands but can become capable of greater understanding, one who judges but can improve his power of discernment (even Supreme Court judges have a learning curve, for they are dealing with new situations all the time). Yes, a thirteen-year-old boy and a twelve-year-old girl do have the ability to judge, but judgment requires experience, among other things, and they are confronting new situations all the time. Experience, additional knowledge, and a few other factors all come into play. Of course they can make decisions, but we have to understand what is affecting their decisions. What are the prime movers in their decision-making process? If we understand who and what is influencing their decision-making, we will know how to speak to them about it.

Once they have decided and know what they have to do, our children face the battle of actually going ahead and doing it. Why is it a battle? What are they fighting against? Having explained the five areas the *Ohr HaChaim* focuses on, we can better understand the difficulties our teenagers encounter in implementing their decisions.

Keep in mind, children are not always aware of certain issues and ideas. They are still processing new information with some childhood notions. It is still difficult for them to understand certain concepts, make certain decisions, and judge certain things, and we can help them in this process. What can be more important for parents than to help their children negotiate the years from thirteen to twenty successfully? Rather than causing them to become more and more rebellious, questioning, and difficult, which is what we often do, we can help them along the path to maturity. With our support, they themselves can learn to recognize their increasing capacity to understand, to judge, to make decisions, and to implement their decisions. Surely that is what we want from them. Surely that is our own goal to help them through this maturation process. But they are still children and they are going to make mistakes. We all make mistakes. They are not wrong when they say, "You had your chance to make mistakes. You are so smart because you learned from your mistakes. Well, let me make my own mistakes."

Chapter Nine
HELPING ADOLESCENTS MATURE

C hildren are knowledgeable today; there is no question about it. But they think they know *all* the answers. Well, we have some answers, too, and one of them is that there are mistakes we should let our children make. It is a mistake to try to protect children from making mistakes, because if we never give them the opportunity to learn to use their judgment, to make decisions, and implement the tools that Hashem gives them at this age, at some point in time they will inevitably make truly major mistakes. If we protect them from everything, always tell them what to do, never let them think things through by themselves, or give them opportunities to make choices on their own, they will grow into adults who lack the tools to manage on their own.

Children can begin to make choices at the age of two and three; even at this early age children are capable of learning through choosing. Obviously we are not going to ask them to set their own bedtime when they are four years old. We are not going to ask them at age six to which school we should send them. Giving them choices means giving choices that they are capable of making. On those rare occasions when I have helped my children get dressed, I have intentionally asked them to make choices: I would show them two shirts or two blouses and ask that they choose between them. That technique contributed to the fact that our eight-year-old and our six-year-old now dress themselves. They don't need someone to choose their clothes for them; they have learned to do it for themselves. Show your young child two items and ask, "Which one do you want?" Allow him or her to make the decision. "I'm going to count to ten while you choose one." He/she chooses one. You have encouraged your child to make a decision and he has also learned not to take more than ten seconds to make it.

These are small choices and they are for little children. Children of thirteen and fourteen have somewhat more difficult decisions to make, for which they don't always feel they need your help. They must make their own decisions and you have to let them make mistakes. So the tie does not match the suit perfectly? That is his problem. Let him deal with it. You don't like the way her sweater matches her skirt? She does. She will learn. She will hear enough comments about it from other people. You must learn to take their unimportant mistakes in stride.

◄ Serious Decisions

On a more serious level, we may be worrying about whether a certain friend is good for our child, and this is not always something we can define clearly. Furthermore, it is not usually something we can control, because our child is not under our supervision twenty-four hours a day. He is in school most of the day and if he wants that friend, he is going to have that friend. We can discuss the friendship, but don't think that we are going to make that decision for him. If we think that he is making some mistakes, we should discuss it with him. He can hear both sides of the argument and decide accordingly.

Sure, he will make mistakes sometimes, and of course we don't want him to make major mistakes. We are not going to let him walk into something that could be, Heaven forbid, the beginning of a downfall. We are not going to let him make a mistake that could destroy the rest of his life. However, there are plenty of things that we can let him do and help him to decide. We should be proud of the fact that he is willing to accomplish things and that he wants to do it on his own. This takes some maturity on our part as well. We need to be able to step back, and we need to trust our children. We need to let them make decisions and we need to believe, really believe, that they understand a lot.

The two prerequisites for understanding are knowledge and experience. You cannot say to a child, "When you grow up you'll understand." But you can say to him, "You know, my decision is based on some things that I have learned from past experience. If you had lived through the same things I have, you might come to the same conclusions as I. I don't know for sure, but I believe you will, because you are an intelligent person. As your father, I am going to try to give you the fruits of that experience. I'm going to try to send you to the right schools and introduce you to the right people so that you'll learn the things that will help you make the kind of decisions that will be most beneficial.

"You are right," you tell him, "our neighbor disagrees with me. Our neighbor has a different educational background than mine. He does not know what I know and I don't know what he knows. I'm not judging whether he is right or I'm right, or whether his opinion is good or bad. He is probably a good person, but good people often make decisions that don't fit our family outlook or the kind of things we do. I truly believe that if you knew all the things I'm talking about, all the reasons for my decision, you would agree with me. Now you really want to go to this place, and I'm saying no. Trust me. Please trust that if I could explain to you everything that is going through my mind right now, you would agree with me. If you don't agree, it is because there are other issues involved in your decision-making. Maybe you want to go because your friends are going, or you want to go because you already said that you were going. I understand this. So why am I telling you not to go? Do you really think I want you to have a bad time, that I don't want you to enjoy your life and have fun?"

That, by the way, is a typical remark. "You don't want me to have a good time." But kids will say that before you have assured them of the opposite. If you address the issue, whatever it is, immediately, and if you show your love, concern, empathy, and understanding of why they want what they want, it will make a big difference. Don't think it will be easy. I don't wish to promote false hopes that your child will instantly respond, "Oh, Imma, you are so smart. That is really what I want to do now." I can assure you, however, that you can develop a better relationship and better communication, understanding, and empathy so that even though you are saying no, the child will not feel as bitter or rebellious. He will not feel as much resentment as he would have if you had said no without careful thought and preparation.

We want to understand our children, and we want them to understand us. Why? Not because we are afraid of them. *Our goal is to help them to develop their ability to make decisions on their own.* We want them to develop the strength of character that is necessary to help them stand up to their friends and not be pressured into decisions which are detrimental to their well-being, and that is why we have to discuss problems with them. We are wrong if we think it is much easier to just say, "No! I'm sorry, that is it. There is not anything to discuss. Anything I say, you are going to say 'no' anyway, so it does not make a difference." We say this because we think it will protect us. Why? What are we afraid of?

A friend of mine once gave me some good advice when I was trying to raise a large sum for a yeshivah. "Before you make the phone call, accept the idea that he is going to say no. That way you can only win. If he indeed says no, you expected it so you have lost nothing; you win. If on the off chance he says yes, you also win. With this attitude you can only win. You cannot lose because you already accepted that you probably lost." My friend is very intelligent. I cannot say it made all the phone calls easier; it is never easy to be refused help in a challenging situation. But it is a true thought. We already have the no, so let us at least try for a yes. That our child will disagree with us is a given before we start. We are telling him not to go somewhere he wants to go. Of course he is going to disagree. But knowing that he is going to disagree does not mean that we cannot initiate a discussion.

❧ Supporting Questionable Friendships

My son had a friend who I did not think was very good for him. I asked him, "How do you feel about this friendship?" My son responded that he believed the boy was a good boy and a good friend, but some people did not understand him. However, they were learning together and my son felt he was helping the boy. Had I implemented my initial parental instinct to protect my son and said, "Listen, you know, this is bad. I see this boy, I know what is going on. I have heard about him. I know the stories. I don't want you around him," I would have hurt my son and I would have hurt another boy. But there was something better to do.

I discussed the problem with my son. "Do you feel you are helping him?" I asked. I figured he would hesitate and stammer and I would be putting him in a corner, and he would have to answer, "Well, not really, but I could. And don't worry, it won't affect me." He did not respond as I expected. He answered, "Yes, Tatty, you know how?" He listed all the things he is doing for this boy. He told me all the things that have happened. He told me what he talks to this boy about when he comes over. He even told me how he persuaded the boy to talk to one of the *rebbeim* in the yeshivah and how the *rebbe* is helping. I had been mistaken. "I'm sorry, son, it all sounds wonderful. Go ahead and continue being helpful."

Sometimes we are concerned about all kinds of things, and when we talk it over, we see that our child was just as concerned.

> *I remember once, many years ago when I was a bachur in Yeshivas Be'er Yaakov, there was a young man who*

would come to the yeshivah once in a while. He had decided he wanted to become frum and we helped him along. We learned with him. We persuaded him to go to learn in Rav Elbaz's yeshivah in Yerushalayim.

A year later he returned to the yeshivah and told us he was getting married. I was happy when he approached me, because I had learned with him once a week. He said to me: "I'm getting married, but you know my parents are not the least bit religious. My kallah's parents are not frum either. My brothers and sisters, and her brothers and sisters — also nothing. I want to have a little bit of a Jewish wedding. Could you please do me a favor and get a few boys to come and dance?"

I did not know what to do. I went to the Mashgiach Rav Wolbe and I told him I felt we needed to allow several some boys to go to the wedding. We used to call such an affair a "meis mitzvah chasunah." He had no one else. If we did not do this mitzvah, nobody else was going to do it. We really had to take care of it. We had to go. The mashgiach said, "Okay, who are you going to take?" I said, "I'll take seven guys who don't want to go. Seven guys I have to beg to go." He smiled. "That is a good idea. Go ahead. Do it."

It is important to note that when a child is aware of the dangers, it is not quite so dangerous. The fellows who are dying to go to that wedding should be kept away. When you find that your child is aware of and sensitive to the issues involved and even concerned about the consequences, then you can trust him more. You will only find this out, however, when you sit down with him and talk over the issues.

If your child is old enough to be facing these more serious decisions, you must discuss them with him. Do you honestly think you can control the situation? Can you forbid your sixteen-year-old child from speaking to someone who is, in your opinion, an undesirable friend? No, he has a cell phone, he has access to a telephone, he is going to talk to him anyway.

If you ask me how far you can trust him, I would say, "What is your alternative?" The alternative is to not trust him. The alternative is to criticize him, to tell him that you don't trust him, that you think he is going to get in trouble, and that you think he is doing something wrong. What do you gain by taking this route? If you are talking about an eleven-year-old child, you can control the situation to a certain extent, but if you are talking about a sixteen-year-old child, you have no control whatsoever over the situation. What will you gain by not trusting him? You have to trust, and only through trust can you adapt or influence the situation so that he may help that friend. Discuss what your child can do to help the friend, suggest things that he should avoid, find out what they talk about, work things through with him. You will most likely find out that he wants your help to help his friend. In any case, he is probably going to keep the friendship. You are not fooling anybody, so it is far better to deal with it in a responsible way.

◄₰ Building a Basis for Decision-Making

Remember, success in *chinuch* means helping our children become individuals who strive on their own to reach their potential. We want them to understand that there are certain prerequisites for maturity. In order to gain understanding, one needs to know certain things. You think a particular relationship is going to have a negative influence on your child. Your child says it is not going to have a negative influence on him. At this point you could raise various questions about the workings of influence in your discussion. Questions like, what is influence? How does it work? What influences us and how do we influence others? You explain to your child that all these things help you form your opinion.

When he says that nothing influences him, ask him if he has taken into consideration all the things you are now discussing. When he says that nothing influences him and that he knows what he wants, you have to tell him that you think there are certain things that influence everyone. You can tell him that you know you are influenced by your surroundings, even if he thinks he is not.

"Well, I'll tell you what," you say. "Right now you cannot go because I'm not letting you go. If you want to, we can sit down and discuss how influence works." He may not be interested. He may not be too happy with your decision. But there is a difference between explaining that your decision is based on knowledge that he does not have and saying, "When you grow up you'll understand."

Sometimes you can share some of this knowledge with your child and sometimes you cannot, because he may require more preliminary knowledge than he possesses to understand certain concepts, and he is surely not going to agree with you. When you have entered into a discussion with him, he will realize that there are some things you are taking into consideration that he is not. You can then say things to your child like, "You were thinking about this one aspect of the problem, right? Well, I was thinking about three other aspects." You can mention the things that you were thinking about that he is not thinking about. Again, he is not necessarily going to agree with you, but he sees that your knowledge is more extensive than his. Hopefully it is, and that is why you are making the right decision for him.

Experience is another level. You cannot say to a teenage child, "When you grow up you'll understand." You can, however, say something like, "When you have a son, you'll understand. When you have a daughter, you'll understand. You don't understand my concern, because you cannot understand how much you can love another person. It is true that you have friends whom you love. You have siblings whom you love. You have parents whom sometimes you are willing to admit that you love. But do you know what it means to be a mother or a father? You don't yet have that experience. I know you don't agree with me, but there is going to come a day when you will understand why I am being so cautious. There is going to come a day when you will understand, because you are going to have as much experience as

I have now. You are going to have the beautiful experience of having a child that you care about so much that you would give anything in your life to have that child safe and sound. There is not anything you would not do to help that child have the best life that he can have. You don't understand that yet, not because you are less intelligent than me but because you have not had that experience."

This is something that can be said and understood. Naturally he or she will not understand it. How could he? How could she know how a mother feels and how could he know how a father feels? Because we know this, we have to evaluate our own feelings as well as his. Are we taking precautions that are a bit extreme? Are we holding him back from something we should allow him to do, solely because of our strong emotions as a mother or father? It is not always a question of right and wrong, or good and bad. We might be doing it because it is more comfortable or reassuring for us.

Of course it may be more comfortable for a valid reason. If this is the case, we would never let a child obtain a driver's license. "Can I have the car?" We hesitate. "All right." You want to call him every twenty minutes just to make sure he is still alive, the car is still in one piece, and the neighbors are still there. It is a challenging experience. Anyone with children of driving age is familiar with it. When we sit down to discuss things like this with our children, we are also discussing them with ourselves. We are trying to recognize what the reason for our decision is and evaluate it. Is this the right decision? Am I being overprotective? Maybe I am going a little bit too far and making my child feel too suffocated and controlled. Maybe I do need to give him a bit more independence. It is an evaluation, though, not a judgment. I have to find out exactly what situation I am dealing with. My decision depends on many different things.

An open discussion enables us to evaluate our own motives and concerns and helps our children understand our evaluations. I am going to repeat this many times in this book. I am not saying that our children have to understand every factor that goes into making our decisions, and I'm not saying they have to agree with everything we do and say. I am stressing that our object is to help them develop a decision-making capability. How can we do this? We show them that the process consists of experience, discussion, and understanding of the many components involved in making any important decision.

The first time an individual makes a particular decision, he thinks that there are only two aspects involved. The second time he learns that there are three; the third time he learns that there are four or five. Eventually one learns to take into consideration eight aspects of the question. When the child goes shopping alone for a pair of pants for the first time, he looks for what he likes. The second time he realizes that when you look for only what you like, you just might spend too much money and you may not be permitted to buy a new pair for another six months. When the second time comes around, he looks at the price too. Then he finds out that he bought cheap pants that fell apart at the seams after a month. Now he has learned to look for quality too.

With each new experience, the child learns.

"You know what? I don't want you to go and get pants by yourself. I would like to go with you."

"Why, do you think I don't know how to buy pants?"

"Sure you know how to buy pants. What are you going to look for?"

"What do you mean? I'll look for nice pants."

"Really? Well, what else are you going to have to take into consideration?"

He will think. He will come up with the answers. He would not have thought about it too much if you had not discussed it with him first. If you just told your child that he is not going alone, what would he have learned? By discussing it with him, you have taught him something. He may think he knows now, but still he will make mistakes. Well, he will learn from his mistakes. He realizes you are not going to provide money for new pants until a certain period of time has elapsed. You tell him, "Listen, if you make a mistake it is on your account. If I come with you I can teach you quality. You need to learn about quality. You don't have that much knowledge about quality in pants. Let me come with you this time. Next time you'll go on your own."

If he still wants to go alone, you tell him, "Go ahead, but you will not get new pants until you outgrow these, not when they started to pill. You'll get new pants for Rosh Hashanah, Pesach, whatever." He may make a mistake. This is not so terrible. He will learn for the next time. You have helped him learn.

Children must learn to weigh the various aspects of a decision, and we have to help them do that. Decisions are difficult, but they are sometimes hard for us too. How long do we spend buying a dress, a suit, or a pair of shoes? Let us analyze some of the things that influence our children's decisions the most. This is important. What are the most powerful factors influencing our children's decision-making?

A. Instant Gratification

A powerful influence on decision-making is the need for instant gratification. Young people want something that is going to give them immediate gratification. We live in a world of raffles, instant lotto, and one-hour photo developing. Our children, who may not see movies, nevertheless live in an environment that sees world catastrophes created in an hour and solved before the hour is over. The world they live in has become a microwave world. Everything has to be "right away." Everything has to be instantaneous. Children don't realize that it is the culture they have been exposed to that impels them to look for instant gratification, and we have to make them aware of that. They don't realize the immense influence their microwave world has had on the way they are making decisions. That is something to discuss with them.

B. Peer Pressure

Children know that this or that just has to be, because their friends all say so or do so. Valid persuasion cannot come from a parent. Only their friends can convince them; we cannot. This is something we have to understand — only their friends constitute reality. We should not belittle friends or disregard the pressure that every child feels regarding his friends. Comments like, "Just because all your friends have it, you think you have to have it?" are not going to get you anywhere. Children see friends as a valid guide to behavior. If everyone else is doing something, well then, it must be the right thing to do. I want to be included; I don't want to be left out. That too is up for discussion.

"Oh, all your friends are doing that? I see that makes it very hard for you."

This comment has just helped him take a step in the direction of self-awareness. Does that mean that he is going to say automatically, "Sure, Ma, and I should not do it, right?"

> Once I took my five-year-old to kindergarten in the rain. I told her to put on her sweater hood. She said: "No, I don't want to put it on." I then asked, "Is your head going to get wet?" She said, "Yeah."
> "So maybe you should put on your hood."
> "No, it looks funny because it's got a shpitz. You know, at the end it's all pointy and the other kids laugh at it."
> "Oh? So if children laugh you should get cold?" I said.
> "No," she said.
> "So what are you going to do?" She thought about it. She did not know. She was not sure what she should do. I asked her if there was a way to push in the pointy part. Together we found a way to do that. Then she put on the sweater and pulled up the hood by herself and held down the point all the way to school.

Friends are their reality. It is true. It is embarrassing to go somewhere and have people look at you. So deal with it. Don't just make believe it does not exist. If you help your child deal successfully with friends when he is five, he will have enough sense to stand up to friends when he is ten and fifteen.

Sometimes it is not even a question of standing up to friends. If "everyone is doing something," find out who "everyone" is, because "everyone" sometimes means 15 percent of his friends and sometimes it means the two other children who are important to him. You have to check out what "everyone" means, and there is not anything wrong with discussing it. Peer pressure is important to your child.

C. Temptation

Finally, of course, a child's decision is affected by what he wants, the *yetzer hara* and *ta'avah*, his desires and temptation. He is thinking about the things he is going to get out of the situation, things he likes, wants, and feels are good at the moment. Fighting the *yetzer hara* in our day is not an easy battle. The *yetzer* is here, there, and all over the place in the lives of each and every one of us, whether we want it there or not. It appears in all shapes and forms; it pops up at every turn and around every corner.

If you have a computer, the *yetzer* is certainly in your home. Our children are fighting a most serious form of *hefkeirus*, total freedom, of total anarchy, where children do whatever they want. At night when I drive along the streets in Yerushalayim, I see really young children hanging out in the street with nobody watching them. Many of those children probably have problematic conditions at home; perhaps their parents don't have any control over them. A few children like that can influence many others. One friend brings another friend. We must be alert to the fact that our children are going to be exposed to many issues and experiences to which we don't want them exposed. Therefore we have to be able to discuss these things with them. We should be able to discuss the *yetzer hara* with them, to discuss their inner battles with it as well as our own battles. It is important that they know that we also have battles. We also have a hard time doing what we are supposed to do.

As we have mentioned before, it is much more difficult to begin having this kind of discussion with them when they are already in high school, but begin whenever you can. It is far too important for your child's development for you to just let things ride.

◄ε *Discussion Leads to Understanding*

The Torah states,[1] "A man must fear his mother and father and keep Shabbos." We were once discussing this passage at the Shabbos table.

"We all know the *Chazal* that states, 'If your parents say transgress the Shabbos, you are not supposed to listen, because you and your father are each responsible to Hashem,'" I said.

"Shouldn't this small child know that he can trust you, his father?" one of our Shabbos guests asked.

"Do you think he does not understand the difference?" I responded. "Watch."

I then turned to my young child, "What happens if I say to you that we are not allowed to turn on the light on Shabbos, but now because of a life-or-death situation, you have to, because Hashem wants you to do that? Would you do it?"

The child said, "Of course." He is only eight years old, but he was able to differentiate between not listening to a father who is telling him to do something wrong and not listening to a father who wants him to do what is right.

Very young children understand many, many concepts. They really do. Fifteen-year-olds understand ten times better, but we have to talk things over with them. My discussion at the table at the time was about a law in the Torah. I wanted to make it clear that I cannot do whatever I want and he cannot do whatever he wants. We all have to keep the Torah. We all have to listen to Hashem. Sometimes I also want to do something that I am not supposed to do, but I am not allowed to do it, right? He answers that I am right, and he understands. He just learned the lesson that the *yetzer hara* is not only his *yetzer hara* but it is my *yetzer hara* too.

---

1. *Vayikra* 19:3.

When we share common ground with our children, when it is clear that we both have the same objective responsibilities to a higher authority, we can have these discussions. We can help them understand a great deal and hopefully, using good *chinuch* techniques, we will be helping them learn how to deal responsibly with the issues they face. This is the way they mature. The teen years are the important stage in their lives, the stage when they develop their innate ability to understand and learn to judge, to decide, and to implement their decisions successfully.

Chapter Ten
LOVE AND BELIEF – THE
TWO ESSENTIALS

One can appreciate the challenge and responsibility of working with adolescents and enjoy this age group by remembering two essential points. The first is the need to view this stage of a child's development as something important and necessary, and the second is to believe deeply in the intrinsic goodness of children.

It is a wondrous and beautiful experience to observe children while they are going through this unique stage in their lives, when their minds, their bodies, and their thought processes are developing. It is the most astonishing stage of growth in any person's life. Parents should view their participation during this time of adolescence as a *zechus*, a privilege.

At the same time, parents must believe in the intrinsic goodness of children, especially during this stage when they could be thinking that perhaps things are not so good. We may find our teenagers to be malicious, angry, bitter, rebellious, or fighting us all the time, but I believe that any negative words the kids may throw at us have no truth or substance to them. I believe that these are good children, children who want to be good and need extra help and support because they are having a hard time. I believe this with my whole heart and every ounce of my being.

Children are sensitive to what parents feel. They connect with your attitude. The *pasuk* in *Mishlei*[1] tells us that just as you can see your face reflected in water, so people reflect each other's feelings. I will guarantee that if you are willing to take the leap of faith required to keep loving these kids and believing in them, you will see immediate results. With just the two elements of love and belief, you will mark a change in your relationship with your own children or with any other adolescents with whom you happen to deal.

◄ᢓ *Loving Our Children*

We are parents. We love our children. Normal, healthy parents love their children. That is the way things are. Even when our children are not normal and healthy, we love them because they are ours. This is something that *HaKadosh Baruch Hu* planted in us and it is a natural, instinctive response. We gave them life; we give them everything they have in life, and there is nothing that is more important or more valuable to us than our children. Of course we love them — most of the time.

Relationships can become strained. When we or they feel discouraged, disappointed, or angry, or even if we just don't understand each other very well for a little while, some level of conflict may arise between us. When we don't understand each other, we sometimes manifest it in a certain tone of voice or a certain irrepressible feeling that we don't really want to admit even to ourselves. We sometimes even "hate" them a little bit for a little while. We don't truly hate them, Heaven forbid, but we can recognize the feeling that we just don't know what to do with them, and we would not mind if for a few minutes they would be somewhere else. We know that it is only for a moment, and we know the feeling will pass, but we do have those thoughts and feelings on occasion.

Well, guess what? Children are perceptive. When they say, "You hate me!" they don't know why they say it but they

1. *Mishlei* 27:19.

feel it is true. "What are you talking about? How could I hate you?" Of course it is not true, but in that moment of anger or frustration or disappointment, maybe a flash of dislike creeps into us for a few seconds. It is not the way we truly feel about them, but that is what we revealed in the way we looked at them, or the way we spoke to them, or the hurtful language we used. They felt insulted by the way we responded. We made them think that we don't really love them. Even though we do love our children, it is also true that we sometimes transmit a mixed message. It is therefore most important that when we do transmit a negative message, which we don't intend to do but which sometimes happens, we must find a speedy way to make sure our message is not interpreted.

Building a loving relationship with our children is not simple. It is difficult enough to build a good relationship with one's spouse, much less one's children. As Rashi points out, the angels asked Avraham where Sarah was "to increase Avraham's appreciation of Sarah." This means that a loving relationship has to be nurtured constantly. It can't be taken for granted. The minute you sit back, assuming that you have such a relationship and you don't have to work at it, you have lost it. If you don't constantly invest in the connection, the connection disintegrates.

You have to invest continually in your relationship with your children too. You assume that your children understand that you love them because you do everything for them. You are awake early in the morning; you don't go to sleep till late at night. Day after day you work, you wash, you clean and cook, you worry, you buy this, that, and the other for them. There is nothing you would not do for them — to the point of doing without some important things so that they can be comfortable. You do everything you can to help them be good, to be what they should be. How can they possibly think you don't love them? They think you don't love them because you take it for granted, but they don't. You have to *show* them your love and concern for them, or else they will misunderstand. There are specific ways in which we can help them understand us better and know that we love them. Let us try a little test.

A. Test Yourself

Two minutes after your outburst of anger, after you have said something hurtful to your child, two minutes after you have said something that you probably already regret but are not ready to retract, can you give that same child a kiss or a hug? He is not going to want it. He sees you are angry and does not want to let you hug him. But can you go over and give him a hug anyway? If you can't, it indicates that he is right and he is sensing a very bad emotion, a negative emotion. He is reading something that you don't want to project or even admit. You should be able to reach out to your child in the midst of and in spite of your anger. If your anger or withdrawal is really for the benefit of your child, if you are doing whatever you are doing for the sake of *chinuch* because you want him to grow, to be good, and to be successful, then you should be able to reach out to him after a show of anger. If your reaction is intended to instruct him, you should be able within seconds to give him a big hug to show him that you do love him.

B. "You Hate Me!"

Reprimands should be acts of love. I would hope that when we issue a reprimand we have control of our emotions, but this is not always the case. Our response to our children's behavior should stem from love and concern and a desire to want what is best for them. I know it is very hard to be able to respond that way all the time, but if we can't do it, it is an indication that other feelings are mixed up in our love and we are a little bit confused about how we feel toward our children. If *we* are feeling a little confused, they certainly have a right to be confused. Therefore we shouldn't be shocked, surprised, or hurt when a child says, "You hate me!" He is verbalizing something that is more real than we want to admit, but it is there and we have to do something about it.

We need to be able to love them even when they are being challenging and even when they may be causing us pain. We can do that only if we understand them and recognize that they are acting this way because they are in trouble. They are suffering at this moment. They are having a difficult time dealing with all the things that teenagers experience. It is a challenge for them, of course, but it is also our challenge to help them through this stage of their development, and we must try to not get angry or upset by their behavior. We certainly shouldn't turn on them in anger.

⋙ Believing in Our Children

We need to believe that our children are intrinsically good. We have to accept that they can understand what good is and that they desire to be good. Let us remember what the *Ohr HaChaim Hakadosh* says: Understanding leads to judgment, judgment leads to making decisions, making decisions leads to implementing decisions. We have to remember that our children, even though they feel the *yetzer hara*, the temptation to misbehave, are Jews. The Talmud teaches us[2] that a Jew's ultimate and most basic desire is to do what is right. A child is really unhappy when he or she is at odds with the family. Children want to get along. They want things to flow smoothly. They want things to work out. They want to feel good about themselves and about their parents, and they want their parents to feel good about them. It does not mean they are willing to do everything necessary for that to happen, any more than we agree to overlook certain things for the sake of tranquility. Sometimes we have to say no, and sometimes we have to demand things of our children that are not always easy for them to do. We have to discipline them and we have to be able to prevent them from misbehaving. But the responsibilities we have as parents shouldn't detract from

2. *Berachos* 17.

our belief that these children really want to do the right thing, even if there are factors that interfere with their doing so.

We ourselves sometimes have to say, "You know, *Ribbono shel Olam*, we want to do what You want us to do, but there is the *yetzer hara* and there is social pressure and there are peer pressures and all kinds of things that stop us from being able to do what we would really like to do." Well, our children likewise want to do what is right and good, but they feel a lot of pressure. They have their own temptations with which they must deal. Children have peer pressure and pressure from their own striving, both of which interfere with the choices they make. Despite all this, we know they are basically and inherently good children.

Every child wants to be good and can understand what good is. He wants to do what is right, but sometimes it is hard for him. There are so many things holding him back and getting in the way of doing what he wants to do.

Just because we are twice their age we can't assume that we are smarter than they and that we are always right. We may have more experience and know more about many things, but we should accept the fact that sometimes they are right and sometimes they are convinced that they are right even if they are wrong. We have to have some insight and understand that, right or wrong, they do know what good means. This is where communication plays its part. Rather than just saying, "Well, you don't know but I do," we have to be able to discuss things and work things through with them. We have addressed the issue of discussion before and we will touch on it again later, but I just want to clarify what it means to love and believe in our children.

A. Empowerment

If children are inherently good, and if they can understand what good is and want to be good, then what can be holding them back? Why is it that they don't behave well all the time? Well, what about all the things that we know and understand and want to do that are good but can't always do? Little things like dieting. We know we need to eat properly and that it is beneficial for us, but we can't always do it. If you are convinced you can't do it, that is negative thinking and it can become a self-fulfilling prophecy. It is the same with children. They want to be good and we know they can be good, so all you have to do is trust them to be good. Have confidence in them and you will empower them to overcome their *yetzer hara*. We have to be the force in their lives that tells them, "Yes, you can do it. You can do what is right. You can overcome this situation. You can be good even though it is hard, and you can do what is right even though your friends don't always want to."

We have to imbue them with strength. We are the parents. We are the ones who are supposed to instruct them how to do what is right. We have an enormous responsibility to help them do what is right by believing that they can do it. Knowing that someone believes in him gives a child the power to believe in himself.

B. Anticipate Success

A basic element in your belief in him is wanting him to succeed. That is not as self-evident as it may seem. Who does not want his child to be successful? Why, then, do we make negative comments anticipating his failure? Perhaps deep down we are hoping he will make a mistake so that he will learn from his mistake. Maybe we want him to make mistakes so he can see that we were right. Have you ever said, "I told you so"? If you ever said the words *I told you so* to someone who made a mistake, it means that deep inside you wanted him to make that mistake. It is hard to admit this, and it seems like a mean thing to say, but the words *I told you so* mean, "I said you were going to be wrong, and I was just waiting for you to fail so I would be vindicated." *I told you so* proves that you really did not want your child to be successful. You wanted him to fail. You wanted him to learn that he has to listen to you because you are right and he is wrong. That is not a healthy wish. If you want to empower your child to succeed in life, you have to start believing in him and honestly wanting him to succeed.

When your child was just learning to walk, you encouraged him to take the first step, and another step, and just a few more steps. You called out joyfully, "Come on, come on, you can do it!" You cheered him on and when he fell, you said, "Okay, get up and try again. You can do it." You were right there with him and he knew that you believed in him. He did not yet know how to walk or how to talk, but when he reached you he smiled and was excited and sometimes would clap for himself. He knew he had done well. He also knew you were rooting for him and that you believed in him. You gave him the power to take another step, and he did.

Our fifteen-year-old is learning to walk too, but he is learning to walk through the difficulties of life. He is learning to walk through decisions. He is learning to walk in the face of the *yetzer hara*, peer pressure, challenges to his growth and self-confidence, and things he does not yet know whether he can or can't do. Our teenager also needs us at his side rooting for him. He needs us to be there — not waiting for him to fall so we can tell him that we warned him, and that if he had just listened to us he would not have fallen; he needs us to be there waiting for him to be right, waiting for him to show us that he can do it. He needs to know that we are right there behind him, feeling proud, knowing all along that he was going to make it.

C. Mistrust Hurts

Unfortunately, we often do the opposite. We don't trust our children. When they want to do something new we take a negative stance. Of course we are concerned for their welfare, and what we really want is what is good for them. But we say no because we don't trust them. We don't let them do the things they want to do, because we are afraid that maybe something bad is going to come of it. They, of course, sense that we don't trust them. We don't want to let them make mistakes because mistakes are embarrassing and mistakes portend — who knows what? Mistakes mean that they are headed for trouble, and we are the ones who will be embarrassed. We can't have our children do anything wrong because we, of course, never do anything wrong, so why should they? What we are doing is clipping their wings. What we are saying silently is that we don't really trust them nor do we have any confidence in them. So why should they try? They don't feel motivated to prove us right or wrong, and so they just take the path of least resistance and do what is easiest for them — which is often the hardest for us.

D. Building Trust

It is difficult, perhaps even impossible, to trust people who don't trust you. If you can't trust your child with big things, trust him with smaller things at first. Build up a feeling of trust. You can tell your child, "I want to trust you. I want to know that if you tell me something, I don't have to worry about it. Tell me what you are planning to do. If your plans don't work out, tell me what you propose to do then. I trust you, and I'm relying on you to tell me what you are going to do if something goes wrong." Place the burden of trust on him; make him think about what he plans to do. If you word it properly, he will say, "If I don't get back at such-and-such a time, you can do this or I will do that ... " and make sure he sets the consequences himself. He is making the decision, and he is going to have to accept the consequence, because he wants to be trusted. Every child wants to be trusted and wants his parents to believe him and to believe in him.

A child loves to hear a parent say, "I trust you to make this evaluation." Sometimes we need to add, "I trust that you are going to be mature about this. Tell me, how are you going to manage coming home on time? How shall we deal with this problem? I want to trust you. Help me trust you." Give him some responsibility. Build up the mutual trust. Show him that you respect him for keeping his word. Let us say that whenever he goes out with his friends he loses his sense of time. Tell him, "I'm trusting you to be back at a certain time." Show him how it feels to be trusted.

This is how it works. When he is leaving with his friends, you say, "I rely on you to be home by 9. But tell me something, if you are not here by 9, what time do I know for sure you will be back? I want you back by 9, but just tell me ..." Talk to him and you will find out that it is not realistic for him to be back by 9. He does not think he will really be back by 9 because he is leaving the house at 8 o'clock. If it takes him half an hour to get there and half an hour to get back, how can he be back at 9? *You* want him back at 9, and that is why he agreed. But of course he can't possibly be back at 9.

Find out why he is not back at 9 each time. Talk to him about it. Maybe he needs until 10. Does he get back at 10? If he always says 9 and he always gets back at 10, then it probably means that he really needs until 10. Tell him, "You know what? I really would like you back at 9, but because I know that you need that time, I'm going to let you have until 10; but at 10 I expect you back." You may be surprised that this child whom you never trusted comes back at 10. He feels good because you trust him.

If we become upset when the one-year-old who is taking his first steps falls down and we walk out of the room, he will just sit there and cry, assuming that that is what he is supposed to do. If we root for him, then he will get up and try again. Our teenagers are no different. Sure, they will fall. Everyone makes mistakes. We have to let them make mistakes. Of course, we don't let them make mistakes that are going to destroy their lives. We don't let them experiment with drugs and learn the hard way, *chas v'shalom!* We don't let them do evil things. You can't build up trust all in one shot anyway. If you haven't trusted your child until now, don't all of a sudden let him do just anything he wants to do, because he will probably take advantage of you. If he knows you don't trust him anyway, he is waiting for the first crack to appear in your stranglehold on him. Once he has it, who knows what he will do. But it is never too late to start building trust between you.

E. Building Confidence

There are many little ways to build up your child's confidence. You can show him that you trust him with money by allowing him to make all kinds of small purchases on his own. Let him make decisions. Let him go shopping for something inexpensive for the house. Let him go out and buy the *nosh* for Shabbos. The worst that can happen is that he will buy the wrong thing and have to go back to the store. But permission to make these small decisions shows him that you trust him.

As you build up his confidence, you will find that you can trust him in more ways than you thought possible. When you believe your children are good, and they know you believe they are good, they are not going to want to let you down. How many times have you heard a child say, "Whatever I do is not good enough for you"? When he says that, it means that he perceives your negative regard for him. When a child says that, he could not feel more hurt. A child's reasoning goes like this: *Mom and Dad don't think I'm good, therefore they think I'm bad. Well, if they think I'm bad, I'll just be bad. I don't have to prove them wrong. They are never going to accept me anyway. Whatever I do is not good enough, so why should I even try to be good?*

This is how we sometimes project negativity and it is the opposite of believing in our children. Loving and believing in our children are the two most basic elements, the really essential ingredients in good parenting. We have to reverse our own negative behavior patterns. We have to empower our children instead.

◆ぅ *Great Expectations*

We all have certain expectations — expectations about what we think our children should do. *There are certain things I expect my son and daughter to do around the house. I want them to feel that they are part of the household. Why don't they help? They see that I'm tired, why don't they see that I need help? Don't they see that one person can't do everything in a house? Shouldn't they be sharing some of the responsibility?*

My *Rebbe* Rav Wolbe says that however many children we may be blessed with, they are not the responsibility of our older sons or daughters. *HaKadosh Baruch Hu* put them in this world for *us* to be responsible for *them*. Children's responsibilities as they approach adulthood are to themselves first. Yes, they have to learn the concepts of *chesed*, of giving and sharing and doing for others, but they will learn these concepts mainly by watching other people share and give to others. *Sure, but don't they see I'm giving to them, that I'm doing things for them? Can't I demand things of them in return? Can't I expect certain things from my children?*

The answer is you can expect anything you like, but if you really want them to share in the responsibilities of the home you have to make them feel like partners in the home. Make them feel like they are part of the action. Make them feel that they have a reason to invest in the home. We should forget our expectations and help them develop sensitivity, teach them to share and care and give, rather than make demands of them that they think are unreasonable. They end up feeling used and taken advantage of. *How in the world can this child feel taken advantage of,* you ask, *when he is always asking me to do things for him?* If he wants me to do so much for him, how can he ask me, "What do you want from my life?"

Let's see how much we really ask compared to how much we give. Is the home one where so many things happen at once that one person or even two people can't cope? Don't these kids see that we need their help and don't they want to help us? The answer is no, they don't see it, they don't want to see it, and they don't want to help.

A. "Why Should We Help?"

Kids think, *Why should we help our parents? What happens when we do? Is our help appreciated? Do our parents show appreciation when we do help?* Parents think, *Why should we show appreciation? Shouldn't we expect them to help around the house?* That is not a reason to ignore *hakaras hatov*, showing appreciation. That is not a reason to neglect the basic response of gratitude. If it were someone else's child who pitched in to help clear off the table, you would definitely show gratitude. You might even call his parents to tell them what a *mentsch* their son or daughter is. Although it is almost an unwritten law that guests should help too, if a guest walks away without helping, we don't criticize. We really do appreciate it when they care enough to help. Why should we expect our children to help any more than a guest?

The difference between our expectations and our demands of children to help at home is a strong factor in creating negative feelings regarding trust and responsibility. Children don't view our expectations in the same light as we do. The gap between the two causes negative feelings, and our children know when we have negative feelings toward them.

B. Sharing

Let us reevaluate our grand expectations and scale them down. We start by trying to teach our children to share, but we actually end up teaching them that sharing is not worth the effort. We can illustrate this best by using the example of young children, though it can be applied to adolescents just as well.

How do we teach little children to share? We say, "Okay, you played with that doll for ten minutes, now it is your sister's turn." We stress that it is the sister's turn. Then we take it away from her and give it to her sister. "Ah, such a good girl, you are sharing." Meanwhile the child is thinking, "Oh boy, I'll hold on to it tighter next time." *Sharing shouldn't mean that we take away from one child to give to the other.* Sharing means that we say to the child, "It is yours, you don't have to give it to anybody. It is only yours. You don't have to give it to the other child, but if you do, he is going to be very happy. Would you like to make him happy? If you do, you can give it to him for a few minutes and when you want it back you can have it back because it is yours." A person can only share if he believes that what he is sharing is his own to share. If I am confident that this is my property and I know that no one can take it away from me, it is easier for me to share. When the younger child starts yelling and screaming because the older child wants his toy back, you have to tell the younger one pleasantly, "It was very nice of Chana'le to let you play with the doll for a few minutes, but it is hers, and now you have to give it back." Then we give it back. The younger child is screaming, but it belongs to the older child. It is hers. And because you gave it back to her, she will learn to share it another time. You know what? When you will give it back to her and she sees the younger child crying, she may very well offer it to her sister by herself, because she is confident in her ownership.

By forcing a child to share, we are teaching him that he can't have any property of his own. Whatever he has, he has to share, and he loses confidence in his right or ability to own anything. That is an extremely basic concept in early childhood development.

This concept is the basis of our expectations of older children as well. We want our older children to share in household burdens. We want them to give of themselves. We have to ask ourselves if we are allowing them to have a self or are we regarding their selves as ours? Do we feel that they owe us everything and whatever help they extend to us is no more than what is expected of them? Are we afraid that if we reward them for helping us they are going to think they are doing us a favor? Well, why not? They *are* doing us a favor, a *chesed*. The more we appreciate the favor that they are doing and show them that we appreciate it, the more they are going to want to do it.

Adults and children like to do things they feel good about; they don't like to do things they are forced to do. *Chazal*[3] say, "Greater is he who does that which he is commanded to do, than he who does it voluntarily," and therefore the reward is greater for the one who does what he is commanded to do. It is the same principle as the one which we have been discussing. When we make children feel that we command them to do something, it is harder for them to do it than if they do so voluntarily.

---

3. *Kiddushin* 31a.

C. Why Don't They Help?

Did you ever discuss with your children the reasons why they don't feel like helping? Could it be that their resistance has something to do with another sibling? Have you ever reassured your child that you appreciate what he does regardless of the fact that another child does more or better? It is important that you communicate your appreciation of what each child does separately so that he knows his efforts are appreciated. Are you sure that your verbalization is enough, or does the child still feel that his sibling is so much more adept at what he does that his own efforts are unnoticed and that is why he does not do anything?

If he has a sibling who outshines him and makes him feel inadequate, you can tell him, "You know, sometimes Mommy does not do some things very well, and sometimes different people do different things at different rates of speed, and that is okay. Everyone chips in, and Daddy and I appreciate everything that each person does." That may give the child more self-confidence even though he may feel less adequate than his siblings. It might be, however, that he does feel appreciated, but something else is bothering him. If children are made to feel demeaned by helping because we don't show appreciation for their help, they would not help.

It does not help at all to tell ourselves that we shouldn't rock the boat, that if we mention the subject the child will notice that he is doing it one way and another child is doing it another way. We want to keep everything under wraps so that family politics will run smoothly. But it is not politics; it is human relations. It is making a child feel good about who he is. This is something that I would bring out into the open. You could say, "Sometimes I feel that you really want to help, but you don't help because So-and-so is around and you just feel like you can't measure up to him. Well, I don't think that way. Do you think you could try to help without comparing yourself to So-and-so?" Make sure your child hears the reassuring words, "I want you to know why I especially appreciate it when you help me. When you help I appreciate it five times as much, because I know that it is harder for you. You would rather sit down on the couch and read, and here you are helping me, and I really appreciate that." You will be surprised to see him getting up and helping. You can start the process just by talking about it openly.

The only reason I can say these things with some level of confidence is that we are not talking about *chiddushim*, newfangled psychological ways of dealing with these issues. These suggestions are so basic to human relations that I know they work.

Communication and human relationships are always *k'mayim hapanim l'panim*,[4] like looking at your reflection in the water. The way you look at a person is the way he will look at you. It is a constant. If your child feels alienated, it means that you are alienating him. There is categorically no such thing as a normal, healthy child who feels alienated from someone who loves him. If your child feels alienated, it means that somehow you are sending the wrong message. A message of respect elicits respect. That is human nature; it is the way the mind works. And when you bring something out into the open and discuss it, explain and share with your child that you are also good at some things and not as good at others, and tell him how much more his extra effort is appreciated. It will make a big difference. After you discuss these things with your child, he is going to feel appreciated and respond to your words of encouragement.

☙ Setting Up a Partnership

We are trying to set up a partnership with our teenager. We create partnerships by being appreciative. We create partnerships by sharing things with our teenagers. We share our thoughts, we share our feelings, and we share our concerns. We get them involved in some of the events that are going on in the house and we ask them what they think about those events. Naturally we are not going to ask a fourteen-year-

---

4. *Mishlei* 27:19.

old the best way to educate our seven-year-old. There are enough things that we can talk to our fourteen- or fifteen-year-old about that will realistically involve him in a discussion. We can talk to our teenagers about various things that are going on in the house so that they will feel a part of it and perhaps feel some responsibility. There are many items we can ask them to shop for by themselves. This is a small thing, but it gives them responsibility.

A. Kids Are Smart

In building a partnership with your adolescent child, you have to recognize that he is intelligent. The *Ohr HaChaim Hakadosh* says that a twelve- and thirteen-year-old boy or girl does have intelligence. It is not fully developed, it is not fully mature, but he or she is intelligent. Well, if your children are intelligent, then deal for real. Accept what they say, accept what they feel, and recognize that what they say and what they feel is real.

How does this appreciation of your child's intelligence apply in practice?

"I can't wear these!" your daughter exclaims. "My friends will think I'm crazy!"

"What do you mean?" you say, taken aback. "Those shoes are very nice."

"Yeah. You think they are nice, but my friends ... are you kidding? I could never wear these. I'd rather die."

Now you could easily answer, "You are just being immature and silly and foolish. Cut it out. There is nothing wrong with the shoes. You can wear them."

Will your daughter feel better when you say that? No, she most decidedly will not. Of course she will not feel better. How could she feel better? You have just told her that what she thinks and feels is foolish, stupid, immature, and not real. How would you feel if someone told you that the way you feel about something is stupid, unreal, and immature? Remember this is a real person you are talking to. And for her, the issue of the shoes is real. Her friends' opinions are real. The way she will be regarded is a real issue. To her it is not only important, it is crucial. Don't ignore her thoughts and feelings. If you want to handle the issue properly, you can. You can even help her deal with the idea that her friends might have different tastes than hers. Think about it for a moment!

The problem here may be that it is not just a question of what her friends think. Perhaps her friends will even notice that the shoe is a one-inch heel instead of a two-inch heel, or that the shoe is a pump and not a sling-back, and that makes those shoes ugly. You can't even tell the difference between the heels on the shoes she wants and the ones she is rejecting. They look exactly the same to you. But she thinks the ones you like are gross and disgusting. Well, maybe you are not aware of the finer points of shoe styles today. Or maybe you are just not sensitive to the fact that your daughter wants one pair in particular. Either she is very concerned about the way she looks, or she is looking for something that is exactly like something she once saw, and nothing else is going to make her happy.

You are now going to have to make a decision whether or not you are going to pay the extra money for the shoe whose heel is a bit higher. So now it is time to deal. Your daughter really is an intelligent girl and really wants to buy a pair of shoes, but she is totally convinced that she *has* to have that pair and no other. What are you going to say? If you are going to insult her feelings by saying something that makes her think that you view her opinions as ridiculous and foolish, then you will miss the boat. You will not accomplish anything at all.

You have to accept her opinion. "Okay, I see the difference," you say. "Yes, those shoes are nicer. I'm not sure what to do now because I'd like to buy you a pair of shoes and I want you to have the shoes that you like, but the difference in price is X amount. We have to decide about that money. Should we splurge it on these shoes, or maybe we should wait and spend it on something else?" You can ask her how important it is to her whether her friends regard these shoes favorably or not. Is her friends' opinion worth the extra amount? And perhaps that is going to leave us X amount less to buy clothes for her siblings? Is the difference in shoes actually that great? Is it more important for her to have those shoes than, let's say, the sweater you were also going to buy her? Tell her you understand this difference, but make it her choice. Include her in the decision. Let her understand clearly what she is choosing between. She probably had not been thinking in terms of a choice at all; she had only been thinking, *I want those shoes.*

B. Embarrassment

Teenagers often feel embarrassed about things that we would never dream could be a source of embarrassment. If they feel embarrassed, however, it does not make any difference what we think. We may be 100 percent right, but still they are embarrassed. Why should they be embarrassed? That is a peculiar question. Should we feel insulted when somebody says something hurtful even if they really did not mean it? Should we feel embarrassed sometimes about some of the things that embarrass us? You know, guests are coming unexpectedly, and there is a mess in the house, so everyone goes crazy trying to clean up fast. You have a house, you have children, so there are some things on the floor; it is not the end of the world if the house is a bit messy. True, but we are embarrassed because we want to present a certain put-together look, a certain facade that everything is perfect. Certain things embarrass us, and certain things embarrass our children. We can't mock the things that embarrass them, whether or not they seem ridiculous to us.

Embarrassment is not an intellectual process, it is an emotion. It is an emotion that should be connected to understanding, but often it is not. There are things we know we should be embarrassed about but are not, and there are things that we shouldn't be embarrassed about, but we are. We have to accept that certain things are important to our children and that is the way it is. We are not going to change their minds by telling them that something else should be important, or that they really shouldn't care about those things. They do care. Accepting their emotions and their feelings is an extremely important part of dealing for real. Our challenge is to direct the transposition of what is not so important to what is truly long-term important.

Adolescents are at the stage in life when they are learning to distinguish between what is important and what is secondary. They are learning how to judge things for themselves. They are beginning to make decisions and to choose. They are beginning to look at things critically, to see that there is another side to most questions and another way to look at things. We have to direct this process. We want to help them develop this newfound sensitivity, this utilization of their native intelligence. We want them to have a healthy sense of self and the confidence to give to others and to share. All these things are a part of their sense of self. What our children think and feel is real. Therefore, if we wish to point them in a different direction, we have to use their own thoughts and feelings as a take-off point.

◄ More About Our Service-Oriented Community

Our children's outlook is greatly affected by the mores and values of the community in which they grow up. As we have already mentioned, we live in a service-oriented society in which we expect people to do things for us. We are a little bit disappointed if we walk into a store and they don't provide whatever it is we want. And we expect smiling, cheerful service along with the provision of our wants, especially those of us who come from what we consider "more civilized" parts of the world. Our money talks, and we are fooled into believing that it is important, but I will not go into that aspect now. We stay in hotels, eat in restaurants, and we are catered to: "Yes, how can I help you? Yes sir, yes ma'am," whatever. They don't really care about you but they want your money, so they will treat you nicely. Nevertheless, we grew up in this social milieu and so did our children. Therefore we just expect good service and if we don't get it, we complain.

> *I was once in the lobby of the King David Hotel when an American fellow was yelling at the bellhop about the taxi that had not arrived when he ordered it. I later chatted with the bellhop while I was waiting for someone.*
>
> *"This guy's crazy," the bellhop said to me in Hebrew. "He paid $180 to stay the night and he thinks he owns the four hundred people who work here. He is screaming that his cab is late. He thinks we control the traffic jam on Jaffa Street. He thinks, 'I pay, so it is coming to me.' This is the way it works, this is what I expect and ... you know, FedEx is going to guarantee that it will be on time for his meeting! He does not care whether there was an accident that is holding up traffic or whether a plane crashed. If he said 10 o'clock, he wants him here at 10 o'clock. It is like we have to get on that phone to FedEx, you know? They guaranteed 10 o'clock delivery, so where is it?"*
>
> *Another incident I recall really drives home what it means to live in a service-oriented society. I was driving in upstate New York last summer and I noticed advertisements for a large new delivery service. They call themselves G.O.D. I don't remember what the initials G.O.D. stand for, but it has something to do with guaranteeing that their deliveries will be made on time. That name says a lot about how people think in service-oriented societies.*

The service motif also extends to what we expect people to *be*, and that includes our children. Children are supposed to be sources of *nachas*, pride-providers. What are parents supposed to provide? Parents are supposed to be there for moral, physical, and financial support, for anything that we need, and whenever we need it. Parents are not allowed to be tired, down, uptight, or run-down. We have to be there fresh and ready to do anything our children need. This is because we live in a service-oriented society. People expect great things from one another. But the truth is — that theory does not hold up. People are not necessarily what they are supposed to be and everyone has needs.

There is no one more human than an adolescent, and there is no one more fallible, more easily mistaken, and more easily fooled — by himself and by his friends — than youngsters in this age group. No one gives up on himself more easily than an adolescent. However, the adolescent covers up his humanness and his weakness with an appearance of exactly the opposite. We see and hear only the obstinacy, the stubbornness, the demanding tone, and his expectations. They are really a cover-up for weakness, fallibility, embarrassment, and discomfort. Our teenagers are in a state of not knowing and are worried and concerned about many, many things.

❧ The Open Society

Children today have to fight the *yetzer hara* in many guises. The temptations they find in their path today are accessible, demonic, dangerous, and lie in wait at all times and in all instances. Our children are exposed to a world that totally opposes the *kedushah*, the holiness, of the Torah no matter how hard we try to shield them. At some point they are going to be exposed to knowledge that we did not have at their age. Our children are really struggling; we shouldn't underestimate the difficulties and challenges that face them.

> *In my office recently I met with a child with whom I've had a connection for many years. I saw he was a little down. He came to visit after the vacation, before he went back to yeshivah. He is in the habit of coming in to see me a few times during the term. He usually comes for a little chizuk, a little encouragement.*
>
> *This is a child who disappeared from his home for three days during the vacation break. For three days his parents did not know where he was. He had been up north somewhere, in an apartment with a friend, living it up. Actually, he was not really living it up too much, because they did not have any money, so it was not as much fun as he had thought it would be. Finally*

I tracked him down and persuaded him to come to my house. We sat for a few hours and shmoozed a bit and learned together for a while. Then I called his parents to come get him.

He told me that his father does not give him adequate spending money when he goes to yeshivah, so he borrows and then his father becomes upset with him. I went out with the boy to speak to his father.

"You know," I said, "this child is not far from deciding three times a day to leave school. 'What am I doing in school? I want to go out and work. I want to have money in my pocket.' What do you think he really wants? He wants to buy himself a Coke and a bag of potato chips. That is one and a half dollars a day. It adds up. It is a lot of money. On Shabbos he wants to have some drinks available and some nosh. He wants to buy a few other things that are important to him because without them there is 'no Shabbos.' Dorm life just is not like home.

"I know it is a lot of money. But do you know what he is really doing? He is fighting the yetzer hara. He is sitting and learning and he is really learning well now. But there is one yetzer hara that keeps on saying to him, 'You idiot, you can't even buy yourself a bottle of Coke. Why don't you go out to work? Get out of here, leave!'

"If money is what is needed to overcome his yetzer hara, then help him quiet his yetzer hara and give him the money. You need to understand what he is dealing with. You have to know that right now these are the choices your son is facing, and these are his options."

In this case it was not just a question of money, which I know is not always readily available. The lesson I draw from this is not that we have to set limits to what children have or do because otherwise they are going to run to the street and become irreligious. Nor do I advocate that you have to give a child everything he desires. We do have to set guidelines and we do have to establish parameters of behavior and of spending money.

But we also have to understand where our children are emotionally. We have to understand what tests they are facing. We have to understand what they are up against and what they are fighting for, because if we understand that, it will be much easier for us to give in on some things that may seem unimportant to us but are extremely important to them.

◄§ Drawing the Line

Parents often ask me where they should draw the line. There is no one answer to that question, because each family's situation is different. One aspect of the equation is the logic or lack of logic in children's requests. Another aspect is that we don't always listen to what they are asking for, nor do we always hear them out. Still another factor is the general affluence of our lives; even those of us who are not wealthy give our children a great many material things, and everything is so expensive today. When you send your child off to yeshivah, you have to be aware of the kind of environment he is leaving. Is your home a place where rules and limitations are clearly defined and the child knows that he has to manage with what he has? Is your home regime slightly permissive in terms of the extra nosh, or buying clothes? Even if he had to split the bag of potato chips with five children at home, when he is fifteen and in yeshivah, he may still expect that the bag of potato chips will be a part of his Shabbos routine, and a can of Coke adds to the cost. If he needs something extra after the meal in the yeshivah, because it is not your home cooking, that involves another expense.

This is reality; we can't ignore it. You have to define the limits of spending based on your comfort level and on your financial situation. It is important that a child realize that not everything is dictated by the fluidity of our bank account. There are times when we are strapped for funds yet we buy what is important. There are other times that we can afford to buy something but we don't because it is superfluous. These are values that you must transmit.

At home he was accustomed to being in on everything that was going on and having many things, not the least of which was your attention, and he felt good about it all. At the yeshivah he feels lonely and whatever extras you can provide make him feel better. A mother can and should always find ways to send along a little something extra. If you are baking challah, bake an extra small one and give it to your child to take to yeshivah. It will make a world of difference to him to take something along from home. Obviously you can't do this all the time and you shouldn't be expected to do it all the time, but there are plenty of little things you can do to compensate if you can't buy your children everything they want. You have to make it your business to show them that you understand that being in yeshivah for Shabbos is not easy when they miss a warm, loving home.

Some children love living in a dorm away from home and don't ask for anything. Maybe they are embarrassed to bring something from home when the other kids can't or don't, so they refuse your offers. Other children love to sit down at the yeshivah Shabbos table and put down their little piece of kugel-from-home, their little salad-from-home, and their little challah. It makes them feel connected: *Mom loves me, and I'm still a part of home.* Children are different, and it is important to know our children. One child is completely happy without store-bought food on his shelf and another has to have his store-bought snacks or he does not feel secure. You have to know your own child, and you have to know your own budget. You have to see clearly what your options are.

And that leads us to the final option: You have to know when you can't say no. I am always concerned that when I say we have to understand our children, people will think I mean that you can never say no. That is not so. When you understand somebody you can say no. It is when you don't understand and you feel you can't say no that you may err. When you empathize with your child and he knows that you love him and are concerned about him, he will know that you would like to give him what he asks for, but you don't have the means at the time. He can handle that.

Please don't respond to your teenager's requests with a flat no or say, "Why do you always want so much? I can't give you everything you want. What do you think I am, a bank?" When we respond this way to a child, he feels that we don't want to give him what he asks for and he feels let down and disappointed. The important point here is not so much whether or not you can give it to him, whatever it is, as it is a question of your understanding and appreciating how important these things are to him. When you can't afford something and you let him know that you are sorry you can't give him whatever he wants, that goes a long way toward soothing his hurt. And when he wants something that you believe is out of proportion even though you can afford it, you can explain that there are values you wish to retain that are beyond money, and it really does not make a difference whether you can manage financially. You need to manage your life according to standards that are important to you. If he sees that you refrain from indulging your own every whim and fancy, he will respect and accept the limitations you set for him. The belief in and love for our children is what allows us to pass on values and set limits.

Chapter Eleven
TALKING WITH
TEENAGERS

W hy is it so difficult to talk to adolescents? Why do they act in such a challenging manner? Why do they seem to question everything we say? Why is it that we sometimes feel it might be better to say the reverse of what we mean because whatever we say, they are going to want to do the opposite?

Several years ago there was a notice posted in my neighborhood regarding a workshop I was going to present on adolescence. A few days before the workshop, I was shopping in a store and a woman approached, took a good look at me, and just turned away. A short while later I received a phone call at home. A woman's voice on the line asked, "Are you the Rabbi Greenwald who is giving the workshop on adolescents?" I said, "Yes."

"How many adolescents do you have?" she asked.

When she saw me in the store, she must have thought I did not seem old enough to handle such a topic. When their children enter their teens some people's hair turns gray, while other people's hair falls out. Since I am in the latter group but was wearing a hat, she wanted to be sure that I had some experience before she went to hear me speak. I told her that I have four adolescent children between the ages of twelve and twenty — and one who is two and a half!

◄¿ The Two-Year-Old Adolescent

The concept of a two-and-a-half-year-old adolescent is not so strange. We all have a two-year-old who we feel is already a little bit of an adolescent. What do I mean? No matter what you say to them, two-year-olds say, "No, no, no!" Would you like a bottle? "No." You want a cup? "No." You want to go to sleep? "No." You want to stay up? "No." Regardless of what you say, they say no; it is an automatic response.

I like to begin the process of instilling self-awareness at a young age. I ask two-year-olds five questions to which they answer no. The sixth question I ask is, "Do you want to say no?" That gets them. The smarter ones laugh; the others stop and think, *Uh oh! What do I do now? If I say no to that, that means I'm saying yes.* This is actually the first step to self-awareness. When you ask children that sixth question, it makes them consider whether or not they really want to say no. When you do that to an intelligent child of two or two and a half and his answer is no, it shows that he sort of knows what he is doing.

Let us try to understand why young children automatically answer no. This *no* is a two-year-old's introduction to his concept of self. When he says no and sees your response, it is the first time he acquires a feeling of self. When his parents tell him, "Do this or that," it comes from *them*. When the child says no, it gives him a sense of *me*. He now knows that he is himself, because if he does whatever it is we tell him to do, it is as if *we* are doing it, not *he*. His ability to say no to us means *I am a separate entity*. His realization that he can do something other than what we tell him to do is proof of this. So at about the age of two a child begins to develop a new sense — an awareness of *self*.

◄¿ A New Sense of Self

Similarly, at the age of thirteen or fourteen a child is exposed to a new capability, one which enables him to discover a hitherto unrecognized part of himself. He now experiences the part of himself that judges, decides, chooses, and evaluates. His developing mind begins to explore these new abilities on a more mature level. At this stage a young person has to define his new sense of self, to identify his newfound skills of judgment and decision. It is his urge to define that new sense of self that induces a young person to say no, because he now finds himself capable of acting, thinking, judging, and deciding for himself. *I must oppose whatever they say*, he reasons, *because I need to say no in order to define for myself who I am.* He has a deep need to separate who he is from the "who" his parents and teachers are. The critical issue for him is: *Who am I?*

Thus for the two-year-old as well as for the teenager, the focus is not what I *am told* to do but what I *want* to do. He does not accept what people tell him he must do; he considers only what he feels is right. With each new issue he asks, "What is *my* understanding, how do *I* feel about this?" Unfortunately, it is this attitude toward the world around him that only too often gives the adolescent his only sense of himself.

How should a young person feel about himself if we try to control everything he does, thinks, and says? The thirteen, fourteen, and fifteen-year-old has all these faculties: He is capable of making decisions for himself. But how much leeway do we give him? How much do we include him in the processes that we want him to be a part of? How much do we think we need to control him and force him to do our will?

We think, *Good communication doesn't help; he doesn't want to hear.* Parents tell me that their children will not hear anything they have to say. That is not really true. Children do want to hear, even though we parents are not so sure they do. Maybe it is a question of from whom they want to hear and how they want to hear it. But they do want to hear. I know this because I speak to hundreds of adolescents every year. They all want to hear — not because someone has told them it will be worth their while to listen to me, or that I know what I am talking about. That does not work because no one knows more than a fifteen-year-old, right? He knows everything. Why then do children want to hear? And from whom are they willing to hear? The answer is very simple.

◄₰ Listening, Not Telling

Children are willing to listen to anyone who is willing to listen to them. I guarantee it. If you know how to listen, you will have to whom to talk.

What are friends? Why do friends talk to each other? They talk because they hear each other. They discuss things. What one says is either accepted or not accepted by the other, but there is a discussion. There is give-and-take between friends. They talk to each other because they listen to each other, and that is why they hear each other. We generally do not talk with our adolescent children; we mostly tell them what we think they are supposed to do. We tell them what we think they are supposed to think. We tell them what we want them to be and how we want them to act.

They are not interested in what we tell them, because they feel left out of the discourse. *Where am I in all this? I am, after all, someone; I am a part of this process. I can define things for myself, I decide, I know, I think, I judge.* How can teenagers feel this personal strength if someone else is always telling them what to do? They do listen, and they listen carefully — to friends. Of course, it frustrates us to see how much they listen to their friends. We feel hurt and we answer, "So who are you listening to, another fifteen-year-old who doesn't understand anything?" We tell our children, "Thank you very much, you won't take even five minutes to listen to what I have to say." We are crushed because our opinion does not have any value to them. Well, what do you expect if your child's opinion does not have value to you? You are treating each other with the same lack of sensitivity. That kind of reciprocity is very common in interpersonal relationships. To respect one another's opinion seems to be such a simple precept, yet it is so commonly ignored.

We know that we would never walk into the boss's office and blurt out, "I want a raise!" The issue and the relationship are much too important for us to act in such a careless manner. It would never work out well if we did such a thing. If I were in the situation, I would first think of how to present the request. I would prepare what I want to say, how I want to say it, how to get him to agree, maybe even how to have him come up with the idea himself. That would be best.

In the many years I have had the gracious ear of my esteemed *Rebbe* Rav Wolbe, I can hardly remember asking a question that did not elicit an answer that began with, "What do you think?" This began when I was just twenty years old and continued until I learned to present my thoughts as part of the question. It holds true even today. The knowledge that my thought process is a real and important part of the equation has forced me to become a thinking, confident individual.

Unfortunately, we usually do not do this with our children. What do we do with our thirteen- or fourteen-year-old sons and daughters? What do we do with our sixteen- and seventeen-year-olds? Do we help them come up with ideas by discussing things with them, by hearing and helping them come to a conclusion, or do we tell them what we want them to think? "This is what we want you to decide. Go ahead and do it, because I said so. I am your mother, I am your father. I have the right to decide for you."

You know what? You are right! *Kibud av va'em* — they have to respect their parents. Sure, you have the right to decide for them — and good luck! But do not be surprised if it does not work. It cannot work because you are hardly giving them a choice. They can't listen to what you are saying because you're telling it to them in such a way that if they listen, they are negating themselves. If they listen to you, it means that they do not have a say in the matter. But how could they not have a say in their own lives, in their friendships, in what they are going to do with their free time, in what they want as their goals? How could they not have a say in all that?

We have to try to define how we are going to approach our youngsters and help them become a part of this process that we want to call communication.

◄ᴢ *Viable Communication*

"All right. Fine. I'll talk to him. But even when I talk to him, he never agrees. Even when I do sit down and have a conversation with him, the bottom line is that he doesn't agree. I don't want him to go somewhere and the bottom line is he wants to go. It just doesn't happen that when I talk to him nicely, all of a sudden he's going to become a little angel who only wants to do what is right, who only wants to do what I want him to do. His behavior is not going to change drastically just because I speak to him differently."

Let us examine this. What do you mean he never agrees? Do you mean he disagrees with everything anyone says? Or do you mean he never agrees with you but always agrees with his friends? Or does he sometimes agree with you and sometimes with his friends? If he *never* agrees with you and *always* agrees with his friends, it may mean that you still have not figured out how to speak to him. If he sometimes agrees with you and sometimes with his friends, perhaps he just has a normal difference of opinion on a particular point.

Now do not misinterpret this. I am not saying that I think children have the right to have different opinions and *therefore* they can do whatever they want with their lives and define for themselves whatever they think they want. No, they do not have this unlimited right, even if they act as if they do. If we do not train them (and ourselves) to deal with this question properly, then the bottom line is that they will do what they want despite their rights or lack thereof, and despite our right to enforce or not to enforce. They are becoming bigger and stronger and older and they will just get up and do what they want. Then it will not be a question of who is right and who is wrong, or whether I think they should be allowed to do what they want. That is clearly not the issue.

The only issue is what works and what is the smart way to handle the situation. How can we become a part of their lives? How can we manage to say things properly so that they will hear us and listen to us because they think it is worth listening? How do we become people they want to listen to and hear what we say? How do we become people they respect? Try to figure out why they will ask a friend's opinion and heed it and ignore a mother's or father's opinion. How can we become people to whom our children will listen?

A. The Underdog

Most teenagers identify with the underdog, because they feel that this is their position. People usually identify with those who they perceive to be in a similar position. Objectively speaking, children *are* underdogs. We sometimes feel that our children have the upper hand, but this is not the way it really is. Think about it for a minute. Who is older, stronger, has more clout, more ability, controls the money, the house key, the car? Who is really in control? Parents are. It is understandable that our children feel inferior. Whether or not we have exacerbated that reality or not is something we have to examine in ourselves. This is a separate question to think about before we discuss the tools we need to acquire to help us become people to whom our children will actually listen.

We want to be people with whom our children can have a real conversation, discuss things, and work things through. We do not want them to feel inferior. We don't want them to feel that they have no say in anything, because it is their lives and they are thirteen now and responsible for their lives. Remember, children from the age of bar and bas mitzvah are responsible to the point that they are *chayav misah*, they are liable for the penalty of death based on their actions. That is real responsibility. And we are responsible at least to help train and develop their sense of responsibility, their decision-making capability.

B. The Basic Tools

What do we need to do in order to become a part of our children's lives? The first step is communication, as we have emphasized. Communication with our children is achieved through the love and respect that we accord them. Respect means recognizing that they are people and that they have the right and ability to think for themselves. They have to believe that we think that what they say might make sense. Their friends respect them as people and as equals. They are not our equals, but they are people. In fact, in a conversation they might well be our equals. They may even have some good ideas. Often they have very good ideas. Respecting them as individuals is basic, that is, *kavod habriyos*, respecting them as human beings. They need our respect, our love, and our support.

Do adolescents really want direction? Yes, they do. They do not want to hear only from their friends. They want to hear from us. Children want to hear what we say, what we want, and what we know. But they want direction with love and respect and a sense of being a part of the action. They want direction with the feeling that we value them and it is therefore worthwhile for them to listen to us.

Although maturity levels and needs differ among adolescents, every child, every single person, needs to feel that he is respected, that he has a place in the scheme of things, that he is necessary. He needs to feel, "I am something." Children want and need to feel that they are equals, because in their own minds they are equal to others. It is not that they think they are superior. They do not. They do not really think that they know more than anyone else. They just do not like to be made to feel that they know nothing. If we make them feel worthless it is a natural reaction for them to reject our opinion. If we listen to them, however, if they know that we respect their opinion and think that what they have to say is worth listening to, they will be interested in what we have to say as well. All of a sudden, what we say makes sense to them.

This really works. Do not just take it for granted. Try it. It works because children need to be heard. They need to know that they are considered equals. As soon as they are treated as equals, then they are not equals anymore. When they are treated as equals, they realize we are smarter than they. If we are smart enough to hear what they have to say, we have got to be smarter. If we are intelligent enough to recognize that what they said is intelligent, we are *really* smart. Suddenly they are interested in what we have to say.

We need to really listen when our children say something. That means asking ourselves: What are they really saying? Why are they saying it? What do they mean? When a child comes home and says he hates someone, what is he really saying? He is saying, "Someone hurt me, someone insulted me." Children do not hate people who respect them. It is a basic rule of human nature. The way you look at a person is the way he looks at you. If you respect a child then the child respects you, and vice versa.

When a child comes home angry at a *rebbe* because of something awful that the *rebbe* did, 99 percent of the time the awful thing was that he put down your child. He did not listen to him. He did not hear him. He did not understand him. When your daughter comes home and says she hates her teacher, it is because the teacher spoke down to the class. That teacher was condescending and made the children feel low. Her attitude is, "I know you don't listen to what I have to say." They "hate" her immediately. Anything she says is certain to be worthless. They are not going to be interested in hearing anything she has to say. In dealing with a young person who wants only to feel that he has value, a condescending attitude is not going to get a teacher or a parent anywhere. This feeling of having value is connected to the teenager's feeling of being in transit. He needs the anchor of feeling that he has value and worth, that he has a mind and intelligence. If he does not have that feeling, the only thing he can do is fight, because that will show that he has *something*. It all comes down to listening, to hearing what he says and how he says it.

When a youngster has an idea, never say, "That's dumb." Say, "Wow, that's a good idea. I never thought about that." After you have said something positive, then you can say,

"One second, though, how are you going to ..." Let me illustrate what I mean with a story.

> Fifteen years ago there was a young boy who was a talmid of mine in the yeshivah. He was living in Har Nof in the home of people who had befriended him because he had no real home. His father, who was not Jewish, was living in America where he had married a non-Jewish woman. His Jewish mother was having a very difficult time financially and lived somewhere out of town.
>
> I had not spoken to the boy in nearly a year and a half. He was no longer in yeshivah. He was working, doing odd jobs here and there, in pizza shops, among other things. One day the family with whom he was staying called me and said, "Rabbi Greenwald, we don't know what to do. Yankel (not his real name) wants to go to America."
>
> "What's the problem?" I asked.
>
> "Well, if he goes to America, we are afraid of what's going to happen to him. He'll go to live with his father because it's the only place he can go, and that's going to be terrible. We'll lose him forever."
>
> "So what did you tell him?" I asked. They said, "We told him that's it's not good for him and we'll lose him, but he's not listening."
>
> "Okay, what would you like me to do?"
>
> "You don't understand. He's been talking about it for a month and a half already. Everyone has told him what a totally ridiculous idea it is, and he's not listening to anyone. His mother is at her wit's end. We are at our wit's end. The guy who he was working for here in the community is also telling him it's not going to be good for him. He's not listening to anyone."
>
> "Listen, tell him that we happened to meet and I asked how Yankel is doing, and let him give me a call," I said.
>
> Sure enough, two or three days later I received a call from Yankel. "Yankel, shalom aleichem, I haven't seen you in such a long time. How are you doing? Come over and visit."
>
> "Really? You mean it?" he asked.

"Yes, yes, come over," I said.

The next day Yankel knocked on my door. I let him in and gave him a big hug. "Shalom aleichem. I haven't seen you in such a long time. How are you doing? What's going on in your life? What's happening?"

"Oh, I'm working now."

"What are your plans?"

"I'm thinking of going to America."

"America? What a brilliant idea," I said. "That's great. Sure. You can go to America."

"You really think so?"

"Oh yes, I think it's a great idea. Why shouldn't you go to America? You know, in America a lot of people make money and why not you? I think you should go. You read and write English, right?" I continued.

"No," he said, "I don't."

"Oh, you don't? Oh. Okay. Right, so you can go to school there. I'm sure that in six months, if you work hard every single day, I'm sure you could learn to read and write English."

"Hmm." He did not really want to go to school for six months.

"Anyway, you have money saved up, right? What does it cost to rent an apartment? You could probably get an apartment in Brooklyn for $400 a month. You have a few thousand dollars saved up. You've been working already now for a year and a half, so that will give you a start."

"I don't know. I don't have any money saved up."

"No? Well, you can borrow the money."

"No one is going to lend me money," he said.

"All right, so maybe ... doesn't your father live in America? Would he ... ? Ah, you don't know ..." I was looking at him and he knew the answer, but he said, "No, that's not a solution."

"Well, I'm sure you'll figure something out." We spoke for another twenty minutes or so and he left.

An hour later the phone rang. The family told me he decided he's not going to America. "What did you tell him? What did you do?" they asked.

"Is that so? I only told him it was a great idea."

That is all a teenager needs — for us to hear the other side. If we want a person to hear our side, we have to hear his side. He needs to be told that his ideas are not stupid; he wants to feel that we are not going to put him down. That gives him the opportunity to think the idea through, with our help in defining the issues. I did not tell Yankel he was crazy to go because he does not speak English. I showed him what the problem was and let him deal with it. I did not tell him what was wrong with his idea or that he could not do it. I told him he can do it. I gave him the belief that someone thinks he can do something. Then he had to wonder whether or not he could do it, and he knew that he could not. After a half-hour conversation in which I only told him that he should go to America, he decided not to go. Whatever I told him he should do, he did the opposite. Why? Because once I told him his idea was great, thus validating his opinion and showing respect for what he said, he had enough strength inside of him to review it objectively and realize that it was a ridiculous idea.

This is not reverse psychology. It is not dishonest. He is not a stupid boy. He wanted to go because he wants a better life. Should I deny him the hope? Maybe he knows something I do not know. No one gave him a chance to think about his plan. No one even credited him with his ability to think. It was very simple.

◄ᴈ Children's Emotions

Children have concerns and fears, and they are real. If you think them irrelevant, you are wrong. Whatever his concerns are, for the teenager they are the most real concerns in the world. You are never going to take away your child's fears by telling him, "Don't be afraid …" This does not work. Why not? Because you are giving a rational answer to an emotional question. His fear is real; he is afraid of something. Talk about it. Find out what it is that he fears.

Once a month I have the privilege of answering a crisis hotline. A young girl once called. She was sixteen years old and said she could not sleep at night. Her father had passed away nine months earlier, and ever since then she has been afraid that a robber is going to break into the house in the middle of the night. A friend of mine who is a therapist taught me how to respond to this problem. I asked the girl to describe to me exactly what it was that she feared.

"Oh, so there are no bars on the window?" I asked.

"Yes, there are bars on the windows."

"Oh, you don't have a solid door downstairs?"

"Yes, we do have a good door downstairs."

"Do you understand why you're afraid?" I asked.

"No, but I am."

"Okay," I said. "I'm going to tell you what to do. Take a sock and fill it with 10-agarot coins until it's the size of a tennis ball. Tie a knot at the end of it and put it under your pillow. When you go to sleep at night, hold onto it. If anyone comes in through those bars, you know, wallop them over the head."

She started laughing, but I asked her seriously if she could do it. She said, "Yes. I like that," and she did it.

Several weeks later the girl called back on the hotline. The girl said to me, "I just want to say thank you. I've been able to sleep for the past two weeks."

What happened here? We cannot tell someone not to be afraid of something he fears. We have to give him the tools to deal with his fear. Our teenager is afraid his friends are going to make fun of him and look down on him. Are we going to tell him, "No they won't!" That is ridiculous. Do we really believe that our assurance is going to change the way he feels?

Communicating is the ability to get a message across. It means that I sent a message and it was heard and understood. Otherwise it is not communication. If we accept our child as a person, we have begun the process of communication, because we have recognized that communication requires two people. Where do we start? Start by talking. Just open our mouth. We will see that our children will respond. They are human beings just like us. They have feelings, thoughts, and concerns; they are smart and intelligent just like us. They are real people. They may be dressed like "lions and bears" at times, and sometimes they act like that, but the bottom line is that they are persons, and if we regard them as persons, they will respond to us.

A. Establishing a Dialogue

Children are not only *nachas* providers; they do not exist solely give us joy. We have to look at them as people and believe that they have a desire for dialogue. If we wonder why our children do not speak to us, it is because we have taught them it is not worthwhile to speak to us. Children want to talk; in fact they need to talk. Taking into account the differences in human nature, there is a basic, minimal human need to share and to express oneself. A normal child wants to discuss things, talk them over with someone, hear and listen. But we tend to think that is true only when it happens. We need to believe that the need is there even when it is not working. If our children are not talking to us, it means that we are doing something wrong. However, we can correct this situation.

Talking *at* a person converts him into an object whose existence is immaterial to the conversation. We can talk at the wall too. That is what happens when we are screaming, letting off steam, and getting everything off our chest. The person we are speaking at, or screaming at, is totally irrelevant. This, unfortunately, is one of the all-too-common ways that teachers, parents, and other figures of authority sometimes speak.

Speaking *to* people does not guarantee that they are listening, either, or that they care. You don't know whether or not they are listening because you are not interested in what they think. You are interested only in what you want to say, and when you are finished, the subject is closed. The conversation has ended. You think you did a great job because you spoke to the person for thirty minutes about such an important matter, but he was just waiting for you to finish whatever you were saying because he was not listening.

When you are talking to people, you may or may not be communicating. When you are talking *with* someone, you know you are communicating, because it is a two-way conversation. In a two-way conversation you know what the other person is thinking and what he has accepted or not accepted. You know where you stand, because you are listening to what he is saying, too; you are communicating.

We think children are closed, but they are not. They are just waiting to open up. In my yeshivah we accepted boys who were not always doing that well in other yeshivos. Registration was always a challenge because we interviewed many children, and we had to figure out what the true story was with each boy. The parents would say, "You can try to talk to him, but he doesn't talk." I would take the boy into another room and ten minutes later I would come out and tell the parents what was bothering the boy. They asked if I had *ruach hakodesh*, Divine intuition. They could not believe that the boy had told me so much.

I have found that most children will speak openly and freely, despite their parents' inability to get them to speak. If this is your problem, I would ask you, "When was the last time you really listened to what your child had to say?"

Now I know you have a problem. You want to listen to what he has to say and you are begging him to tell you, but you think he is not interested in talking to you. I'm telling you that he really is. When this "closed" boy sat down with me, we had a real conversation. I started out by telling him a little joke about myself and that made him a bit more comfortable. Then I asked him a question. He answered me and I showed him that I was impressed. I said, "Oh, I see that you understand. I'd better watch what I say." The boy thought, "Oh, this guy understands that I know what I'm talking about." Then this same child who "won't say a word" did not stop talking for twenty minutes because he found someone who thinks that what he has to say is intelligent. I asked him a question and he answered me, and the whole transformation took thirty seconds. Thirty seconds to establish one crucial thing:

I like you — you're smart. That is all I communicated to him. That is the only message I gave him.

If you think that happened because it was the first time I met the boy and I was someone new to him, someone willing to listen to him, you are wrong. The first time you try it you will be new and fresh to your child, and it will be like the first time he is meeting you. If you can adopt this attitude toward your child, you will find that he is definitely interested.

You can even say, "I don't know" or "I'm sorry." That is basic honesty. I know there are people who disagree with this and claim that if a parent says, "I don't know" or "I'm sorry," it breaks down the barrier and your children will not respect you because they will know that you made a mistake. In all my experience I have found that when you say, "I'm sorry, I made a mistake," children know and appreciate that you are an honest person and that they can trust you. If you never admit to a mistake, it means that you think you never make mistakes. Well, if you never make mistakes no one is going to want to talk to you. You yourself do not like to talk to someone who knows everything, because nobody knows everything. The greatest doctor is even more respected when he seeks a consultation.

Regarding the *mekoshesh*, the one who gathered wood on Shabbos, the *pasuk* says[1] that Moshe Rabbeinu requested that the man be placed in custody until Hashem would tell Moshe what to do. The *Targum Yonason ben Uziel* says,[2] "This is one of four places where Moshe Rabbeinu said he did not know, in order to teach the heads of the Sanhedrin in later generations that they should not be embarrassed to say they don't know and require further investigation. If Moshe Rabbeinu could require additional information, surely they can as well." This clearly tells us that we should not be afraid to admit our mistakes, nor should we fear to apologize. We should confidently assume responsibility for our own lack of knowledge.

---

1. *Bamidbar* 15:34.
2. Ibid.

Parents should aim to feel what their children feel and recognize that what they feel is real. Make sure that they hear you when you admit a mistake or tell them something, because it is not enough just to say it. Having placed food on the table, you cannot be sure the child ate it. You can make a speech, but you cannot be sure the child heard it. If you want to know that your message is accepted, make sure that you follow through — discuss it to find out whether he really understands or if he is simply nodding his head without having heard a word.

More than anything else, adolescents need to be listened to. They speak for hours with their friends, in person and on the telephone. (Most parents who have teenage children do not even expect to receive personal phone calls anymore.) Why? Because friends listen. They hear what the teenager has to say about anything and everything: silly things, stupidities, and foolishness as well as intelligent, philosophical, emotional subjects, and even family matters. They will talk on and on as long as someone is listening. Sometimes friends argue, but they never judge each other. We parents feel we have to judge and to explain how wrong our children are. And we do not argue with them as equals, we argue because they have to know that we are right and they are wrong. This does not get us anywhere. Criticism and bashing their opinions will cut off conversation. Interest in what they have to say will open up a conversation. If we listen carefully, we can hear things they only hint at and in this way learn what is important to them. Let them repeat themselves over and over again, but do not respond negatively, do not criticize, push, or judge. Just listen. You will learn a lot that way. Then you will have to find the best way to take the information and bring it up for discussion at another, more suitable time.

"You know, I was thinking about something you said the other day. You mentioned it a couple of times. Is it something that bothers you?" If you do not seem to be threatening, you can usually find a way to discuss the problem and work it out. Their fears, which we tend to think of as foolish and immature, are real. I cannot repeat this often enough. If we belittle their thoughts, we have no way of getting into their world and thus no way of directing them into ours. When they are concerned about how their peers will perceive them with a new item of clothing and we belittle this fear, we are belittling something that is important to them. We must give legitimacy to their worry. This does not, however, mean that when they say they "need" a certain item of clothing, we have to buy them something that we cannot afford or that we feel is inappropriate.

"Listen, because it's so important to you, it's going to go to the top of the list of priorities. I can't buy it right now, though. Maybe we can make a decision about postponing something else, so that we can buy it? Perhaps we can buy this or that instead?"

Recognizing and understanding the practical side of dealing with adolescents is based totally on understanding their point of view. We need to note what is important to them and why, and with what they are grappling. We will aim to give them what they need: love, respect, strength, and support. We will listen to them, and we will work with them. Hopefully, we will help them move from childhood to successful adulthood with less pain and a brighter future.

B. More About Lying

You have to believe what your children say, even when they are not telling the truth. When you call someone a liar, you are cutting off all lines of communication. You can say instead, "Please tell me only what's really true." If the child says, "I am telling the truth," don't respond, "No, you're not." Try saying, "I'm happy to hear you are telling the truth, because it seems to me that something else happened." You can ask him a question, but do not turn him into a liar. When your child feels that you think he is a liar, he has no reason to tell the truth anymore and no reason to say anything more at all. He reasons that if he does speak, he does not have to tell the truth because you are not going to believe him anyway, so why should he speak?

In the Gemara there is a concept known as *"migo."*[3] A Jewish court of law will accept a person's questionable claim and give him credibility, "since" he could just as easily have presented a more plausible claim. This logic is based on the fact that you trust the other person. "I trust you now and believe what you're saying because I trust whatever you say." But if you are not going to trust anything he says, he does not have to tell the truth. The truth emerges only when a person knows that he is expected to tell the truth and knows that he's going to be believed. If you are not going to believe him anyway, why should he invest in the truth which might put him in a tight spot?

Children are not really liars — most of the time — unless we have trained them to be.

"Who broke the plate?"

"I did."

Wham!

If it happens again and you ask who broke the plate, he will blame someone else. Why should he admit that he did it? You have just trained him to sidestep the truth so that he can avoid punishment. It is not worth his while to tell the truth. That's how we train our children to lie. When they do vent their feelings and tell the truth: "I think you hate me!" then we yell at them, scream at them, or worse. They will never tell us their feelings again. Why should they tell us what they think if we are going to punish them for telling the truth?

How should you have responded?

"Who broke the plate?"

"I did."

When we have established lines of communication, it is probable that your child will add, "I'm sorry." At that point simply hand him the broom and shovel and ask him to clean up the mess. Allow him to accept responsibility for his mistake and to make amends.

Your daughter is going somewhere you do not want her to go. You know that she is going there. Find a technical way to

---

3. *Bava Basra* 55b.

stop it before you confront her. Right now she is not telling you the truth because she does not want you to know, which means she is embarrassed. She loves you. She does not want to hurt you. She does not want this to get blown up out of proportion. And if you confront her, it will certainly blow up out of proportion. Once you turn it into an issue by confronting her, she has nothing more to lose. Sometimes it is better "not to know."

This story of a *gadol* is one of my favorites.

> *Harav Meir Chodosh was in Tzefas (Safed) in the middle of the winter term when he saw two bachurim from his yeshivah there. He was walking with another rebbe and he immediately grabbed that rebbe's arm and pulled him into an alley.*
>
> *"What's the matter? What are you doing?" the other rebbe asked. "You caught them! That's every mashgiach's dream. You caught them red-handed."*
>
> *"Now that I know who these boys are," explained Rav Chodosh, "I will be able to deal with them. If I confront them now, I won't be able to talk to them for another six months. Every time I'd try to talk to them they'd be worrying about what I think of them. Now that I know what they're doing, I know what the problem is. I can go and talk to them freely and say all that I want to say, because they don't know that I know. Now I know what they need, and I can give them what they need."*

As a parent you have to be aware, but you do not have to know every little thing. You do not have to know about every fight they have with their friends. You do not have to know every time they say something wrong or do something wrong in class. If you do not know the truth, you can talk about it objectively and deal with it without a confrontation, and without making them feel low about themselves and denigrating their worth. We have to take a positive approach, because when we are positive with them, they have reason to trust us and communicate with us. That is what communication is all about.

C. Some Words Are Best Not Said

Do not give grand ultimatums: "If you go there or do that, I won't let you into this house," or "I'll never let you have the car again," or "I'll never let you go shopping by yourself again." Grand ultimatums are senseless, because most of the time you cannot stick to them. Of course you will let him in the house again. You know you will let him have the car again (especially when you want him to run an errand for you). You only said it because you wanted to get a message across at the moment. If you do not mean it, do not say it.

Say what you mean instead. Say something like, "This is not acceptable. I'm sorry it is so difficult for you to understand this, but in this house it's just not acceptable." If he insists that he wants to do it anyway, you can repeat such a statement fifteen times. It is strong but it is not an ultimatum. It is foolish to think that your statement will stop a teenager from doing what he wants to do. You have to tell him clearly that you disapprove and make known what you expect of him. Even if he dares you: "And what if I do?" you can answer, "Do I have to respond immediately? Must I tell you now what's going to happen if you do? I've said I don't want you to do that and I expect that you won't do it. In our home this is not acceptable. I don't want to deal now with what I'll do if you don't listen. I'll deal with it then. In any case, I don't believe that you're going to do what I don't want you to do. And I'm anticipating that you won't." "And if I do?" "Then I'll decide what kind of response to make when that happens." Do not promise to do something you will not be able to fulfill. Do not say things that you do not mean.

There are two more phrases that it is wise to refrain from saying: "You always ..." and "You never ..." These words are powerful and hurtful and most likely not true. They cancel out every good thing the child has ever done and indicate to him that you do not appreciate anything he has ever done. Why should he want to accede to your request if you are not going to appreciate it? You can say, "You know, sometimes I feel you could be more sensitive to my situation. Sometimes

I feel you could be a bit more helpful. I do appreciate and thank you for all the things you do, but sometimes you just don't notice that there's a difficult situation and we could use your help."

☙ Sending and Receiving

Aharon HaKohen was always seeking *shalom*, peace. We can learn from his tactics. He would come to the person on one side in a dispute and he would say, "The other fellow is so sorry, he feels so bad about what he did. He really wants to be your friend." The fellow would respond eagerly. Then Aharon would go to the person on the other side and say, "You know, that fellow is so sorry, he feels so bad about what he did." When the two parties would meet, they would already be predisposed to good feelings toward each other. Why? Each one knew the other person was sorry, that he accepted responsibility; therefore they could both be forgiving.

When we cannot do something for our children, when we understand them, recognize what they want, and explain to them why we are unable to do what we really want to do for them, it is much, much easier for them to deal with the situation. When we scold them, they do not understand, but when we are apologetic, they can be very understanding. It works the other way, too. When they say, "Oh Mommy, I'm so sorry I forgot to take out the garbage. I feel so bad," we answer, "That's all right, it's already taken out." That is the way human nature works.

Remember Harav Yisrael Salanter's example of the child whose paper ship sinks in the bathtub? In real life almost everything is replaceable, and change is always possible. An adult who loses $100,000 can eventually turn things around and start over again; life has not ended for him. But adults assume the only things of real importance are the things that they value, while children have a different perspective on what really counts at the moment.

An adolescent is somewhere between an adult and a child, and Harav Salanter's lesson must be applied to him, too. Understanding his feelings, getting a real perspective of what he is like, will be of great practical help in learning how to build a good relationship with him.

In regard to acquiring communication skills, the fact that we live in a service-oriented society places a certain pressure on us. We do not look at people as individuals, but as providers of things that we desire. As our children get older, we demand more and more of them because of this outlook. Our children are providers of *nachas*, of true parental pleasure. Of course they must also abide by the mitzvah of *kibud av va'em*, because it says so in the Torah. As they grow, our expectations grow too, our demands on them become more complicated, and we just assume that these demands will be fulfilled. When they are not, we are very disappointed and we do not know why the "system" is not working. Why are they not doing what they are supposed to do, and why are they not reacting in the way we expect?

We pray, "*Avinu Malkeinu, zachor ki afar anachnu*, Our Father, our King, remember that we come from the dust of the earth." You know we are fallible; Adam came from the *adamah*, the earth. We are not *malachim*, so please do not expect perfection from us. If human beings are not angels, then an adolescent is even more human!

A young child is a receiver, he accepts. We instill a tremendous amount of information and values into our children. From the time they are born, children are in a receiving mode. They learn to speak and to deal with the world, but their minds are not actively "sending." They do not project anything because they are too busy receiving, sorting, and putting everything into place according to their understanding.

Adults, however, have to be in both the "receiving" and the "sending" mode. We take in information, feelings, and experiences and we project them to our children. We also send out messages to our surroundings, to our students, to our co-workers, wherever we are, in order to accomplish the things we should. Obviously an adult always has to have his "receiving" mode turned on as well, because someone who stops learning, accepting, and understanding stagnates. Although a child is active and does productive things — and even tries to affect people and situations around him — his basic mode is "receiving."

An adolescent is caught in between. When we receive correct information and act on it, we do the right thing. If we get the wrong information and base our actions on it, we do the wrong thing. At our child's bar mitzvah, we say, "*Baruch shepetarani mei'ansho shel zeh*," meaning that we are no longer responsible for our son's actions. Until that age we assume that if our child does the wrong thing, it is because we have sent him the wrong information and we are therefore responsible for his wrongdoing — until he reaches the Torah's legal adulthood.

An adult is totally responsible for himself and his deeds. When this child becomes an adult according to the halachah, he begins to make his own decisions. In essence he is what we describe as an adolescent, and he is no longer making decisions based purely on information that he has received. He now takes an active role in trying to effect, accomplish, or attain whatever it is he thinks is important at the time. Deciding what is important is in itself an active decision.

A baby's emotional state is totally honest at all times. In one moment he can go from crying hysterically from hunger to laughing at a funny face, or a lollipop, or some other distraction. If you take away that object, he will cry again, and if you give it back, he will laugh. He is not making decisions about whether to be happy or sad or about what is important to him. If he feels good at that particular moment, he expresses it. Adults do not operate that way. When we are unhappy, even after the situation that caused us to be upset disappears, we very often decide to remain that way for the next two minutes, two hours, two days, two weeks, two months; it is a decision. We decide to remain with the anger, the fear, the pain, the suffering.

Children do not make those kinds of choices, but adolescents begin to make them. And because they are new at it, they are going to make mistakes. Just by virtue of his transition from child to adult, from the receiving mode to the sending mode, the teenager's inexperience is going to cause him to make many mistakes.

The needs of an adolescent are really the needs of all human beings, but since we cannot always manage to see them as such, we are going to discuss them one at a time.

◀ঽ *An Adolescent's Needs*

We react to our children's actions with our emotions and our intellect, based on who we are, how much we have worked on ourselves, what set of character traits we started with, and so forth. But when we are not happy with something he has said or done, and there are often many things to be unhappy about, our adolescent child will get the clear message that we are dissatisfied with him. His new insecurity may cause him to seriously doubt that he is loved. We forget to give him this all-important message because we are busy giving him other messages: what he should be doing, what he should not be doing, why this is important and that is not important, why he should not be going here or there, or complaining that he should spend more time studying. This happens in every home as soon as the first child reaches adolescence.

We are probably getting messages like these across three, four, five times a day, but how often do we stop and think, "Wait a second, have I been sending other messages too?" Have I been telling him that he is important to me, that I love him and care about him, that I want what is good for him, that I respect him? An adolescent needs to know this because he is in a very volatile stage, more often than not in the line of fire. Often we foolishly assume that he should know the positive things that we are thinking. How is it that we do not depend on this intuition when it comes to criticism?

Respect is a most basic human necessity. The adolescent is not sure of himself, of his identity, of what is his real place in this world. Because he is now questioning all values, trying to sort them out, getting information, trying some new things and testing others, he very often has a low level of self-esteem. When we question his ability, his fallibility, or his honesty, therefore, he feels as if we are not giving him respect and then the slightest doubt sets off a hydrogen bomb. One who is confident about who he is and feels good about himself can handle it when someone doubts him. One who feels insecure and has no self-confidence feels challenged and not respected when any of his weaknesses are touched. We show our children that we respect them by listening to what they say, by giving them the right to have their own opinions.

A fourteen-year-old today has a lot of information and a lot of ideas of his own. Because he is our child, however, we want to tell him what and how to think; we want him to see things the way we do. But it does not work that way. Showing him respect means that we have to allow him the space he needs to think for himself, even if he is wrong. We also come up with wrong answers sometimes. How many mistakes do we make every day? Being wrong is not the end of the world. Making a mistake is part of being human, but he is not going to see it that way unless *we* see it that way.

"Okay," we can say, "let me hear what you think."

Adolescents always seem to be sure of themselves. Do not disagree with his surety. The minute we give him the benefit of the doubt, he will be ready to back down. He is not so sure, after all. His constant need to exude confidence comes from his need to have his opinion respected. When we disagree, he feels he has to fight us so that he can be right and respected. He *has* to be right. On the other hand, if we agree that he may be right, that we did not consider it from his point of view, he can be wrong without losing his self-respect. We considered it, we actually heard what he said; now he can back down with his self-respect intact.

Of course there are things we have to insist on; there are certain limits we have to set in our homes. We need not be afraid to impose this important aspect of *chinuch* on our children. But we have to say what has to be said with firmness and understanding.

"I know you disagree, and I understand that this bothers you. G-d willing, when you have your own home, you'll do it your way, but this is the way we've decided we want it done in ours. You're a part of this family, and we love you and care about you. We know you love and care about us. Since we want to live together, decisions have to be made. In our house this is the decision. When you get older you may agree with me or you may not. I don't know."

Let me remind you once again, never say, "When you are older, you'll understand." If anyone would say that to us, we would be insulted. There is a middle road between saying that this is the way things have to be, even though you do not agree, and saying, "Well, you can't understand and you don't have to understand."

There are no guarantees, but experience shows that *usually*, if we give an adolescent the right to make decisions, he will more often than not make the right ones. If he feels that we are interested in what he has to say, and we listen to his opinions, he will be more accepting of what we tell him. If he feels he has to fight us every step of the way, most of his decisions will be the wrong ones even when he *wants* to do what is right. Surely there are times when your spouse says something that you know is true, but because of the way he or she said it, you do not want to listen. (The classic case is where the husband has lost his way en route to a *simchah*.) You would rather continue doing something the wrong way, go the long way around, because no one is going to tell *you* what to do in that tone of voice. You are an adult and *you* are supposed to be beyond that sort of pettiness, but if *you* are not, how can you expect more from your children? We have to be very sensitive to what they are feeling and to the way we demand things of them and tell them things.

An adolescent who is questioning himself, his parents, and his teachers sends the message that he knows everything, but in truth he does not feel strong in his position. He says, "I can deal with anything," but inside he wants the support of his family and of the people around him. Elderly people sometimes are insulted when we offer help. "Do I look like I need help? Do I look that old? I'm strong, I can do it myself." We do not always want to admit it when we need help. But if somebody casually gives a hand, we are grateful. We appreciate it. We do not feel infirm when somebody helps us in a respectful way. When our ability is questioned, it is harder to accept.

Our child needs someone to tell him, "You know, the way you've been helping your friend lately is just great. It's really beautiful." It is not easy for a youngster to give of himself. He sometimes questions whether he is being a sucker, if he is really doing the right thing, because in today's society giving is not always considered "cool." Give him credit when he does something good, at home or elsewhere.

- *"I noticed that you helped your friend with homework a couple of times."*
- *"I noticed that you've been going over to So-and-so's house and helping out."*
- *"I can't tell you how great it is to have another pair of hands that we can depend on."*

Those few words provide support and give strength.

Sometimes we worry about one or more of our teenager's friends. Maybe he even wants us to open a conversation about it. "You know, sometimes you don't seem so sure about that friendship." Of course, if we want to make sure that they become best friends, we could say, "I absolutely forbid you to meet with that kid at any time. His house is off-limits; his family is off-limits." This is guaranteed to work every time. Children usually know when they are doing something wrong. By saying, "I can tell sometimes that you're really not sure how far you should go with that friendship," you are giving him the strength he needs to deal with the decision properly. If he feels that we encroached a bit too far into his private life, he might not open up. If he feels, however, that we are being supportive and respect him, he will probably say, "Yeah, he's a good kid, but certain things bother me about him." You will then have a basis for a discussion and may be able to work out the problem together.

Adolescents tend to side with the underdog, because that is how they perceive themselves — on the receiving end of criticism, questioning, and constant distrust. When a teenager hangs out with a boy whom teachers and parents do not like, he sees the boy as an underdog just like himself.

All too often we mistakenly interpret this identification as total agreement with everything that is wrong with the other boy and assume that our son likes "bad" people. This is not necessarily true. He does not always agree with the wrong things this boy does, but because so many people are "on his case," the identification takes place. This does not mean that he is going to do whatever the other boy says or does, but we can help him turn the underdog into the greatest man on earth simply by continuing to criticize, telling him how bad he is. Since that other boy is probably going through his own set of difficulties, our son thinks we just don't understand. "He's not a bad kid," he thinks. "He's my friend. My parents don't know what his parents do to him at home. They don't know what he's going through in school. They just don't know." He thinks we just do not understand, because he knows this boy does not intend to do everything wrong. "He's having a hard time, that's all. I'm also having a hard time. I hate it too when they get on my case and tell me what to do, what not to do, how much to do, and how much not to do." The more we fight the friendship, the more the identification will grow; the more it becomes an argument, the more his friend becomes an important part of his life.

With today's wide-open information frontiers, a fourteen-year-old has much more data about things that we did not even know existed when we were his age. I heard a five-year-old say to his mother in a store, "I'm depressed." Obviously it was a borrowed term and he did not know all of its connotations, but depression was once a condition kept hidden. It was the most private experience of a person who was going through deep levels of suffering and it was never brought out into the open or even discussed. But today a five-year-old has heard of it and can use the term more or less in context. Fifteen-year-olds have opinions about why their teachers feel the way they do about many things, and they are right most of the time. My children come home sometimes with psycho-analyses of their teachers — not their peers, their teachers! — that are mind-boggling.

"Oh yeah," one of my children told me, "of course he is short-tempered lately. He's got a lot of financial pressure because he's marrying off his ..." My son was right. My eleven-year-old once told me that the reason his *rebbe* acts the way he does with the class is because when he was a child of eleven he was thrown out of the house. I was incredulous.

"Who said so?"

"Everybody knows."

"How does everybody know?"

"They know."

Their level of awareness is frightening, and therefore when they have something to say, we have to give them credit. We cannot just assume that because they are young, adolescents they do not know anything. Not only do they know, they understand and interpret, and very often they are right.

We would be shocked if we knew how our children have analyzed us. Our adolescent children have an idea why their parents behave as they do. They know what goes on between their parents. This awareness goes way beyond anything we imagine. They are sensitive to friction, to give-and-take, to the smallest nuances in relationships, and they watch, inter-pret, and *judge*.

We often ask siblings, "Can't you speak nicely to each other?" And they are thinking, "Can't *you* talk nicely to each other?" They judge us and understand relationships on levels that would surprise us. Obviously we have to give them more credit and more respect than we do. When we want them to make sensible decisions, we have to hear their opinions. They clearly have something to say. They are smart.

I have a son not yet fourteen who talks about politics. He has a less mature understanding about events than I have, but he definitely has more detailed information. We do not buy daily newspapers because, among other reasons, I do not have time to read them. But he hears the radio on the bus going to and from school, and he listens to the news because it interests him. He absorbs it all and talks about it. Since politics does not particularly interest me, he talks about it with other people, with other adults, and he certainly has opinions — about certain politicians, who they are and why and what they think, whether they are responsible, and in what ways they are irresponsible. Were I to negate his opinions, I would be losing his respect, because my son knows that he knows more than I do in this area. I keep quiet until he comes to conclusions that have nothing to do with the information he has culled.

The teens are critical years. If we deal with our teenagers as real people and respect them, they will respond in the same way. Hopefully, during the twelve to fourteen years that preceded their adolescence we did many things right alongside the many things we mishandled. These are years when we can change things and turn them around. We have to work hard at it, but we can do it. All it takes to build sound relationships is love, strength, motivation, and respect.

◄ℓ Look Ahead

We can do everything we have to do and we need not fear doing it *if* we understand that an adolescent is a highly intelligent, informed human being who has many real difficulties. His mind and emotions are in transit. He is in limbo between childhood and adulthood. We continue to consider him a child because he sometimes acts in childish ways, and we fail to recognize that although he has a great deal of adult information at his fingertips, he has thoughts and feelings that he needs help to work through. As parents we have to try to direct the transition. This is our challenge. Try not to sit back just marking time until it will be over, but rather rise to the occasion and enjoy participating in the phenomenal metamorphosis of your child into adulthood and responsibility. In a few years he will be an adult. If you do not recognize his present stage as a period of growth and tell yourself, "Okay, this is who he is now," the transition will take much longer and be more difficult. Understand that the child is still there but recognize the adult that is budding, and you can make it a much shorter and less painful period in both your lives.

If we look at a flower that is just beginning to open, we would be foolish to say, "See how closed this bud is. It's not pretty at all. It doesn't have any color." Give it another day or two. Do not stop giving it water just because it has not yet opened. It has not bloomed but it is on the way. Give it a little bit more water, or put in an aspirin, or do whatever it is your florist told you to do to make your plants flourish, and it will soon be a beautiful flower. Your teenager is on his way, too. Do not look only at the negative stages he is going through now, but rather rejoice in his progress on his journey toward full maturity.

Chapter Twelve
DEFINING GOALS

G oal-tending usually refers to watching your team's basket and not allowing the other player to put the ball through it. I use this same expression to describe what happens when an adult helps to modify a child's goals so that he can realize them. Our first concern should be helping our children define their goals. However, our goals for our children and our children's goals do not always match.

One of the most important things for us to achieve in our lives and in the *chinuch* of our children is the sharing of the same goals. For some reason, we find this difficult, so we need to figure out how to coordinate their goals and our goals. I call this process goal-tending because we have to tend/nurture our children's goals in life — they will not tend themselves. We must help them develop goals that are in consonance with our aspirations, and help them develop their goals to fit those things that we are spending so much of our lives working toward.

We will begin with a question. Why should their goals be the same as our goals? We are confident that our goals are the most important goals in life because they contain the *Emes*, the truth of Torah; thus we know what *HaKadosh Baruch Hu* wants. We therefore believe our goals are good, and we want our children to share in those same goals. Still, it is an impressive level of self-confidence that assumes not only that our general goal, which of course is *avodas Hashem*, fits every single person individually, but also that our particular goals are exactly what they should be for every one of our children. Are we so sure that all our goals — like, for instance, wanting our child to be a *talmid chacham* (as everyone in our community does) or wanting him to be successful or wanting him to do exceptionally well in school — are appropriate goals for each and every one of our children? Many of our goals for them have more to do with how we expect them to spend the next few years of their lives rather than with the ultimate goal of becoming *ovdei Hashem*, servants of G-d.

Of course, we know that becoming an *oved Hashem* is the goal of every one of us, and that it is important that each of us aspires to have a good connection with *HaKadosh Baruch Hu* and to do His will. These are clearly important goals. But how to get there amid the multitude of paths and obstacles that exist is a little less clear. It is precisely in the navigation of these paths and methods that we have to be very, very careful and question whether or not our goals and our children's goals need to match 100 percent. Perhaps there are some things that need to match and others that might vary. We have to ask ourselves what we really want them to achieve and then see if we are getting the message across clearly. Perhaps we are confusing the ultimate goal that we have for all our children with the individual way in which each child is going to reach that goal.

Let us first take the time to define our general goal, for ourselves and for our children, and for the moment leave aside specific, individual goals. I am sure that each of us knows what our own, personal goal in life is; we know what we need to achieve in this world in general. Therefore, we also know what we really want from our children. For they, too, need to live their lives in consonance with the same Authority to Whom we bow.

Let us try to differentiate between the goal itself and the way we will transmit it to our children. Are we giving them the message we wish to give them? Are we telling them what our goal is, or are we perhaps dealing so much with the details of how they are going to get there that we lose sight completely of our target? That is, unfortunately, why there is so much confusion between our perception of our goals and our children's perception. At this point we have to clarify what our goals should be and what message we ought to be giving to our children. They may not be receiving the message we think they are.

◄? Are We Saying What We Mean?

Here are some points to consider. Is my goal attractive to my child? Am I presenting my *derech*, my path, sensibly? Does it make sense to him? Is it something that he will respect and therefore be able to share? Maybe I have very lofty and important goals, but they are somewhere deep inside my heart and I am not getting them across to him. My goal can be *avodas Hashem*, for example, but my presentation can come across as anger, frustration, or nervousness. My goal may be to have a strong connection with *HaKadosh Baruch Hu*, but my presentation may transmit disappointment, negativity, and bitterness. If my presentation has nothing to do with my actual goal, my child will look at me, hear the words I say, and perhaps understand that I am speaking of something lofty and fine, but the only way he can identify with those beautiful words is by observing the way I act and behave. He also carefully compares my words with the way I interact with him. He sees a conflict between the word pictures of my lofty goals and the real picture he sees of the way I am living my life, which are not the same. This conflict confuses him.

We are all, unquestionably, *mechanchim*, educators, but what does that mean? It means that we want our children to share our ideals. We want them, as individuals, to aspire to achieve everything that is important, each one in his own way. That is what *chinuch* entails. Our job is to help a child want to be what he should be. Helping to prepare a child for life is exactly what *chinuch* is all about.

Let us be salesmen for a moment. How would we present something we wanted to sell in a way that piques the customer's interest? I am not talking about the hard sell that many advertisers succumb to these days. I saw an ad recently of an unhappy but trendy-looking boy, the caption of which says, "Do less, live longer!" I cannot think of a more negative, non-Jewish, antieducational, antihuman message. Obviously, this advertiser is addressing the baser part of the human being. Certainly some people will find such ads catchy, but we want our message to attract the loftier side of our children to the higher side of life. We want to attract them to live a life of Torah.

What are advertising and sales all about? How do we sell something? If we want to sell a vacuum cleaner, we have to make it attractive to the buyer. We have to show him how this is going to help him, how, once he buys it, he will never have to work hard again. Well, even without the lies, it does make life easier. Why? It is lightweight, it has strong suction, it is easy to move around, it has versatile attachments. Then all the salesman has to do is convince the buyer that his vacuum is better than any other vacuum. We are bombarded today with advertisements wherever we go and wherever we look, supplying a thousand reasons to do or to buy. The technique of course consists of persuading the buyer to identify with the cleanliness, the health, whichever quality of life they say comes along with their product. And the pictures! Just see all those beautiful blueberry, strawberry, and upside-down cheese cakes with fifteen different types of fillings and toppings. You take one look and, even if you do not go right out and buy it, it has captured your interest.

We understand that that is basic salesmanship. The Sages call it *Mitoch shelo lishmah, ba lishmah* — through initial ulterior motives one achieves appreciation of the essence. It is a way of attracting the interest of a person who is not yet ready to buy into the lofty ideal of *lishmah*, doing something for its own sake. *Chazal* explain that this means you must first give a little child sweets; after the sweets you give him a toy; and after the toy you give him something else, until finally you give him *kavod*, honor. The idea is to build a person up continually until he eventually reaches the point where he recognizes the beauty, loftiness, and the *shleimus*, the wholeness of Torah. Then, he is ready to take off on his own.

Before we can even talk about the preliminary stage of *shelo lishmah*, doing something for the sake of an ulterior motive, we need to provide our children with a role model to emulate. If the salesman who comes to sell us a vacuum cleaner arrives at our door looking like a *shlump*, looking like he himself could use a good vacuuming, we are going to take one look at him and not trust him. Maybe he has a great product, and maybe he is able to wax enthusiastic about it, but we look at him and, because of his personal lack of good grooming, we cannot bring ourselves to trust him. One cannot sell something when he is not in some way identified with the product.

We want to sell Torah and mitzvos. Are Torah and mitzvos a good product? Of course they are. We know they are good, but do we personally reflect that? How do *we* obey the Torah and mitzvos? With what kind of *simchah*, with what kind of joy, do we do the mitzvos? What kind of *simchah* do we show our children when we are getting ready for Shabbos, when we have to build a *succah*, when we have to do whatever it is we are obligated to do? Do we show anger, frustration, bitterness, and stress? This is often what the child sees when he watches us doing the mitzvos, and he says, "I am not so sure this is exciting. Yes, we heard all the stories about it and all the good things in school. It is supposed to be so nice, but it does not seem that way. It does not look that way at all."

If we want our children to share our goals, then maybe we should first clarify what our goals are and determine whether we are making those goals attractive. Our kids are watching us very, very carefully. They are looking at us and listening to us, and they are comparing what we say with what we do. They are judging whether what we *say* is important is that which we treat as important. They hear us say that one should not be angry and one should do the mitzvos with *simchah*, and then they see how we behave *erev Shabbos*. The manner in which we bring Shabbos in defines for them how happy they are going to be when Shabbos arrives. These are not such lofty ideas. On the contrary, they are very simple.

We are like salesmen trying to introduce our children to the idea that *HaKadosh Baruch Hu* is our Father, that the mitzvos are our way of life, that the Torah gives us fulfillment and joy, that it fills our lives with meaning. In the meantime, the children are looking at us, watching what we do, and deciding whether our words match our actions. Clearly, we cannot sell something that we do not have a connection to or that does not make sense. We have to be honest with ourselves and with our children.

◄֑ Our Children's Goals

How do we influence, direct, and, if need be, change the goals of our child and our teenager? We say that it is important to us that our child be a *ben Torah*, that he live a Torah life, so let us say that this is our goal. We want our son to be a *ben Torah* and our daughter to be a *bas aliyah*, to live a life of striving upward. We want them to have spiritual aspirations. What do they want? Well, how old are they? They are fourteen or fifteen years old, and they want to be successful — whatever that means. Depending on which school they are in, success can mean different things. First, they want acceptance by their peers, which makes sense. Then they want respect as individuals. These things are important to them. Is what we want contradictory to what they want?

Obviously it should not be. Even if their peers are not always precisely what we would prefer, there is no intrinsic contradiction between being accepted by peers and wanting to do mitzvos. Being accepted by peers is a valid aspiration for a young person. Adults also want to be accepted by their peers. Being accepted by peers does not have to be and should not be a contradiction to long-term goals.

The difficulty lies in integrating our children's aspirations with ours. We want them to be accepted into that yeshivah or seminary or high school. We want them to do whatever it is that will make us feel successful if they do it. But they want to go where their friends are going; they want to be accepted and successful. Do we accept their goals as realistic, important, or at least something to consider, or do we say: "One second, you don't understand. You've got it all wrong. Your goals are short-term goals. My goals are long-term goals. You have to ignore what you want and listen to me, because I am going to tell you what to do. If you listen to me, you'll be successful."

Okay, let us assume we have done everything right: Our children see that we really do have good lives and are happy people; we are well-adjusted, we are happy with our Torah and our mitzvos, we are happy with the way we live. We are fulfilled people. We speak to them with respect. We communicate with our children effectively. Now they are about to make a decision and the decision has to do with what they want. Their goals are immediate goals. It is now a case of *Mitoch shelo lishmah, ba lishmah*, of not ignoring the young person's immediate goals so that they will come to understand and buy into your long-term goals. Your long-term goal is beyond them at this point. It is too lofty; they do not appreciate it. They may admit that it seems wonderful, but right now they are looking to fulfill their immediate needs. And we have to recognize, accept, and respect their short-term goals.

This means that we have to be able to speak with them about their goals. We have to hear them out. We have to be able to work it through with them to see what it is that they really want. Then we have to find a way to show them how their goals and our goals are really not so far apart. As a matter of fact, we really do share the same goals, because we too want them to be successful and accepted by their peers. We also want them to do well and feel good about themselves. We just have to understand their goals and somehow fit them into the bigger picture. Sometimes we get caught up with our own personal goals and forget that we really want our children to succeed.

◄≀ Which Yeshivah? — What Your Child Needs Vs. Your Needs

I once knew a student whose parents were having a hard time. They had to send their son to my yeshivah, where most of the boys were not particularly high achievers. These parents felt that it was beneath their dignity to send their son to us, because what were they going to tell their neighbors? They wanted to be able to say "My son goes to X," and name one of the superstar yeshivos. Everyone wants that. We all want people to look at us and say, "Wow, you are successful!" so that we can agree with them. But I am telling you that not every child belongs in a superstar yeshivah or seminary, and not every child has to do exactly what all the other children in his family are doing.

> The parents who did not want to send their son to our school were really saying, "We know we have to do it. We know we have to do it, but we cannot. What are we going to do? We are afraid."
>
> The principal of the school surprised me. He called me and said, "Rabbi Greenwald, I do not know what to do. I finally told this boy's parents that it is cheaper to get themselves a psychologist to figure out how to deal with their problem than to try to figure out what to do with their kid. 'Send your child where he belongs and then

you go get help dealing with your own insecurities,' I told them."

His outburst actually pleased me, but it did not help us persuade the parents to send their child to our school. Evidently he was not able to get the message across. But that is the fact.

Sometimes we need help dealing with our own frustration, but the bottom line should be that we have to do what is best for the child. It helps to recognize and accept the child's goal and find a way to help him fit that goal into the bigger picture.

◄ẓ *Using Short-Term Goals*

When you define your child's short-term goals, you can see if they are really different from your long-term goals. These short-term goals are the catalyst that will bring him closer to the long-term goals. Once you are communicating, respecting each other, listening and talking to each other about things that are important to both of you, you can figure out how to make the required adjustments to fit both goals into the same picture. Ultimately we want the same things, even when the kids say they do not. Their goals are minimal and narrowly defined, and we know that those goals in themselves are not going to bring them closer to what we want for them. But unless we work within their goals, they will never even hear what our goals are. Only if we clarify what their goals are and talk to them about them can we possibly find the common denominator.

Do you recall the major premise in my story about the boy who wanted to go directly into the army from *yeshivah ketanah* (in Chapter 7)? What caused him to alter his plans? All we did was recognize that this child did not want to be a nobody. He wanted to be somebody. He never buckled down to learning because he was amusing his friends. He was good with the *chevrah*, with his pals. He did not have to study hard in that yeshivah where the standards were not the highest, and he got away with it. He never dreamed that he could become a high achiever in learning. I told him he could be the one who gives the *Daf Yomi shiur* in the army. That made sense and was important to him. He would be somebody. We used that as the primary goal, the short-term goal. The secondary goal was to get him into a better yeshivah. The third goal was to move on, and the fourth goal was to marry well. *Baruch Hashem*, he went from goal to goal and did very well for himself in every aspect of his life.

Because he was smart, he had been getting by with little effort and never had the chance to prove himself to the point where he could feel good about himself. He wanted to be "someone" in learning, but did not know how or where. He looked at himself and at his friends who had been learning seriously for three years in high school. How was he ever going to measure up to them? He ended up surpassing them. But that only happened after he saw a goal that made sense to him, after he was able to identify with some part of the goal. I am not saying that this is a solution for every child. That is what this child thought he wanted. If we had reacted negatively, told him it was a dumb idea, that he would become irreligious if he went into the army, he would have been left with nothing to cling to. We had to give him something to look forward to, to believe in, to feel good about. If I had told him his goals were meaningless, why should my goals be important to him? When I told him that his goals were important to me, he could begin to listen to my goals as well. That is really the secret of goal-tending.

Buy into your child's goal. That is what happens when we buy the vacuum or the steam iron. Our life is going to be easier. "But, it is a very expensive item; we do not have $100," we say. Then the salesman counters with: "Do you know how much money you are going to save? You are not going to need a cleaning lady for the next six years because of this steam iron." Have you ever fallen for that, or was it just me?

And let us not forget the vacuum cleaner. The salesman knew my weak spot. He bought right into my sensitivity. I was ready to buy that vacuum cleaner. It cost $100, but he was selling something that does everything. It cleans your couches, does your dishes, diapers your babies. It does everything. It is a vacuum cleaner, but it is a super-deluxe model. Thanks to my wife I did not waste my money, but I remember him telling me, "You will not need a cleaning lady ... "

We need salesmanship to help our child. We need to latch onto something that speaks to him, that is important to him. When we find it, we can discuss it. We do not put him down. We see the good in what he wants. He wants to be successful. Is that a good goal? Is it a good enough goal to show him that we respect it? Is it a good enough goal that we can say to him, "You know, I see you really want to make it. I see you really want to be successful. I am going to help you be successful." You are buying into his goal rather than knocking it. When you buy into his goal, he will listen to you. He has to. Who else is going to listen to him? Who else is going to help him? Every child wants to succeed. If there is someone who listens and is willing to help and wants him to be successful, then of course his goal becomes valid to him.

There is a phenomenon I frequently encounter when parents come in to see me with a child who is not doing well in school. The parents say, "He does not want anything. Everything is *no*, he is against everything, and everything is negative." The child sits down in front of me and I immediately ask him three questions — any three questions. What is your name? Where are you from? How old are you? Tell me something about a friend. Anything. No matter what his answer is, I respond, "You are a smart kid, I'd better watch what I say in front of you." The child is taken aback. He thinks to himself, *I am smart? You have to be careful? You have to watch what you say in front of me?*

Now, what is the child going to say in response? He has to say something that makes sense and — I have seen this happen every time — he does. He tells me something that is true, that he would not even say to his parents. He will not tell it to his parents because his parents would seize onto his words and drive him against the wall and pressure him to carry out whatever it is that he is dreaming about doing. He will tell me something and I say, "That is easier said than done, isn't it?" He catches my meaning. "Yes, it is easier said than done."

So I ask, "How do you want to go about it? What do you want to do?" You would be surprised. These are the children who are telling their parents that they do not want to do anything, because they know that whatever they tell their parents they want, their parents are either going to knock down or force them to do. To me, though, these same children start talking real sense. It does not make it easier, by the way, but their parents do not even know what these children really want to do. So many times I have heard a child say, "All I want is to be at school like everybody else and be a normal kid." That is what they say. That is what they want. These children have been asked to leave school or they are not doing well, and they are fighting everything. But when you ask them, "What do you want?" their true desire is not to be looked upon as different. They want to be normal, to go to a normal school and to do well there.

At that point you should reinforce their goal. "That is a very, very important goal. How can I help you do that? Which normal school is going to accept you now? Why would they accept you? Why wouldn't they accept you?" We talk about it and the children come up with all the answers. They know the answers, but that does not always mean that they have the ability to implement everything they know. There is often a difference between what they know and understand and what they are capable of doing about it.

Our next step should be to consider what we can do to help — one step we can take to start. Offer this "problem child" one idea, one thing you could do to help him strengthen the things he says he wants. I have found repeatedly, amazing as it may seem, that after twenty minutes of discussing one idea to help him implement his goal, you have a friend for life.

Whenever the child sees you thereafter, whenever he talks to you, this child is going to consider you his friend.

You, his parent, can do the same thing that I can. Your child does not need to go to someone else. All you need to do is invest in him, show him that you believe in him. In the matter of achieving goals, just as we discussed in the matter of his doubting your love, *your belief in him will empower him.* It is a matter of catching on to what his goals are and then helping him to achieve them. Once you understand where he is headed, you can direct him more subtly in smaller things by constantly giving positive advice and reinforcement about whatever he is doing. Your encouragement will give him the strength to continue the good things he has begun. When you think he is ready for the next step, praise him for how well he has done thus far and inspire him to take the next step.

◄◄ Moving On

A friend of mine told me a joke about the last convention of the Reform movement: It was decided to change the theme of *Parashas Yisro* to the "Ten Suggestions" instead of the "Ten Commandments." Of course, as parents, we have the right to "command" our children and tell them what to do. But it works so much better if we make suggestions instead. When we think they are ready to move on and take the next step, we should talk to them about it and try to give them a picture of what the next step looks like. Discussing it with them makes the suggestions work so much better. As I have pointed out repeatedly, parents sometimes have to command and say no, just as they can say yes. Our parental responsibility is to direct our children. But it is so much smarter and easier to achieve results when you work with them rather than fight them. When you work together toward the same goal, with you gently directing, you are in a sense investing in each other. This is, in a nutshell, what we have to do to help our children define and achieve their goals.

◄? A Word About the Wayward Sibling

What should we do when there is an older child who is already out of the house and has chosen a different way of life from ours? We maintain contact with that child because we want to be a part of his life and we want to influence him. At the same time, however, we have to recognize that there is a risk involved. We can minimize that risk by doing all the things we have been speaking about with his at-home siblings. Of course this older sibling may have an influence on his younger siblings, but so can we. We have to ask ourselves what this older sibling is providing for the younger ones that we are not. Why do the younger children feel more loyalty to and respect for the older sibling than they do for us? What can we do about it? How can we make the younger children feel as loved, accepted, and wanted by us as they feel loved, accepted, and wanted by that sibling?

This is a special problem, because the older sibling makes no demands on the others, nor does he hold out values as conditions for acceptance. Therefore it requires no effort whatsoever to be accepted by him. We will have to work harder and make a real effort to create an attractive environment in our house for the younger siblings.

We must also make the younger siblings a part of our attempt to maintain contact with the older, straying one, because they should understand that we love him even though he is not doing so well. If the younger children feel we are at odds with the difficult sibling, they will realize that we must therefore be at odds with anyone who communicates with him, and they will be pulled in two directions. Therefore, it is our job to try to include the younger siblings in our efforts by creating an atmosphere wherein they know they can speak to us freely and work these things out with us. They will respect us for this. We can include the younger ones in our wishes and prayers for the older one's return. We can all *daven* together for his (or her) success. We are thereby showing them that we truly want this older child to acquire *ahavas Torah* and *yiras Shamayim*, the love of Torah and fear of G-d, and to do what is right. Even though he may not be making all the right decisions at present, the younger children should see that we are all rooting for him to do so in the future and that we wish him well. When a younger child feels himself a part of this positive effort on behalf of that older sibling, the latter cannot wield as strong or as destructive an influence as he might otherwise have done.

Chapter Thirteen
THE MECHANICS OF DISCIPLINE

Discipline is probably the most challenging issue of all those we have to contend with in relation to guiding our children's behavior. We all have standards that are important to us, but we are often unsure of how to enforce them, because what we have been doing so far does not seem to be effective. Let us examine what alternatives there are.

I am going to begin with the most vital and powerful factor of all in enforcing discipline. This factor is the main cause, about 90 percent of the time, of children rejecting discipline at home and in school. Children have a hard time with discipline because one thing is lacking at home: a united front on the part of their parents. When children know that their parents work together in *shalom bayis*, in mutual agreement, they accept discipline. If there are cracks, even small ones, in the front their parents present, children do not accept discipline. Children see everything; they observe that Mommy wants one thing and Tatty wants something else. When they see that Abba says yes but Imma says no, or the reverse, they will find a way to wheedle themselves into that crack and end up getting what they want. In most cases, they find a way to get out of doing what they are supposed to do.

I want to clarify an important point. When parents do not present a united front, children's emotional needs go unsatisfied. Children will not admit it, indeed they often do not even know it, but they want to be disciplined because it provides the structure they need. They know exactly how to play Mommy against Daddy, because by playing us against each other they emerge blameless.

Picture this scenario: Esther wants to go out with friends, some of whom are not a particularly good influence on her. Abba says it is important that Esther go to the tryouts for the school play, but Imma says she does not think participating in the school play is really that important. Both parents are not happy about Esther's friends. Esther, being the smart girl she is, knows that instead of asking, "Can I go out with my friends?" she will ask Imma, "Do I really have to go to tryouts?" This clever distraction will leave Imma and Abba arguing about whether it is or is not important that she go to the tryouts, and Esther will be free to do what she wants. She can argue the point with Abba, knowing that Imma will back her. Because she knows or senses that there is a weak link, she will take advantage of it in order to get what she wants. Had Abba said, "No, you cannot go out with your friends," and Imma agreed, that would have been the final word, and Esther would have had a very hard time fighting it. Had she fought it anyway, she would feel bad about arguing with both parents. But when she ends up doing what she wanted because her parents did not agree with each other, they are not in a position to complain.

This is the bottom line. If we parents are not in harmony, it is extraordinarily difficult to present any kind of cohesive guidance for children. It is difficult to present anything at all that they will understand and accept, because they know that there is always an alternate opinion. This of course makes us look hypocritical or dishonest in their eyes, or at the least, shows that we do not really know what we want. This is a dangerous way for parents to behave. Sometimes parents are not even aware they are doing it. In our home we go out of our way to show a united front to our children. When they ask me for something and I am not sure whether or not they have already asked their mother, I will say, "Go and ask Imma and see what Imma says." Then they say, "Imma said to ask you.' Their next question is, inevitably, "How come every time I ask Imma she says to ask Abba and every time I ask you, you say to ask her?"

"Well, maybe because we want to say the same thing," I tell them. "We agree, so isn't that good? When we don't agree, it is not good, because if one parent says one thing and the other parent says something else, we are stuck."

Then I will say, "Well, maybe Imma did not understand your question. I will go discuss it with her and we will see."

If your children see you both go into another room and hear that you are discussing the matter, they know you were not fooling them. Make sure you do not! Then you come out together and say, "Well, there was a small misunderstanding. *Now this is what Imma and Abba say: This is what you can do and this is what you cannot do.*" This gives your children security. They know that this is what both Abba and Imma want. That is the way it works in our house. We can say those words because those words have meaning. If they would see us bickering and disagreeing, they would not have that same sense of security, and they would pit us against each other in order to get what they want. Parental unity is the first element of good discipline.

◄ε *Responsibilities at Home*

One of the biggest sources of frustration for both parents and children is the matter of doling out and accepting responsibilities at home, which definitely fits into the category of discipline. You have to define your children's responsibilities at home — what they have to do and what they do not have to do. Behind all the complaints and frustrations lies a serious misconception regarding the role and function of children in the home.

To whom do our children belong? They are *our* children, but what does that really mean? It means that we were able, with the help of Hashem, to bring a family into the world. We have accepted the responsibility of raising these children, of providing for them and taking care of them. The children had no part in that decision. They were born, they turned out to be boys or girls, and we are their parents. So, because we have a large family, *baruch Hashem*, does that mean that they have to become mother's helpers? When a mother has a hard time taking care of so many little ones on her own, she looks to her older children for assistance. Fine. But is this fair? Is it right that the oldest daughter becomes the drudge, a sacrifice for the family?

"You are the oldest; you have to help."

"Why?"

"Because you are the oldest. That is the way it is."

"I did not ask you to have six children after me. I wasn't part of that decision. What do you want from me? Just because I'm the oldest and I'm a girl, why do I have to have all the responsibilities of a mother?"

This girl should not be pressured into assuming such a role. True, we have the right to expect things from our children. We all agree that helping is important. When children are not willing to do what we ask of them, we become upset. We want our children to share in our responsibilities. We think: *They live in this house so they must share part of the burden.* Still, we might want to keep in mind something Rav Wolbe advises. He writes that "a parent is not allowed to expect his or her children to do things to make life easier for the parent."

We must honestly evaluate our motives in asking children to assume responsibility. If we want kids to develop the desire to help and share in running the household, we can help them by sharing things with them and letting them do the chores they enjoy. As you show them over time that you really need them and you share that need with them, they will grow up wanting to help. But if they feel that you are unloading your responsibilities on them all the time, when they get older they will not want to do anything at all.

Let us differentiate here between communal household responsibility and helping Mom. There are certain basic tasks that people living in the same house are required to do in order to function. Children can be taught to feel a partnership and responsibility in these areas. Everyone eats and dirties dishes, so everyone, including you, is a part of the team to see that the dishes are washed and put away. Everyone wears and soils clothes and everyone generates garbage, so everyone should put their soiled clothing in the laundry basket and take out the garbage. When everyone contributes to making a mess, everyone should help clean it up.

When a parent does not invest too much time in building a reciprocal relationship, a child feels naturally that he does not need to do anything for the parent. But if a child feels that his parents are always looking out for his good, for what is best for him, it usually follows naturally that the child is willing to do things for his parents' good.

Now do not get me wrong. Obviously we would like our children to want to baby-sit and to want to cooperate and be a part of creating a warm family atmosphere. But in order for that to happen we have to do something to make it happen. We need to do something to make our children feel like they are a part of this one big happy family where everybody does things together.

Let me give you a simple example. Your neighbor's child comes to play. After the children finish playing, they put almost everything away. You tell the neighbor's child what a *tzaddik* he is, what a good kid he is, how thoughtful he was to help put the toys away. You compliment him from today until tomorrow. But what do you say to your child? "Don't you see all that stuff that is still under the bed? You didn't put everything away." That is the difference. The neighbor's kid picks up toys at your house and you let him know that he is doing you a favor, which he feels good about. The same thing probably happens when your son goes to the neighbor for dinner and helps clear the table. They thank him profusely and he feels good. When he cleans off the table at home he does not get this kind of response. He removed the silverware but he forgot the glasses. "Oh, there is only silverware on the table today?" you ask sarcastically. We do not even think of thanking him for removing the silverware. *Why should we? It is his responsibility. That is the way it is. This is family.* Is that the right attitude? Is that the way to instill motivation?

A. Showing Appreciation

It seems fairly obvious that the best motivator for good behavior is showing appreciation, *hakaras hatov*. Every wife and mother wants to hear that the food is tasty after she worked so hard to prepare it. There is no such thing as hearing too many times how delicious the food was. Every husband wants to hear that his wife or guests enjoyed his *dvar Torah*, or how great it was that he was able to fix whatever it was that he fixed or did whatever he did. The need for recognition is a basic part of our nature, indeed of our survival. It is the factor that makes us feel good about ourselves and motivates us to move on and do more. It is the greatest pleasure in the world to help someone who is certain to say thank you every time we do a small favor for him.

At the same time, we have to realize that often when our children do things in the house, they are doing us a kindness, performing a *chesed*. You cannot inspire an act of loving-kindness with anger and with bitterness; that is contradictory. And you cannot force someone to do an act of loving-kindness. You cannot force someone to do *chesed*, and if you do, it is not *chesed*. *Chesed* comes from within, from the good part of a person, and it needs *chizuk*, strengthening. When we accord appreciation, acceptance, respect, and recognition to an individual, his *yetzer tov*, the good part of him, receives an input of energy that enables him to repeat the *chesed*. If we make our children feel good about the good things they do, they will be energized to do more and more.

B. "I Need Your Help"

We have already pointed out that confrontation, which invariably causes bitter reactions, is rarely good *chinuch*. We have to convey our point of view calmly and politely. Instead of abruptly giving orders, we can say, "I see you are in the middle of doing something. I know you are at the computer now, but I need your help. How much more time do you need?" We are not talking about the occasional, desperate situations when we must say, "It is an emergency. Ruchie's diaper is falling down and Moishie, Shloimie, and Dovie are in the tub! I need you right now!" These are the times when we can say, "Come now! I do not care what you are doing, or whether you will feel bad about this. This is an emergency. I will deal with everything else later. Right now I need you."

There are, however, one hundred and one daily situations that we can utilize to teach our child to help in the house. It is our responsibility as parents to teach our child that he cannot play at the computer all day. Sit down with him and work out a schedule of when he is free to work on the computer, and when he has to help us. How long will we need him? Ten minutes, twenty minutes, half an hour? Decide on an amount of time we can consider to be educational, how long he can help without becoming resentful, and try to build up the amount of time gradually.

Decide beforehand how we are going to go about getting them to help. Why do we always act at the last minute, without forethought, and then have to worry about the consequences? Do we want our son or daughter to help on a regular basis, to contribute to the family? So prepare them for it. Talk about it first. Do not suddenly pull them out of an activity they are enjoying and then wonder why they are upset.

Suppose we and our child discuss the issue of helping once. But what happens the second, the third, the fourth, and the fifth time, when we find we are in the same situation, the same confrontation? How can we do it differently? We can give the child time to adjust. Instead of saying, "Okay, everybody in bed now," try saying, "In two minutes it will be bedtime." This works better, even with a younger child. He is probably engrossed in doing something and does not want to stop. Give him at least two minutes to prepare himself to cooperate with this new instruction. In other situations, we can give the child half an hour. "Do you want to help me now or do you want to finish the game and then come and help?" Asking for help does not have to be confrontational. We create unnecessary conflicts by not giving our children a minimal amount of respect and consideration for their needs and by not allowing them to feel good about themselves. This approach should help to improve the relationship we have with our child.

Another small example: Our child is playing with two balls. His brother wants a ball. We say, "Give him a ball!" He says, "No, it is mine!" So we try again. "Give him a ball. You have two." What would happen if we were to say instead, "You have two balls. He does not have any. He would be so happy if you would give him one of yours." Most of the time, the child will hand over one ball. Ah, but what about the rest of the time when he does not? If we just take the ball away, they are both going to be upset and cry, so what have we accomplished? Most of the time, if we think ahead a second or two and present the situation to him carefully, we will achieve our goal.

C. To Pay or Not to Pay?

Should we pay our child to help us? The final answer depends on a variety of factors. My feeling, however, is that we should not have to ask that question, because this is our child. We should be building a relationship with him to the point where he would refuse an offer of monetary payment because he is our child and it is his house too. We cannot tell him to feel this way, though. There is nothing wrong with saying to a child, "I know you are not going to take money for baby-sitting because we are your parents, but we would like to buy you something because you do baby-sit for us so frequently and it is such a big help to us. We would have to pay someone else to do it, and although we are not figuring out what it would come to per hour, we want you to know that we appreciate all the time you give us and the great job you do with the children." How often do we say thank you to our own child the same way we would to a neighbor's child?

Recognizing and appreciating the help that children give us is the only way I know of that works in developing a child's feeling of belonging, his sense of responsibility and of caring about the family, over and above the distinction between things that are joint responsibilities and those that are not. Nonetheless, tasks done in regular rotation by everyone in the house also deserve a word of thanks.

Children are no different from us. Can you imagine how a wife would feel if her husband came home to a delicious dinner and said, "Well, it is your job to prepare a meal that I like and have it ready for me ..."? That would be the last time he would get supper! How could we live with each other if we talked to each other that way? Although we discussed the question of showing appreciation in an earlier chapter, it is also part of the issue of discipline. The simple wisdom of *hakaras hatov*, showing appreciation, is a *middah*, an attribute, that we should think about more often.

D. Doing Favors

Why is it so difficult to speak to our children about helping us? Perhaps the answer is that we are afraid the child is going to say no. When we demand immediate compliance, we really mean that we are not going to accept no for an answer. This type of communication with our children is not effective, as we all know. Even if it does work in the short term, it will not work in the long term. If you force a child to do a task, he will come to hate doing it, but he will cooperate until he is old enough and smart enough to just say no. But right now we are talking about persuading an older child to take on regular responsibilities at home, not about asking him to go to bed on time. Aside from emergencies, it is so much better to make the child feel he is trusted, respected, and appreciated. He will then want to help you from the heart and he will feel good about doing it.

When we ask our fifteen-year-old daughter to baby-sit one night because we want to go out, we are asking her to do us a favor. She can say no and we would have to live with it. She is choosing whether or not she wants to do us a favor.

We are the ones who have to go out. Let her know that we understand that she is doing us a favor. She will want to help us if she sees that we recognize her decision to baby-sit as a kindness. But we must acknowledge that she does have the right to say no sometimes, even to her parents.

"I have a test tomorrow and I am sorry; I just cannot do it," or "I'm sorry, I have to go out, I promised someone I would ..." Well, even if we really need her, if she cannot, she cannot. We must allow her that space. Hire a baby-sitter for that night. It is the only way we are going to have the services of this young lady, our daughter, as a baby-sitter for the next five years. I know children who baby-sit for others, while their own parents have to hire a baby-sitter. It is obvious that the parents in this home never communicated the proper attitude to their daughter with regard to this topic. Baby-sitting is a *chesed*, a favor. Helping someone, even parents, is a *chesed*, and *chesed* begins at home. But first we have to recognize that it is *chesed*.

◀֎ Applying Discipline

Long-term discipline requires self-awareness. Self-awareness is, of course, a basic component in all phases of education, but especially so with adolescents. If we are trying to educate our children to become independent and learn how to achieve their goals in life, both we and they have to cultivate self-awareness. In the matter of discipline, too, we need to promote self-awareness, for that is what gives our children the tools they need to accept discipline. When we want to say no to a child, we might find it helpful to ask a question first, like, "What do you think I am going to say?"

This is not a comfortable position for the child to be in, because he has to find an answer. This kind of question forces him to recognize and admit what the issues really are. It is much easier for him when we just say no, and he answers yes, and an argument is under way. Why do we have to argue? What about discussion? Ask the child, "What do you think I am going to say? Why do you think I'm going to say that?"

Sometimes a child will say, "Because you always say no."

"Oh? Do I *always* say no?"

If he answers yes, be careful. It means we have a lot of work to do, because perhaps we have not really wanted to know his views on things. Hopefully, he will say, "No, you do not always say no, but whenever it comes to this question, you say no."

Then, if we really care about his views, we can inquire further, "Why do you think I would say no about this issue? What is the problem you think I have with it?"

Adolescents are old enough to participate in the disciplinary process. We want them to understand. We do not want to enforce discipline by telling them what to do and what not to do. We have to knock it into our heads and remember that our purpose is not just to get our children to do what we want. They are in the midst of developing their minds, their senses, and their judgment. They are developing their ability to make decisions, and we want them to make the right decisions. We want them to refrain from doing things they know are wrong, and we want the initiative to come from them. Sometimes it will not come from them, and we have to put our foot down. As we have already pointed out, our ability to control them is limited both in scope and in time.

◀‍₹ The Consequences of Control

There is a fine line between discipline and control. One of two things happens to children over whom we exert too much control: Either they rebel or they become incompetent, indecisive, insecure people. I have seen eighteen- and nineteen-year-old boys and girls who are bright, creative, and talented but are insecure and incapable of making the smallest life decision on their own. They are truly incapacitated people. I do not know how in the world they are ever going to build a home. They do not know what it means to make a decision. They do not know what it means to think something through. They have been controlled their whole life. Being passive worked well for them while they were students, because all they had to do was what was expected of them. When the time comes to start their own family, however, they do not know where to start. They can neither decide nor think things through, and in addition they do not even know how to make mistakes. Mistakes frighten them. They were never allowed to make mistakes. Their parents taught them that if they make a mistake, they are out of the game. They became perfectionists, and because things rarely turn out according to plan, they are insecure. It is a sad thing to witness.

People cannot really be controlled. Not only do we not want to be controlling parents, we cannot really control others. It is not possible. Once the child grows bigger and stronger, any power or control we had is gone. If he has learned that one controls others by force, we will be helpless when his strength of will matures. When he is smart enough to answer back and knows what to say, his answers will be better than our questions. What will we do then? What tools are we left with? The only way we controlled him was with superior size and strength, but we no longer have that means of control. If discipline and *chinuch* are going to be a contest of who is stronger, we know perfectly well that he is eventually going to be stronger. This is something to think deeply about while our children are young and we can still plan the kind of discipline we want to enforce in our home.

We have to discipline teenagers with wisdom, not with battles. We have to discipline with discussion, understanding, and sensitivity — not with control.

A. When to Fight

When do we fight? The first rule is never to fight when we are going to lose. Do not ever put your foot down on an issue on which we will not be able to pick it up again. We cannot afford to lose. The only time we are allowed to engage in a battle is in those rare moments when our child is really about to do something dangerous and nothing else works. If we are fairly certain he is going to do it anyway, be careful not to give an ultimatum ("If you do, I will never ..."), because we will be painted into a corner when he does it anyway. The only time we ever speak in this manner is when, Heaven have pity on us, all is lost. All is almost never lost, but in the sense that right now we are dealing with an extraordinarily difficult situation wherein the child is already doing things that are truly dangerous, then we have to call out forcefully so that he will know we love him and care about him, and that we absolutely cannot let him do it. This is an extreme situation, and Heaven save us from having such things to confront. (We will consider this problem in more depth in the next chapter.)

The way to handle a fight that we know we are not going to win is to establish our disapproval clearly. Tell him that we cannot and will not try to stop him physically from doing it, whatever it is, but that he does not have our blessing and that we do *not* think it is good for him to do it; it is wrong and/or harmful for him. And do not give in afterwards — do not relent! We will see that the child will be affected by these words, and they may often help him decide not to do it, because he really does want our approval. Fighting will accomplish the opposite. If we tell him, "I understand what you want. I totally understand how you feel, but I believe it is wrong," we are not fighting him. "I cannot support that. Do you want me to pay for you to go somewhere that I do not think you should go? Do you want me to give you the money to spend on doing something that I do not approve of? I cannot do that. I don't believe that it is right, and I'm not going to support it. I am not going to let you go. If you do go, I am not going to throw you out of the house. I do not want you doing those things while you are in this house, but you are my son, you are my daughter, I love you. What should I do?"

This approach is heart-wrenching for the child, because the child does not want to fight his parents when his parents aren't fighting him. It makes a difference when the child hears us say in the same breath, "I love you and I care about you, and therefore I am saying no." These words are not appropriate or even believable when we are yelling and screaming at him and fighting with him. Emotional confrontation makes him positive that we hate him and that he hates us and encourages him to storm out of the house and do it anyway, or go wherever it is we do not want him to go. It gives the wrong message.

Discipline has to be applied very firmly, but not as a threat. Act firmly with complete understanding of why we are saying what we are saying. "This is what I believe and this is what is important to me, because I love you and care about you." Children have a very difficult time fighting that, even those who are accustomed to fighting. This type of dialogue replaces fighting because children do not want to hurt their parents when they see that their parents really do not want to hurt them.

B. When to Put Your Foot Down

I tell my children in advance that my decisions regarding safety may seem arbitrary to them, but that I am basing my decision on the current situation and the way I understand reality. I may be wrong, but compromise is not possible when it comes to a decision about safety, because it concerns life and death. It is not a question of whether or not I like it or do not like it. The issue of safety is a weighty, serious question and though they may not agree with me, I make it clear to my children that this is a question on which I am going to put my foot down.

I will say the same thing if a serious question arises involving the *ruchnius*, the spiritual condition, of our family. Just like those rare occasions when I think a question of life and death is involved, there are times when I have a serious concern regarding my child's spiritual condition. At those times I will say to the child, "Listen, you know that normally I involve you in the discussion, but the reason I'm not including you in the discussion in this case is that I cannot. I know that you really want to do this, but there are just certain things in life that not only threaten one's physical safety but also can threaten one's spiritual well-being. As long as I am able to watch out for you, I can tell you that you are not going to do this, and it is not going to be done in our home."

With the connection, the communication that we have been hopefully building all along — and this is of course basic to every aspect of discipline — our children are not going to question it when we do actually put our foot down. My children understand that this happens only rarely and they do not question it.

C. *Tefillah* — Whose Responsibility?

Another issue that is a common problem for parents of teenagers is their *davening*. *Tefillah*, prayer, is a very emotional topic because it shocks parents to see their fifteen-year-old child who attends yeshivah not get up in time for *davening*. Whose responsibility is it for him to get up in time for *minyan*? It is clearly his problem. He is fifteen and a bar mitzvah. We are not responsible for his praying and not even for his *chinuch* anymore. We are, however, his parents and we want to do what is best for him, but are we aware that the responsibility for his education is ours no longer? All we had to do was bring him to the point that when he becomes bar mitzvah he will want to *daven* on his own.

So we know it is his responsibility, but we cannot handle seeing him sleep through *Shacharis*, so what do we do? We wake him up. Who is responsible when we wake him up? We care, we are the ones who are worried, so we are making it our responsibility. This is the opportunity to apply the technique we spoke of in an earlier chapter. We place the responsibility squarely on his shoulders. At most, we can agree to wake him up at a time that he specifies, making it clear that we will only wake him once, twice, or three times as agreed, but no more.

As long as we are going to get upset about his oversleeping, we are teaching our son that *davening* is our problem. As long as it is our problem, he is not going to worry about it. Even if we get him out of bed, are we going to go with him to shul and watch him put on his *tefillin* and then make him *daven*? No. He is fifteen years old. We can speak with him about *davening*. We can tell him that we know how hard it is for him to get up and that we are sure he feels bad that he missed the *minyan*. How can we help him? *Make it his responsibility*. If he needs an alarm clock, help him get him an alarm clock.

We should help him develop the personal concern that makes him wake up on time. When he misses, when he leaves his room at 9:15 or 10:00, we should look at him and say, "Tomorrow you will make it. It was hard today. You probably feel bad." He does feel bad. When a child decides that he wants to wake up for the 8:30 *minyan* and he does not make it, he feels bad. Well, feel bad for him and bad with him. If we make fun of him or put him down, it is going to remove any desire he had to improve, while sympathy and empathy could actually help.

We may find out, much to our painful surprise, that he is not interested. Then what are we going to do? Are we going to force him? Oh, that is going to make him *love davening*! If a child is not interested in getting up in time for *davening* at the age of fifteen, we have to think about what happened during the previous ten years. We are not going to change his attitude now by forcing him. We have to reevaluate how we presented the *davening* to him until now. Maybe he is just going through a rough time and he is temporarily not interested. But we are not going to change him by forcing things.

If a boy has not been inspired before the age of bar mitzvah to want to *daven*, it is going to be difficult to inspire him now. Whatever negative association he has with shul, with *davening*, we have to show him that our concern now is for him, not ourselves. We have to convey to him that we know he wants to fulfill his responsibilities. We, however, do feel responsible, because the fact that he does not want to *daven* probably has something to do with the way we handled his shul experience during the seven or eight years before his bar mitzvah. We must try and figure out if his attitude has something to do with the way we treated shul or the way we treated him.

Maybe it is just one of the ways he is using to get back at us for perceived slights.

And maybe shul is something he just does not feel a connection to. How do we develop his connection? Not by pushing him, but by making a greater effort to speak to him about *davening*. During family discussions, the Shabbos table is an ideal venue, speak about your experiences with *tefillah*, the experience of *klal Yisrael* with *tefillah*, and the feeling of everybody being together in *tefillah*. The positive aspects of *tefillah* have to be brought out, but it is difficult. It is not going to be a one-day process, either. It is going to be a new, long-term process of making *tefillah* beloved to him.

D. Being a Mitzvah Salesman

Children do not live in a vacuum, find inspiration in a vacuum, or react to things in a vacuum. We are very much a part of their lives and we have to make sure we know what is going on in their lives in order to inspire them and pique their interest in doing what they should be doing.

If you were given a business opportunity that paid $100 for every vacuum cleaner you sold, you would sit right down and make plans: how you would approach potential buyers, what you would tell them, how you would convince them to buy this wonderful vacuum cleaner. You would map out a campaign before you start, allowing for the different quirks of a variety of potential customers; you would not just blunder forth and hope to sell vacuum cleaners off the cuff. You would think about it, you would prepare a plan. The money issue would appeal to some, so you would tell them how much money they would save with this vacuum cleaner. Another person might have allergies, so you would talk to him about how this vacuum will remove all the mites embedded in the mattresses and carpets. By dealing with each person individually and using everything you know about this vacuum cleaner, you would hope to make many sales.

To convince children to do mitzvos, you are going to have to sell those mitzvos. You have to be able to tell them all the good things about it, not just say, "Well, Hashem says this is the way we are supposed to live and this is what we have to do." We live in a world where there are other options and other choices. When children are five, six, and seven years old, we can take advantage of their natural responsiveness and involve them in the mitzvos with good associations. They like to do good things; they accept them as part of their daily life, and because they are comfortable with them, they will continue doing them for the rest of their life.

However, if we have not implanted those associations by the age of thirteen, fourteen, or fifteen, and it appears that we are going to have trouble doing so, we have to take a different approach — one that sells. Maybe we can motivate the child with prizes — at thirteen or fourteen he is still a child — or other incentives. At fifteen, financial incentives for going to *minyan* are probably not going to work. $10 will not impress him as much as buying him something he really wants. You can tell him that you know it is difficult for him, and you cannot pay him for his cooperation, but you can give him something for which he has been saving, or really would like to have. It will be an incentive for him, and part of your sales pitch.

E. Setting a Curfew

Another difficulty that is fairly common among parents of teenagers is setting a curfew. It is prudent to set limits on the time to come home at night for a child who keeps most of the rules (this does not apply to a child who is not obeying any rules). Decide what the rule is in your house, present a united front, and be consistent. In our house, the door is closed at 11 o'clock at night. In your home, you can make it 11:30 or 12:00, as you see fit. If you know your child is a good child and only going to do good things, you have no problem. If you are worried about what your child is doing late at night, speak with him about it. Explain to him that in this house it is just not acceptable to either parent that he stay outside until he thinks it would be a good time to come home. He will not test you when both parents have made it extremely clear that the door will be locked and bolted at that time.

This is a rule you will have to begin imposing long before the child starts to stay out until 3 o'clock in the morning. If he has reached this point of irresponsibility and you try to impose a curfew, he will just sleep at a friend's house. You can always make exceptions to the rule when it seems reasonable. That is why you talk things over with him and arrive at a good set of working rules. Children can understand reasonable rules. If he is going to be late, he can always call in and you can accept that with understanding. If parents say firmly, "This is what we accept and this we do not," and a child sees that his parents mean it, it solves most of the problems. The first time he comes back late without notifying you and finds the door locked and bolted, it sends an extremely strong message, and he realizes that you mean it. When you come out of bed to open the door for him, looking rather stern, he has to realize that he has just crossed a red line. This is it! You made it clear that this cannot happen. Children do not want to break the security of a well-defined environment. (Once children are breaking all the rules all the time, they are beyond your influence and that is a different story. But initially, children really do not want to break the rules of the house.)

"In our house we want everyone home at 11 o'clock. That is our rule." If you have defined this curfew from the very first time your child wanted to stay out late at night, he knows that he has to be back on time. You have told him that at 11 the door will be locked and you will be in bed. If you have not done this and the staying out late has already snowballed, you have lost control. And that is a totally different situation. It is beyond the realm of good communication and setting rules. It is now a discipline question, where the child is already out of control and you have to regain his cooperation, or at least try to become a part of his life in a way that you know where he is going and what he is doing.

Some parents know that their child is really fine and that they can trust him to be out until 12:30 at night, because he is seventeen or eighteen and he is doing good things. He is likely to be at a friend's house studying or learning in the *beis midrash* or, with regard to a girl, she is helping her grand-mother bake challos for Purim, so that is fine. If a parent does not know where his child is and he is not so sure whether the child is doing good things, that parent should start to find out and become more of a part of what is going on in his life. If our child stays out late, we need to know where he is and what he is doing. Then we will know whether or not we can continue to trust him. The more we trust our child, the more worthy of being trusted he will become. That is an ongoing, reciprocal process. Remember, however, that there is not one answer for all children. Every child is different.

What are our chances of getting older teenagers who have completely disregarded curfew back to keeping a curfew? Most likely curfew is only one of the many issues with which we are dealing. Before we even attempt to discuss curfew in this case, we have to go back to the beginning and rees-tablish a relationship of trust, love, and interest, because the curfew right now is a symptom, not the problem. There is no way we are going to reestablish a curfew for a seven-teen- or eighteen-year-old after curfew has been ignored for three years. The first step will be to find out where we have diverged, where it is that we have parted ways with our child, what the misunderstanding is between us. Perhaps we can start by letting him know that we no longer expect him to be what we wanted him to be when he was thirteen. He is long past that, and this might be a good time for the two of us to start anew.

How can we now help him be what he wants to be within the parameters of what is acceptable to us and our home? How are we going to help him achieve the good things that he wants? After we have reestablished a relationship and we can talk to each other, we can begin to talk of particulars, whether it is curfew, clothing, Shabbos, or whatever the issues may be. We cannot start by dealing with a specific issue, because the specific issue is not the problem. The problem is that a child who has been ignoring and disregarding a curfew for a number of years has already diverged in many other areas.

Maybe the curfew bothers us the most, but it is futile to try to modify the behavior of a nineteen-year-old in relation to only one issue such as curfew. Even if we are successful, and we might be, our aim should be to get to the root of the problem, to reestablish communication and find a bond with this child.

I know one smart mother who told me what she did when her child began to come home late every night. She tried various measures, none of which worked. Finally she decided to do the following. The boy would come in at 2 in the morning and find his mother sitting on a chair in the living room with her *Tehillim* in her lap. When he walked in, he could see the tears in her eyes, but all she did was close the *Tehillim*, kiss it, say "*Baruch Hashem*," and go to her room. This happened a few times until the child could not face her anymore. All the fights and all her arguments had meant nothing to him, but when he saw her waiting up for him and realized that all she cared about was that he come home safely, he too began to care. She did not tell him how bad he was, what a *rasha* he was, how guilty he should feel for everything he had done wrong. She just showed him that all she wanted was to know he was safe at home so she would have peace of mind and be able to sleep.

This mother's response worked to correct a specific problem, because it reflected a parent's best desires. She sincerely wanted her son to do what was right and that is what discipline is all about. She did not compromise her behavior — it was her righteousness that helped him to choose the good and improve.

Chapter Fourteen
TROUBLED TEENS

The phenomenon of troubled teens presents a grave challenge to us all, parents and educators alike. First we will present a behavioral overview of these children at risk and define the symptoms. Then we will analyze some of the issues involved.

Every child in our community is, in a sense, somewhat at risk. This is due to the proliferation of access to the *yetzer hara*, the bad influences — the freedom and permissiveness — that penetrate even the highest levels of our society. Despite our strong educational framework, every one of our children is vulnerable to exposure and attraction to the world outside, and to the very challenging tests these influences place before him.

There are four identifiable groups of children who are at higher risk than others as their adolescent years crest:

1) children who come from homes where *shalom bayis*, domestic peace, is an issue;
2) children who have various forms of learning disabilities or difficulties at school;
3) children who are perfectionists; and
4) children who are socially challenged.

❧ Shalom Bayis

Let us begin with *shalom bayis*, domestic accord. We touched on this subject earlier in relation to establishing discipline in the home, and now we will attempt to explain why the home environment has the potential to put a child at great risk. The home should be a place of security and stability. The home is what gives a child the sense that he belongs somewhere, that he is a part of something, and that he has a place to go. At home he is safe.

When a home lacks *shalom bayis*, the child suffers a deep emotional deficiency, for he has lost the safe place that he needs. He lacks a place he can come to under all circumstances and feel secure. We mentioned the fact that children need structure. Without *shalom bayis*, there is no structure in the home. A child needs to trust people who are honest with him, and naturally his parents are the ones in whom he should trust. When a child loses trust in his parents, it is often difficult for him to develop trust in another adult, if he ever does. The home is that special place that gives the child the feeling that this is *me*, this is who I am, this is my identity, this is where I belong.

If there is a strong, warm relationship between his mother and father, the child knows that he has a place to go, even if he is rebelling against the rules, which he does mostly just because he is an adolescent. Even if he is fighting with his mother and father — and, as I have pointed out, it is not so easy to fight when the home is functioning in good order — he knows that there is a solid, healthy, and strong relationship in his home. He knows that his environment is secure and he can rely on it, because his parents are united. The foundation of the house is the relationship between the mother and the father; if that goes awry, the entire structure founders.

That is why discipline becomes almost impossible when parents do not listen to each other or are disrespectful to one another. Where is a child going to learn respect and discipline if not from parents who speak to each other with *derech eretz*? When one parent speaks to another parent disrespectfully or harshly, the child learns that he does not have to respect that parent either, that he can cross that parent and look down on and even hurt him or her. Worse yet, he learns that he can act contrary to what the parent says; he does not have to listen. Where is a child going to learn to treat his parents with respect, love, compassion, and concern if he does not see them treating each other that way? Thus the child has no concept of discipline, because he has no concept of what it means to listen to someone. The child observes that his mother does not listen to his father or vice versa, and he thinks, *so why should I listen to what either of them says?* Children look down at their parents when that happens. They lose respect for authority — all authority.

When a child sees that his parents are not a solid refuge for him, that he cannot rest his confidence in them, he does not trust anyone who is older. A child's parents are his first and prime example of authority. He is introduced to them first; he gets to know them first and best. Just as we know other children through knowing our own, identify teachers by those who taught us as youngsters, and appraise rabbis by the rabbis we know, children assume that other adults are like the adults they know. When there is no *shalom bayis*, we become our child's role models in a very negative way, which undermines his ability to accept all authority and all discipline. As a result, he simply does not understand the need for rules or for listening to elders. School therefore becomes a challenge, the neighbors become a challenge, and he becomes a difficult child. He is at risk of becoming a challenging child.

I was once involved in setting up a meeting for about twenty people who wanted to discuss various problem in educating children who were having a hard time in school. Many of these children had already dropped out of the educational system. There were Sephardim, Ashkenazim, Americans, and Israelis in the group, and the children were boys and girls from all walks of life who lived in Jerusalem. We were hoping to form an umbrella organization to help troubled teenagers, but unfortunately, it never came to be. At one point in our discussions I raised the question of the single most common denominator of all these children who are having difficulties. The consensus was that these children, *almost* without exception — there are always exceptions — came from homes in which *shalom bayis* was absent.

One educator told me that he believes the number one challenge to a child's discipline in school is a lack of *shalom bayis* at home. He said that you can almost always recognize which child in school suffers from this. If you have an eye for it and you get to know your pupils, you can see it from the way they interact with you and with each other. This is the most prevalent cause of trouble for teenagers.

◄ఽ *Learning Problems*

Children who are learning disabled in any way and for whatever reason are also at risk. Whether the learning disability is severe or minimal, whether it is only that they are not as good at some things as other children or if they are having a hard time in only certain areas of learning, take heed! It is cause for concern.

Many parents do not realize that a child who seems to lack only *zitzfleish,* who has a hard time sitting still, can also be having a very difficult time. Our religious school systems today are very demanding, and do not have the luxury of providing individualized programs for children who cannot perform at their best in the standard curriculum and methodology. Usually, there are only very slight variations across the board from school to school and from class to class. By the time a child is eight years old he's expected to sit still and learn until 4 o'clock or even later. When he is ten or twelve he is expected to sit in class until 4 or 5 o'clock. At fourteen he is expected to stay in his seat during an evening session as well. We must realize that any child, boy or girl, who is having a hard time at school is potentially a child at risk. Unfortunately, any child who is having a difficult time learning or keeping up with the class is not going to be respected by his peers. Unfortunately, scholastic excellence has taken on a disproportionate level of importance in determining what makes a child successful or not successful in life. School has become so competitive, so difficult and challenging, that literally hundreds of graduating youngsters — both boys and girls — every year are not accepted into any secondary school.

Hundreds of children right here in Jerusalem are not doing well in school and are failing out of the system. *A child who is not doing well at school is in a high-risk category, and it is our responsibility as parents to do everything we can to help him. We cannot leave any stone unturned in helping him feel good about school and do better in his studies.*

A. Tutoring

If you have a child who cannot read properly, do absolutely everything you can to help him improve. If you have to involve the school, do so — and keep at it until your child is receiving the help he needs. If you need to get special help, a tutor, a specialist teacher, stop at nothing. Make sure that your child feels good in school, because a child who is not doing well will eventually feel bad, left out, and dumb.

Although a child can be intelligent, even brilliant, it can happen that he or she does not do well in school, in which case he or she feels stupid. If the child does not do well on tests, for example, his entire sense of self-worth is damaged — often for life. Where school plays such a pivotal role, parents want their boys to become superstars, *talmidei chachamim,* and their girls to do well academically and to acquire the skills necessary to support a family. The pressures to get into a "good" high school, then a post-high school seminary, and then to earn a degree or a certificate so they will be able to support their families, builds and builds. Many of the pressures in our *frum* society are focused on education. A resumé of the schools attended by a boy or girl has become the prime mover and the prime definer of who's who in our community. With success in school playing such a crucial role in everything we expect the child to accomplish in the future, we cannot ignore it if he is experiencing learning difficulties. We must do everything we can to help him feel good about his school and his studies; we must convey to him our belief and confidence that he can achieve.

Some schools are more open to tutoring than others. In general, extra tutoring is a good idea, but it usually means that the child who is already suffering in school comes home to suffer another hour or so with a tutor. Personally, I have always made a point of trying to set up tutoring for my children during school hours by prioritizing which subjects they can miss and which they cannot. For example, I arrange tutoring for them during class time in the subject in which they need tutoring. If a child is weak in mathematics, I take him out of class during the math lesson and arrange tutoring in that subject. If he is weak in Gemara, I have him learn Gemara privately during Gemara class until he catches up and can learn with the class.

Even where this is possible, it must be done with extreme delicacy, lest the child feel embarrassed by being removed from class. Will he or she be stereotyped as a dummy? A school will often work with you if they see that you know what you are doing and have a clear picture of what you hope to accomplish. It is essential, however, to plan this carefully with the school, which may object to disrupting a class routine by permitting a "revolving door." Excellent teachers may find this disruptive of their routine and may legitimately feel that it is not in the best interest of the child. Even though it may cost another few shekels or dollars to get the tutor to come to the school, and it may be a little bit harder to work out logistically, anything you can do to help your child succeed in his studies is worth every penny.

When your child comes home from school and must spend extra hours studying with a tutor, it will only help if the child himself really believes he can improve. I know this from experience with my own children. Our son needed extensive tutoring after we discovered that he had a serious learning disability. When he himself realized how much he gained from the tutoring and how it helped him get ahead, he asked if we could arrange for more help on his own time in other areas where he felt he needed help. Because we had always considered his feelings and tried to arrange the tutoring during class hours, when he realized there were certain things that he was not going to achieve in this way (because many schools, unfortunately, are not ready to set up a school-coordinated P'TACH program), he requested that we send him to a different, after-hours P'TACH program. I was extremely punctilious in picking him up a little early on those days and explaining to his teacher that he would be missing some class time, but that he was going for extra help. And I took great care that he should not feel he was losing out by having extra work. A child needs to know that though he is getting help, he is not going to be penalized by suffering both in school and when he gets home too.

B. Transition Periods

Many boys begin having a difficult time in fifth grade. Many of us can look back and see a significant turning point in our son's attitude toward learning at that time. We remember that he was the smartest boy in his class until fourth grade. Then suddenly he started to change; we don't know what happened, but he stopped doing well. And what did we do when this happened? We pushed and pressured the child, because we could not understand what had happened. We forgot or did not realize that this is a common occurrence. In fifth grade, boys start learning Gemara, which is an abstract, theoretical, highly logical subject that is extremely difficult for students. Brilliant men, who have successfully gone through university, sit down in front of a Gemara for the first time and have the utmost difficulty for at least a year or two before they can begin to read on a beginner's level. And we expect our children at the age of ten to sit down and start learning Gemara immediately. *Baruch Hashem*, most kids succeed.

But it happens that some bright children, who were at the top of their class until this point, suddenly cannot get their minds to bend around the abstract thinking necessary to master Gemara. They learned many *mishnayos* by heart; they knew *mishnayos* inside out. They are accustomed to get 100's in everything, but on the first Gemara test they get a 70. Do you remember how you reacted when your son brought home his first low grade? Your reaction may have made a difference that will affect his entire life. It is vital to be prepared for this turning point before it happens. If it has happened already, there are steps you can take. But it is an important turning point in a boy's life and we should be prepared to monitor how he gets through this stage in his education.

We often see these changes in our children at certain transitional stages of learning. The child who did very well with *Mishnah* cannot understand the Gemara with *Rashi*. Then they have to start dealing with *Tosafos* and *Rishonim*, with *machlokos* (disputes) and different *girsa'os* (nuances in wording), and the child who understood the Gemara with *Rashi* may now be the one who is confused. There are many different levels in learning, and there are many different stages in our child's progress through them. If a child is having a hard time at one stage, it does not mean he cannot overcome the difficulty. It merely means that *he may need help at the beginning* in order to adjust to the new stage his class has reached.

A delicate transition in the case of young girls occurs usually in second grade, when the teacher begins to demand reading comprehension. Later, in about sixth grade, some girls are thrown off-track when they begin departmental, where they suddenly have to deal with several teachers instead of only one. Any serious changes in either structure or content in the syllabus give us reason to be concerned and watchful and to make sure that we notice what is happening in our children's education so that we can help them over the humps.

In all these transition periods, some children who did well until that point stop doing well. Parents bring their child to me and say, "Listen, I don't know what happened. Until fourth grade he was the genius of the class. He was number one. Then in fifth grade all of a sudden he became lazy and disinterested, and he couldn't do the work. From fifth grade he went to sixth grade where he sat just like a piece of furniture. In sixth grade the *rebbe* didn't even look at him. They passed him up to seventh grade because he was the biggest child in his class and they couldn't leave him back. In eighth grade they really wanted to get rid of him before the school year started, because no one could be bothered to worry about which high school would accept him. The truth is that he has been a piece of furniture altogether in the classroom for the past three years."

This of course is a fallacy. Children do not become dumb overnight. Nor do they lose all their motivation and aspirations from one day to the next. *They can be broken overnight, though, because the first time they come home with that 70 they get it over the head!* The parents say, "What? You got a 70? Why aren't you learning?" The child really was trying, and he does not know what happened. He's embarrassed. He does not even want to show you the 70. Many children are so embarrassed that they do not show their parents their first three Gemara tests. The father comes to the parent-teacher meeting and hears about four Gemara tests that the child has failed.

"What's going on?" he asks the child.

The child truthfully answers that he does not know. He does not know how to explain it.

The parent asks, "Well, are you trying?" The child says, "Yes."

The parent gets angry. "Well, you can't be trying. You didn't even show me your test. You didn't even talk to me. You didn't tell me ..." and so on. Now, on top of the poor grades the child has just begun to receive, he has earned his father's disapproval.

If we first become aware of this when the child is already in high school, this self-defeating process is extremely difficult to reverse, because it has now been in place for a few years. The crisis in this child's progress happened in a lower grade. It happened at a point in time when, if we think back, we can remember that he began to have difficulties. If we were not paying attention and did not notice the problems as they surfaced, it is still not too late to take notice and discuss the problems and help him overcome the obstacles.

High school (*yeshivah ketanah*) is an enormous transition in itself. At this point he does not believe in himself, and at this point he often has already given up on himself. We are going to have to do some serious work here in order to get him back onto any level of faith in himself and/or in the system. Although there are various concrete things we can do (i.e., choosing the correct school, which we will discuss in a later chapter), we can begin with the effort to recognize that there is a problem and watch out for possible sources of risk as they come up. It is extremely important at this point to be alert to these problems and handle the pitfalls as they occur.

C. Testing

Sometimes it is hard to discover the source of the difficulty because there is such a wide variety of reactions to transition. One child may have trouble with abstract thinking, which makes the Gemara difficult for him. Another child may have trouble with long-term memory: His difficulty may be the language barrier that never surfaced until he started learning in Aramaic. When all the learning was in Hebrew, which he has been dealing with since first grade, he was able to compensate for his poor memory. Now that he has to learn a new language, we suddenly find that he is challenged.

There are objective standards by which to assess the problem, and therefore we can have our child tested. When we see that he has got problems that we cannot solve by ourselves, send him for testing. Testing is a little bit expensive, but it is a good investment. The earlier we test our child, the better. Then we will know what it is we need to do in order to help him.

The results of these tests should be taken seriously and acted upon. We will need to develop a suitable program to help our child succeed in spite of his challenge. Please listen carefully to this next sentence because it could save our child's life. *There are situations in life where we must not calculate cost and expense.* If Heaven forbid a child is deathly ill we will do ANYTHING and EVERYTHING to help him get better. Well, the situation we have been discussing is of the same crucial importance. A child who does not get the help he needs when he is young is at a tremendous risk. This is life and death. Do not take it lightly! And if you are concerned about the expenses at this point, let me tell you that the cost of special "programs" for older children who are in trouble are unbelievably prohibitive and the chances of recovery so small, that you would regret not having spent every penny you could have spent earlier. At that point you would do anything to get your child back. Please do not save money on education!

◄₹ *The Perfection Syndrome*

The child who by nature is a perfectionist is also at high risk, but the perfection syndrome is a little tricky to analyze. The youngster is used to demanding 100 percent of himself. The problem arises when something changes and he now has trouble meeting this new demand. His parents also demand 100 percent "success" from him; in fact they have become accustomed to it. Parents think there is no reason not to push children to do well. *Why not? Don't we want our children to do the best they can? Don't we want to make sure they are not slacking off, that they are not lying back, and that they are doing what they are supposed to be doing as well as they can?* I guess the answer is somewhere between "yes" and "but be careful." When we cultivate perfectionism in this fashion, we are really nurturing long-term disappointment.

The world is not a perfect place, and no one is perfect. Any of us who are the least bit perfectionist in our own lives know how much we suffer from it. Whether it's cleanliness we require, the need to receive 100 on tests, the need to be perfect in the cakes we bake, the letters we write, or however we demand perfection in ourselves, we know that we suffer from these self-imposed demands. Life situations arise that challenge that perfectionism. We need to let some things go. We need to leave other people alone, even though they're not the way we really want them to be. If we cannot do so, we are the ones who will suffer, and seriously. It is self-defeating. People who are perfectionists are people who suffer.

The Gemara[1] says, *"Sheloshah chayeihem einam chayim* — There are three categories of people whose lives are not lives, and one of them is *aninei hada'as." Aninei hada'as* is a form of self-imposed perfectionism. In it, there is no life. If you need everything to be just so, your life will never be satisfactory. Children who demand of themselves perfection because they think that that is the only way their parents are going to be satisfied with them, often come to a point in their life where their efforts are not producing. Then they simply give up. I cannot count the number of children I have seen and worked with who, even though they are really bright children, never received a mark over 60 on *anything*, because they suffer from this syndrome.

I have found that when children think they cannot succeed, they will say, "Either I can get 100, or I am not even going to try." To try and then to receive an 80 is unacceptable for this type of child. An 80, he thinks, is embarrassing because it is not 100. Why? Who turned it into an embarrassment? Did the child try? If he tried and achieved an 80, is it really an embarrassment?

As a parent, are you embarrassed if your child gets only an 80 when other children in the class received higher marks? Do you ask yourself, "Did he try? Did he do his best?" Did you see him putting in the hours of study on Shabbos? Did you study with him? Did you see that he did his homework, and when he got only an 80, did you say, "I'm proud of you, you got an 80. I know how hard you worked for that. Maybe next time you will get a higher mark, and if not, that is okay. You keep on trying and doing your best, and as long as you do your best, I'm with you." Or did you make the grave mis-

---

1. *Pesachim* 113b.

take of saying, "An 80? Why did you get only an 80? The average in the class was 90."

What messages are we giving to our children? Children reach high school: The schedule is challenging; it is demanding. Our schools are more competitive scholastically than ever before. The competition and challenges are on a different level from those of elementary school and not every child can keep up on the new level. How can we cope with this? Let us scrutinize our goals. Are we promoting self-esteem in our children or are we cultivating perfectionism? Don't we want our children to feel confident because they know they have done their best and that is all that really matters?

A. Success

We should want our children to succeed. This is axiomatic. However, is it possible that we are waiting for them to fail so that we can say, "I told you so"? We told them to do it our way, but they did it another way and we are almost hoping they will fail. That feeling is disastrous. Surely we do not want to do that.

What shall we do, however, when we tell them to study and they study and still they fail? Now what? Are we there for them? Do we stand behind them? Do we tell them that it is really, really all right, because we know they tried, we saw them studying, we saw them putting their best foot forward? Sometimes the feeling of trying and failing is worse than not trying at all. We have to understand this. After such an experience there are those children who say, "That's it. I can't do it anyway so I'm not even going to try. To try and then fail means that I am no good, but if I don't even try I have nothing to lose because I can say I didn't even try."

I have seen so many smart children who just say, "I don't want to learn. I don't want to do well. I'm not going to try. I am not even going to study." This is perfectionist thinking and leads to utter discouragement. It just is not worth the effort for them to try if they are not going to get 100 on the test. Our job as parents is to teach our children not to be perfectionists.

We do have to nourish their self-esteem, which means: *You are who you are and we like who you are.*

B. Accepting Our Shortcomings

When I was in high school, it was that lucky year when the New York State algebra Regents Examinations were stolen. My class was euphoric. I was terrible in algebra; I could not begin to understand the subject. Yet I learned later that I have a very good head for math, if I understand it. But I was one of those children who needed to understand. I did very well in geometry, except that I always got marked wrong for using a theorem we hadn't "learned" yet. The teacher would say, "You can't do that." I would say, "But is it correct?" He would say, "It is correct, but you don't know that yet so you can't use it." Algebra was just formulas. Memorize the formula, use it, and you will arrive at the answer. I could not memorize formulas. It did not make sense to me. If you add minus x and y, why do you get z? I could not follow the logic, and nobody explained it to me. Now I understand it, but then I did not.

When the Regents were stolen, everybody was delighted that we would be subjected to the citywide rather than the statewide exam. I do not mean to impugn the general intelligence level of New York City citizens, but the citywide exams were known to be less stringent. At the time, everyone in my class achieved the mark of 100 on the examination. Everyone, that is, except me, who had been tutored for two months before the test and received an 80. An 80 was like a dream for me.

My parents looked at my mark and did not consider it worth a discussion. They knew that I suffered through math from fifth grade through eighth grade. They did not expect that I would become a mathematician, and their expectations were borne out. I use a calculator now to figure out anything remotely connected with numbers.

The point is that nothing bad happened to me, and I was able to accept the fact that I am good at a lot of other things even though I am not good in math. I joke about my math skills all the time to my students, who have to have high averages to get into my school — except for math. I have no problem with this policy because I sincerely believe that doing poorly in one area of your life is not a problem, if you try and if you make an effort. I did. I had a tutor who was a friend whom my parents paid. He studied with me every single night for two months. It was almost hopeless, but **I did not give up hope** because my parents believed in me. They backed me. They gave me full support with no feeling whatsoever of being a failure, even though I did not do well in one subject in high school.

Parents are afraid that if they accept the shortcomings of their children, the children will take advantage of their forbearance and will not do well in other things. I do not believe this is true. I have said it before and I do not mind repeating that children want to do well, to be successful, and to be good. They want to give us *nachas*, parental joy. *Children want to be successful, but they have to believe they can.* They have to stop being disappointed in themselves because they think everyone else is disappointed in them. When a child is reluctant to try something new, it is because he fears he will not be good at it.

This is where self-esteem plays such an important role. Any difficulty a child is having in school should be held up against the mirror of perfectionism, because sometimes the difficulty is not really a difficulty but rather the child's need to excel in everything. Perfectionist children grow up in denial of issues in their own life because they assume that if they look closely at a problem, it will reveal their own shortcomings. They are not capable of dealing with anything that goes wrong because when something goes wrong, it means there is something wrong with them. After all, they have to be Miss Perfect or Mr. Perfect (and this is what I call the Perfection Syndrome). It is probably the most damaging factor in the lives of successful people, for it does not allow them to face up to shortcomings, limitations, difficulties, or challenges. In order to cope with life, the perfectionist child needs everything to be fine, perfect. The result is that he moves on and ignores things that ought to have been dealt with at the right time.

✌ Obeying the Rules

Some children are just not good at keeping to the rules. Some children have a hard time with frameworks, standards, and structure. We know they want structure, but they also need to test it. They feel insecure until they are sure of exactly what their place is and who they are.

Parents do not always agree with all the rules the school establishes. To be smart parents, we should not be at odds with the school our children attend. It is decidedly not a good idea to oppose school regulations. If you happen to disagree personally with certain things or prioritize them differently from the school, you have to be careful and clever about how you present your opinion and your reaction to the things your child brings home. I do not subscribe to the belief that the teacher is always right. Teachers can be wrong and they do make mistakes, sometimes even foolish ones. Teachers have even been known to do things that we may perceive as petty. While we do not have to agree with the teacher all the time, and we can understand that our child may have a legitimate complaint, we do have to recognize that there is probably another side to the story the child tells us. If we must complain, it should be done in a private discussion with the principal or teacher, not in front of the child.

Schools have to deal with extremely difficult and challenging issues. Rules are made by the school administration to avoid potential problems. However, by establishing a rule the school seems to be saying, "This is the way it is, and if you don't like it you don't belong here." The rule does not have to make complete sense to us; it does not have to make sense at all times in all cases. By making a rule, the school avoids having to deal with complications arising from that rule. If the standard is to wear a hat and a jacket, students have to abide by that rule. In general the staff cannot make exceptions. This is the rule and teachers should not have to deal with problems caused by it because it is the rule and it has been clearly stated. Obviously there are exceptions to every rule but we must recognize that all semblance of structure in the school will be destroyed if everyone does as he wishes. Therefore we have rules.

A. Uniforms

The inordinate amount of rules for girls' dress codes can be understood better in light of the above. Yet all the variations in dress code from school to school are established in the name of *tzenius*, modesty. In one school white socks are allowed, in another white socks are not *tzenuah*, while in a third only blue stockings are considered modest enough. Children come home with questions, and we parents also wonder about some rules. Last week my wife was at a parent-teacher meeting for my second daughter who is in a different school than my first daughter, and she had to make an effort to remember what was considered modest in which school. The nitpicking nuance can be annoying and I suppose this lends itself to poking fun at, but it helps alleviate our frustration to do so.

Schools create standards so that they will not have to address each situation on its own merits. The students must conform and the school cannot allow deviations from the standards. Here is a case in point. A girl comes to school ready to learn, but is sent home because her sweater is not the right color. She wore a blue sweater as she was supposed to, but it had a white splotch on one sleeve. Perhaps this seems nitpicky, ridiculous, even foolish. But there are seven hundred girls in the school, and if each child were to deviate even slightly from the basic dress code, it would destroy the system. Then the school would be back where it started, that is, where everybody dresses as she wishes. That is why schools have to be very precise about such things. I am not saying that these rules are right or wrong; I am not sure I would be able to implement such stringent rules, but I believe that it is necessary to implement the institution of school rules in a healthy, educational way.

We also have to realize that the school is dealing with hundreds of children in addition to our child, who is of course an angel and always wants to do the right thing. The parents of some of those children think that uniforms are ridiculous and/or unnecessary, while others have children who cannot function well without an organized framework and the pressure that it entails. Schools have to deal with widely differing situations. We cannot judge the schools from a limited perspective.

Recently I had a discussion with a close friend. He said to me, "I'm telling you, the school system here is destroying my child."

"Why do you say that?" I asked.

"My daughter likes long skirts. Now, since when are long skirts not modest? The longer it is, the more modest, it seems to me. Why is there a problem with her wearing long skirts?" he replied.

"Well," I tried to explain, "with very long skirts there are two problems that make it a challenging question. One is that when children run and walk fast, which they do a lot, they sort of pick up the skirt to gain freedom of movement, and that could result in immodesty. Second, sometimes the long skirt is part of a nonchalant, streetwise look that is actually rather shlumpy, messy, and takes away from the kavod of a bas Yisrael."

He became angry; he was livid. He questioned me. "You ... you're defending the system? Are you just saying this to play devil's advocate with me? You can't believe this! You're telling me that you are going to turn long skirts into immodesty because you want to protect some crazy ..."

"My dear friend," I said. "I'm not being ridiculous and I'm not saying this just to have a good argument. I am saying this because I have children in the system, and if I have children in this system, I intend to find sense in what the system does. Because if my child comes home and says something about this, and I respond the way

you respond, then it will not be the system destroying my children but I."

Systems do not destroy children. Systems are systems. They have their good points and they also have their problems. When you or your kids are in a school, you have to go along with that school. Every institution has its limitations. Are you going to harp on the limitations? Are you going to take those limitations and turn them into a symbol for the whole school? Are you going to let those limitations become the focus of everything you do and everything you say and everything you live for? If you are going to do that, you are going to destroy your children. I suggest you try to figure out the reasoning behind the rule. You do not have to agree with it. You do not have to think it is the finest decision of all the decisions the administration has made, but there is enough sense in it that you should defend it.

You can say to your daughter, "Listen sweetie, I don't know if I would make that rule, but I understand where they're coming from. We know they have the students' good in mind." Even if somewhere in my mind I think that some of the things are a bit extreme or a bit far-fetched, I know I must present these rules to my children in a palatable way. I can say, "Listen, when we open the school that we want to open one day, we'll decide whether we'll do it this way or not; that will be our decision. But as long as you're in this school, and this is where we have decided to send you, you have to focus on the good things while trying to accept some of the things you don't like so much." You can point out that it is not bad, it is not evil. No one is making these rules with any sinister intention.

If you cannot sincerely respond this way — maybe your child does not belong in that school.

B. When in Rome ...

Americans and other English-speaking *olim* living in *Eretz Yisrael* are aware of the challenges of raising children in a society that is precisely the same as the society in which they grew up. Whether you come from Houston and move to Brooklyn, or come from Flatbush and move to Monsey, or the reverse, when you grow up in one system and then raise your children in a different system, you are going to find conflicts. You will have to come to terms with the fact that you have to send your children to schools that will not be like those in your former community. You and your children have to adjust to the society in which you are currently living, and you will have to make peace with it. This might include making a few changes in your approach to certain things. It might even mean making some changes in your own appearance. You should keep your children out of any conflict, however, and make sure that they are not getting a mixed or contradictory message as to what is right and wrong, good and bad. This is especially true when children begin to question who they are and what life is all about, as they often do in their teens.

◄₹ Social Acceptance

Returning to our list of children at risk, the fourth type of child you must take pains to help is the child who is not socially accepted. Every child needs to feel himself a part of a larger group; every child needs friends. Friends accept you for who you are and spend time with you, play with you, and speak with you throughout the day. A friend does not judge you; every child needs a nonjudgmental peer. A child who is not accepted, who feels left out in school or at play, will try to find another group that will accept him. This is when the sharks come along.

Children out on the street are leaders who know how to make these left-out children feel good about themselves. They feel an indefinable empathy with another child who is "out" because they themselves feel "out," so they understand him. The frightening part of this scenario is that these street-wise children — and this is why I call them sharks — are themselves needy. They need to find unsophisticated children that they can use to their advantage. Even these sharks can be helped, of course. They are children who are basically good but need help, and we will discuss this type of child later. But the child who feels left out suddenly finds peers who accept him and are nice to him. He does not realize that this sympathetic, apparently nice person might want to take advantage of him. Sweet, innocent children who just never found their place in their *chevrah*, in their group, are often easy prey to be taken advantage of in many ways, some very harmful, and it happens over and over again.

When the child realizes he has been taken advantage of by someone who is a bit older, he loses his self-respect completely. He loses trust in everyone and that is when he becomes seriously and totally at risk. The only way we can help the child who has no friends and prevent a catastrophe like this is by investing heavily in helping him develop social skills. The most significant thing a parent can do in this instance is to find this child a "big brother" or a "big sister." For a fifteen-year-old boy it could be an *avreich*, a young married man. For a fourteen- or fifteen-year-old girl it could be an older girl whom we may have to pay for her time without our child knowing it. Somehow a parent has to find an older friend whom this child feels accepts him — someone good, someone positive. Whoever it is, whatever it takes!

Some time ago I helped to found a group program called "Achoseinu" in Monsey and in Detroit, in which girls just out of seminary volunteer two hours a week to befriend younger girls, in the grades right before high school, who are potentially at risk. The girls give one hour on the phone and one hour meeting with the child. The group representatives try to identify these girls in sixth, seventh, and eighth grades and match up an older girl with each of the younger ones. The change in the younger girls is almost instantly noticeable. Instead of feeling left out, the child begins to feel she has a friend, someone she can talk to, someone who cares about her. When a child has a problem and has no one to talk to about it, it will eat away at her until either it explodes or she talks to the wrong people about it. With a "big sister" on "her side," the girl has someone to turn to; she finds she can talk about her problems and suddenly she sees that they can be solved. The group provides guidance for the big sisters, indicating how they can help, what they can do, and what they should not do. It is a very simple system. It is very small at the moment — maybe thirty or forty children are involved — but it is a program that we hope to develop and expand.

If we realize that our child is socially inept and does not fit in, the first step is to get the child involved socially with a big brother or sister. Sometimes, however, that may not be enough to turn things around. In that case we will need to involve a professional, because the reasons the child is holding back or feels inadequate are probably deeply embedded.

◄₂ Warning Signals

A. Belligerency

When our child gets unusually contradictory in an active, aggressive, and adamant way about whatever we ask or expect him to do, or about school, it is a warning signal that flashes, "Watch out! Take care! Something is going on that you need to be aware of." We must think about what we can do for him at this point. See if we can understand him better and reopen a channel of communication with him. We will have to look carefully to detect where our relationship has faltered and how we can reestablish closer ties.

B. Apathy

Another warning signal is apathy. If our child has lost interest in just about everything, does not seem to care about anything, and just sits around doing nothing, this child is in danger. Apathy is a sign that he is very unhappy. It is a sign that he has no interest in life. He does not want to get up in the morning because he feels like he has nothing to get up for. This child is soon going to be at risk.

There are children who find their lives so meaningless that they literally disappear and we cannot find them. Children today, unfortunately, have access to areas of society that we do not even want to know exist. There is a subculture of adolescents out there who will absorb a child without a trace. It is no longer frightening to a child to be threatened with being sent out of the house. If we had threatened him with that punishment years ago, the child had nowhere to go. He could leave, he could run away from home, but after a while he would realize that he had nowhere to go. There was no one else on the street. There was nothing to do. He would come creeping home. Today, unfortunately, a child can leave home and disappear for days or weeks without a trace. There is a subculture of young people out there who will take him in, help him, find him a job, give him food, take him to the movies, give him status. It is frightening to think about what is out there.

If your child starts disappearing from home and you do not know where he or she is, you should be highly concerned. There is no need to panic or overreact, but you do have to find out what is happening. You must know where your children are. You cannot always assume that your children are in good places, especially if it is a child who is not doing well in school or socially. When a child disappears for long periods of time, it is a sign that it is time for you to react. You must get the message across to him that parents must know where their children are and that you care about him. It should not be happening in the first place, but if it is, you must try to put a stop to it immediately, because there is no way of knowing where children can end up today.

C. Secretive Phone Conversations

When a child has a lot of secrets from you and begins making phone calls at odd hours, like late at night, you had better take a closer look at your phone bill. You can order a printout of numbers that have been called. He or she may have friends you are not supposed to know about, especially of the opposite gender, and this of course can result in many difficult challenges, including being expelled from school. I am not suggesting that you have to quiz your child on the details of his conversations with his friends. But you have to know what is going on in your child's life, not so that you can come down heavily on his every move, but so that you can help him deal responsibly with his problems and work them through.

D. Eating Disorders

The phenomenon of young girls' eating disorders has reached staggering proportions in the United States and is on the rise in *Eretz Yisrael.* This is partially an offshoot of the Perfection Syndrome and partially the desire for social acceptance, and it is also something that should exact our serious concern. Girls as young as eleven focus on their physical appearance to bolster their lack of self-esteem, thinking that the only way they will be accepted is if they look thin. Parents should be aware of their sensitivities on this issue, and part of that awareness is not making a big issue about weight. Be careful not to arouse bad feelings about the way our daughters look, especially if they are a bit overweight before they reach the teen years, or it will mushroom into an all-consuming interest in their lives. We certainly do not want to be the cause of an eating disorder.

If you question them, most girls with eating disorders will say they have no idea how such a thing happened. If their worry about their looks snowballs into something they never intended, let us not aggravate it. Most girls who have developed eating disorders never in their wildest dreams did so intentionally. If the child is eating too much or not eating at all, either one is a danger signal.

I do not want to be an alarmist, but this is a situation that exists in our society and has even reached crisis proportions. Therefore, in regard to all these warning signals we have mentioned, we should keep our eyes open for behavior that does not make sense, that does not fit with what came before, or that does not seem to be as it ought to be. If your daughter is "helping" a friend with an eating disorder, be very wary.

Many young women who develop eating disorders began by sincerely trying to help a friend.

◄◊ Intervention

Let us talk now about a child who is already troubled, who is displaying some of these signs, and we are feeling challenged. I would like to offer a number of elemental considerations. Children at risk are "troubled." We parents may think that it is we who are challenged, that we are the ones who are suffering. Well, of course we are. It is very hard to deal with a child who is having a difficult time. It is painful, scary, and embarrassing, and we have many conflicting thoughts and feelings at such times. But I think we have to realize that until we develop a close rapport with the child, the child is suffering more. Even if your child *looks* happily in control, remember that looks can be deceiving.

Every child wants to be a part of his family. Every child wants to be loved and accepted by his mother and father. No child wants to be at odds. There are some children who fight us tooth and nail, who threaten us, whose condition is, *Rachmana litzlan*, already so volatile and so dangerous, that we cannot manage to live in the same house anymore. That child really wants his parents to love and accept him. He looks like he wants to kill his parents, *and sometimes he does*, because he believes they do not love him and accept him. The only thing that satisfies a person's elemental needs, child or adult, is the love and acceptance of his parents.

Even adults want to be loved, appreciated, and respected. But children need that love so desperately, they will fight us to the bitter end until they get it. It is unfortunate and sad that there are so many children whose parents do not have sufficient insight to show that they love their children with no strings attached. Sometimes it takes a borderline situation (when the parents realize that they may very well be losing their child) to make them show their son or daughter the unconditional love the child needs. Once the child runs away and disappears for two weeks, and the parents are on the phone with the police, the organizations, the VIPs, and so on, it is probably too late to begin to show love for that child.

Unfortunately, I am only too familiar with such a scenario. I have been on the phone with parents in this situation countless times, when we did not know where their child was. The parents' fears at that point are overwhelming. I am used to hearing parents say, "Just come home. We'll do anything. We love you. We don't care what color shirt you wear. We don't care if you wear your *tzitzis* in or out or what kind of haircut you like. We will take you with the friends, even those of whom we do not approve. *Just come home.*"

Only then does the child learn something that was true all along, but which the parents did not know how to express. Because it is hard to express to a child your love for him when he is doing everything that goes against what you have taught him. How can you love and show a child that love, when he is doing things that you do not believe he should be doing? Well, the only way we have a chance of changing our children, and we have mentioned this before, is if we are a part of their lives. If we are not a part of their lives we will not be able to change them or even influence them. Shunting them aside, cutting them out of our lives, is counter-productive. We have to keep them in and part of our lives, and we have to go on loving them. *No matter how bad it gets, we have to maintain an unconditional concern for our children and we have to let them know that we are concerned.*

If it really seems as though our children do not want to be part of our lives, then we must look at ourselves and figure out what we possibly could have done to create the situation with which we are grappling. We have to find out why they do not want to be a part of our lives, anymore. If we look carefully, we can inevitably find something to adjust or change that will help them rejoin us. Do not be discouraged when this child seems not to want any part of what we are selling him, even when we tell him that we will accept him this way and we still love him, because if we can get him to believe us, he might take a chance on coming back. He is afraid to believe us and then be disappointed. He is afraid to believe it and then be rejected. He does not really think it is going to work. We do know, from experience, that if he finds a *rebbe*, a neighbor, or a big brother who gives him the unconditional love he needs, he can be brought back.

When he finds somebody who respects him and who treats him like a *mentsch,* he begins to trust in someone again. This is not easy for him, and it takes time until he builds that trust. When he finds someone whom he believes in and who believes in him, then our child is okay, but we have lost out. We have turned our responsibility over to someone else. Do we really want to lose out? If we have been involved in our child's world all along, there is a much better chance we will be included in it when he is having a hard time too, and we will not be just spectators during his struggle to return.

◄ℰ *Getting Help*

Being involved all along with our troubled teens today could mean, unfortunately, helping children who have become involved in drugs, crime, or with other children who are hanging out with bad people. If this is the case, we are really at a loss and simply do not have the tools to cope. At this stage, just loving the child is not enough. These kids are in trouble and are doing bad things. We have to get them help. Ideally we should get help even before it goes this far, sometimes just for them and sometimes to supervise us in coping. We have to look for someone who has a proven track record with such matters.

We have to be prepared for the process to take a long time. We should not be tempted to bounce from one professional to another if we do not see instant success, or if we feel insulted by criticism or if we do not like what the professional is saying. Our child is already having a hard time. Parents have said to me, "I've taken my child to five different psychologists. No one has been able to help him." If we have taken our child to five psychologists, it was because we didn't trust one to help us through the whole process. Whenever we heard something we did not like, we took the child out of therapy and gave neither the therapist nor the child a chance. Obviously the child learns from this not to trust people. He is not going to open up more than once or twice. He is not going to express himself all over again to yet another person whom he expects he will never see in a month anyway. This behavior on our child's part is totally understandable.

If we cannot cope on our own, we should find someone to whom our child can talk that he can trust, and leave him in their good hands. But we have to find out before we begin that the professional is trustworthy. When we do not know what to do, we must let other people get involved to help us. It is better to receive help in the very beginning stages when we sense something is wrong and are checking up to find out what it is. Then, whatever his approach, we should continue with the same person through the entire difficult process, whether he is working with the child or helping us deal with the child's problems.

May we not have to deal with extreme situations. May we have the understanding and the *siyata diShemaya* to bring up our children properly from the beginning and be able to help them through the hard times so that they never have to be dealt with on this level.

Chapter Fifteen
THE PARENT AND THE SCHOOL

The title of this book is *Preparing Your Child for Success*, and we have been talking about the responsibility of parents in this process called *chinuch*. In this chapter we will be talking about the parents' relationship with schools. With this in mind, please understand that the mention of any shortcomings in relation to our schools is specifically intended to make us as parents aware of where we have to be more careful and responsible. It is not at all my intention to judge our school system harshly; if anything, I would be harsh on us as parents, because beyond the built-in limitations of any system, there are many problem areas that more dedication on our part would resolve. It is not the fault of the system that teachers are overworked and underpaid in many schools; that is our fault as a society. We place a very high value on many different things over the schooling of our children. If the education of our children were the highest value in our lives, we would not have to face so many of the issues that perforce we will be dealing with in this chapter.

Creating a good school system is one of the most important phases of preparing our children for their future. We, as parents who are interested in the *chinuch* of our children, must recognize, however, that the school's sole function is to *help* us educate and guide our children. *The essential responsibility of educating children is ours.* Assuredly, we need the school as a supplementary aid to our own Herculean efforts in child-rearing. The challenge of fully educating all our children is mammoth and nearly unattainable. *But we must never forget that the basic responsibility of chinuch lies with us, the parents.* That is the first line, the bottom line, and almost all the lines in between.

Our Sages say we should praise the name of Yehoshua ben Gamla until today for instituting schools in the Jewish community about 2,000 years ago.[1] Until then, every parent educated his own children. Fathers sat and studied with each son, and as the child grew older, brought him up to the highest level he could reach. As the *galus,* our exile, continued and the pressure to survive mounted, it became increasingly difficult for parents to educate their children alone. Schools of Torah learning were created in order to ensure the continuance and stability of our *mesorah,* our tradition.

At the same time, if we neglect our responsibility to educate our children properly, the school can become an "evil" place. If we are not aware of the shortcomings in some classrooms, we will not realize the limitations that some of our children will be facing. A school cannot always address the specific needs of all children. It often cannot recognize exactly what every single child is capable of or what his or her needs are. With close to thirty or forty children in a class, even the best teachers can't always be on top of every pupil's progress in every subject in addition to catering to his psychological and social needs. *We* have to be aware that when our Dovid needs some help in one area, and our Sarah needs a little more challenge in another, it is *our* responsibility.

◄§ The Individual and the System

Most schools by their very nature inadvertently breed mediocrity. Every child is a world unto himself and therefore has different needs, capabilities, and interests. When capable parents studied with a child before the advent of schools,

---

1. *Bava Basra* 21a.

they did it in accordance with his nature, requirements, abilities, and talents. Clearly, in a class of thirty to forty children there is little, if any, way that individual needs can be met. The most intelligent students are often bored, and less intellectually motivated, slower students are often left behind. The median students are addressed, but who in the class is challenged? Only the child for whom the median level is exactly one step above his comfort level! He will grow in a most beneficial way. All the other children are over-challenged or under-challenged. It is true, of course, that the better and more experienced the teacher, the more children will be challenged, but even the best teacher cannot challenge every student, certainly not equally. In the whole class, only some will be learning at a pace properly suited to them. This situation is obviously not ideal, but few things are in this world, and we have to deal with what we have. When we send our children to school, we have to understand that their individual needs may not be met. After all, the classroom cannot be tailored to suit thirty-five children simultaneously. Nor can teachers implement a special program for each child. This is neither criticism nor condemnation, but a realistic understanding of one of the practically inevitable limitations of schools and the classroom. Schools are the best way to teach our children today, even with these limitations, so it is important that we face the facts and think about how to deal with them.

The fact is that in each class there may be some gifted children and a few under-endowed. There will be a percentage that fits in just below the former and a similar percentage just above the latter. The school can only provide an average, middle-level education — unless it is large enough to have special classes for each need. Rare is the school that can attend to the progress of each and every child in his or her schoolwork and relationships. I say this as the principal of a relatively small school with an almost homogeneous group of high-achieving post-high school students whose special educational needs are almost non-existent.

A competent teacher will usually recognize a problem and notify the parents when a child is not challenged enough or when the child finds the work too difficult. We must then thank the teacher, look into the problem, find out what our child needs, and try to help him. The following is a story that may seem extreme, but it is a true story that indicates our need to be on top of the situation and not wait for the teacher to notify us of our child's standing.

> My father was the sixth-grade rebbe in Toras Emes-Kamenitz many years ago in Brooklyn. The parents of one student were both prestigious people, the father a great Torah scholar. The boy's father called my father, who was going to be the child's rebbe for the coming year. "I don't know what to do," he told my father. "The secular studies teacher said that my son is retarded, and I'm very concerned."
>
> My father spoke to the boy for a while, learned a few passages with him, and called the father back.
>
> "If anyone is retarded, it's not your son. Your child is brilliant!"
>
> The boy skipped my father's class and went into seventh grade. By the end of the year he was in eighth grade, and by the age of thirteen or fourteen he was in Lakewood Yeshivah. Today he is a very well-known talmid chacham and Rosh Kollel.

What had happened with this child through the first five grades? He was suffering such boredom that he retreated into his own little dream world and no one noticed. This is frightening. At home the boy acted normally, seemed fine, and did not complain. Parents have to be aware of what is going on with their children in school. The above story is not so common. More often, painful situations arise because a child is having a difficult time. A child might have had a hard time with only one aspect of one subject, and there was a lack of recognition of the seriousness of the problem. The symptoms may then spread to other areas. It would be ideal if the school were able to recognize each and every problem earlier on and help him or her. But schools cannot always fulfill the many functions expected of them. Not every *rebbe* and teacher has the necessary training and experience to identify all the difficulties children have, given that the identical difficulty may impact differently on different children. A problem that one child shrugs off as nothing may loom ominously over a second child. The broad abilities of our children's schools and teachers are not perfect. In an ideal world they would be perfect, but we do not live in an ideal world, and we must work with the schools and teachers, and respect them.

Furthermore, children today need to grow up within a social setting. The nature of our society is such that social norms play a very powerful role in the development of identity and self-confidence. Under healthy and normal circumstances, a child's self-confidence is determined almost completely by his initial years at home, yet today, with the child spending eight or more hours a day in school for twelve years in a row, his social standing in school will strongly affect that self-confidence. That is why even parents who are capable of home-schooling their children should, in most cases, send them to school. A child needs a social structure. Generations ago, when all children learned directly from their parents, an outside social framework was less important; whatever needs they had were defined for them during their free, non-learning time. That worked in another era. Today, however, when everyone else grows up within the school system, it may be a disservice to our children to make them stand out from the rest by choosing to home-school. Serious consideration must be given to the issue before making such a decision.

Another aspect of formal education, which is really the principal function of the school, is that of transmitting information. The main purpose of the school is to teach *Chumash*, *Navi*, Jewish history, the three Rs, and so forth. Although this is the *raison d'etre* of the school, the individual who has a problem in absorbing this information may, unfortunately, be ignored. More often then not, this occurs when the underachieving child is not disruptive. Although most schools are trying their best, recognizing this child demands a response, and responses generate expenses. This is not to say that most schools are unwilling to spend money to benefit your child, it is simply that they *do not have* the extra money. Even if the solution entails moving only one child into a different group, it might necessitate far-reaching changes in schedule or other complications. All change is difficult, but it is especially so when it involves the dynamics of an entire school. As a parent, you are the one who must take notice if the school is not taking action on such a problem or is addressing it only minimally. It does happen that a school will move the child forward automatically through the grades, regardless of his academic shortcomings or strengths. By the fourth or fifth grade, the *rebbe* and the teachers already know that "Oh yes, little Chaim Yankel or Esther'ke is a very sweet child, but let's just be nice to them and not rock the boat." The child continues to go through school as a piece of furniture, because everyone "knows" there is nothing to be done.

Parents occasionally ask me, when their child has not done well in elementary school, whether they should assume that he or she just does not like school and that the same will apply in high school. My answer depends on what has transpired during the elementary school years and what has been done to ameliorate the child's dislike of school or to help him do better. If your child is finishing eighth grade and dislikes school and has not done well, then yes, you can assume this trend will continue. Unless you ensure that the child will be dealt with on an individual level in his new school, or you send him to a school that better fits his needs, you (and he) could be in for trouble. You have to deal with the facts, and the facts are that your child does not like school, and that so far he has not succeeded. There's no reason to assume that when he reaches high school, everything will suddenly straighten out. Unless you see some newfound motivation, excitement, or willingness to improve, you can assume it doesn't exist. If the child has made a turnaround in eighth grade and he's started to try and work himself up, by all means, back him up. You must believe in a kid like this and you have to give him a chance. But if you don't see any change, make sure the high school you send him to is one that will deal with who he is.

I've seen fifteen-year-old boys who went through eight years of elementary school and two years of yeshivah high school and never learned how to read properly! No one can tell me that these children compensated for their inability to read through ten years of school. One, and only one, child I knew proved to have such a phenomenal memory that it propelled him through ten years of schooling before we discovered, in the second year in yeshivah, that he could barely read. He could hear something once and repeat it almost verbatim. He actually made it all the way through elementary school with no one the wiser, but he suffered socially because he never could learn with a *chavrusa*, a study partner. In our high school we had study partners take turns reading aloud, and that is when his problems began to surface.

That boy was unusual. Most fifteen-year-olds who are not functional in school have a history of learning difficulties. In speaking to this particular student's former teachers, *rebbeim*, and principal, I found out that they were not even aware that the child did not know how to read. There were behavioral issues that we now understood were related to his avoiding reading in the classroom. In most cases a child like that will give up on himself, thinking of himself as "stupid," and go into a dream world as he moves from class to class.

❧ Teachers

A school is only as good as its administration and teachers. Obviously, with hundreds of schools and thousands of teachers in our communities, we cannot expect each one of those thousands to be successful, perceptive, and talented. Let us address some of the difficulties schools face, starting with teachers.

1) The first of the many challenges and limitations our teachers confront is poor training. How many of our teachers have received proper training? I wonder if there are courses in a teachers training program that can train one to *be* a

teacher. They train people who want to *become* teachers. They train people to maintain a certain standard of learning, but teaching is a personal art. Most training programs teach technical methodology: how and what to teach, how to formulate and build a lesson. Teachers are taught what to write on the board, what to assign for homework, and so forth. These are important tools, and I am not in any way trying to belittle them. It is important to learn methods, but it is at least as important to be a fair, honest, caring human being. One cannot learn to teach without learning methods, but the first prerequisite for being a successful teacher is a love for children and the ability to express it in the classroom.

2) While there are many skills one can learn, many skills cannot be learned. An individual can graduate with several degrees in education and still be a terrible teacher. If his (or her) skills in human relationships are not well honed, if he is not sensitive and caring, how can he be a good teacher? If he does not love a child for himself, and if he does not want to give, he will not be a good teacher despite the most extensive training. One would have to be a mind reader to tap into a potential teacher's inner thoughts and feelings. Since this is an impossibility, many training programs never address this aspect.

3) With trepidation I say that we as a community suffer greatly from the fact that we don't pay our teachers adequately, which explains to a certain extent why there are not enough supertalented, capable, charismatic, caring, fine, loving, good, intelligent, bright, successful, and exciting people who go into teaching. With the aforementioned traits they can find employment in areas that will afford their family a better standard of living. A talented individual who becomes a teacher must be idealistic. Therefore, how many phenomenal teachers are we going to have in any school system? How many superb people are we going to have in any one school? Although many teachers are wonderful individuals, they are not all adequately prepared and capable of fulfilling the requirements of their job. As many idealists as you will find, you will find many more who simply need to earn a living for their family. Even those

wonderful individuals who are really idealistic often burn out when they are undercompensated year after year. The blame is not the teachers'. We as a community need to prioritize our values properly to place education in the highly professional and respectable position we understand it needs to be. When tuition for a four-week summer camp equals that of four months of our children's education, we need to question our priorities. When there are people who go on Pesach vacations that cost more than a full year's tuition and then give the tuition committee a hard time and request scholarships, it is time for some of us to reorganize our values.

Principals are the individuals who have the most influence on our children's education. They define the level of professionalism, organization, and education. It is the principals who choose the teachers, who should be able to coach the teachers and help those who require training. A principal who is concerned for the welfare of the children in his school has input in every level of their progress. He can help develop good resource rooms and make sure that the individual student gets what he needs. He creates the atmosphere in a school. His attitude will define if teachers and parents can discuss questions or problems without fear of being labeled incompetent or troublemakers. Parents must feel that they have an open line of communication with the school, as we will discuss at length in Chapter Sixteen. And students must believe that even though their principal may be strict, he is fair and truly wants to help them. Many difficult students have survived and thrived because a principal supported them rather than their teacher and sometimes even their parents. We must make sure that we are the parents who appreciate that kind of principal; but even if the principal is not living up to the above, we must do whatever is necessary for our children's welfare.

◄ε Challenges Old and New

Our children's teachers are challenged in the classroom with difficulties beyond preparing and giving over a good lesson.

We put thirty to forty children in a classroom. Even the most capable teacher, the most exciting, charismatic, happy, well-balanced, loving, caring teacher is faced with an almost impossible task: to teach forty children, all on different levels; to manage, accept, and deal with all these children and to keep each of them interested is indeed a challenge. It is not for naught that *Chazal*[2] in the *halachos* of *chinuch* say that there should be no more than twenty-five children in one classroom.

The following is a fable. Though it is not the original version, it reflects the immense challenges that face our teachers and our schools. In transmitting to teachers the awesome responsibility of recognizing individual needs of students early in the educational process, I personally use this fable as a syllabus for six hours of teacher-training in noticing, understanding, and helping all the individuals a teacher will encounter in a classroom.

> *Once upon a time the animals had a school. They had to create a curriculum that would satisfy everyone, so they chose four subjects: running, climbing, flying, and swimming. All the animals, of course, studied all the subjects. The duck was very good at swimming, better than the teacher, in fact. He received passing grades in running and flying, but was hopeless in climbing, so they made him drop swimming so that he could practice climbing. After a while he was only average at swimming, but average is still acceptable, at least in school, and nobody worried much about it except the duck.*
>
> *The eagle was considered a troublemaker. In his climbing class he beat everybody to the top of the tree, but he had his own way of getting there that was against the rules. He always had to stay after school and write, "Cheating is wrong," five hundred times. This kept him from soaring, which he loved, but schoolwork comes first.*
>
> *The bear flunked because they said he was lazy, especially in the winter. His best time was summer, but school wasn't open then.*

---

2. *Shulchan Aruch Yoreh Deah*, Siman 245, *Seif* 14.

The zebra played hooky a lot because the ponies made fun of his stripes, and this made him very sad.

The kangaroo started out at the top of the racing class, but became discouraged when was told to move swiftly on all four legs the way his classmates did.

The fish quit school because he was bored. To him, all four subjects were the same, but nobody understood that because they had never seen a fish.

The squirrel got an A in climbing, but his flying teacher made him start from the ground up, instead of from the treetop down. His legs got so sore practicing takeoffs that he began getting Cs in climbing and Ds in running.

The bee was the biggest problem of all, so the teacher sent him to Doctor Owl for testing. Doctor Owl said that the bee's wings were too small for flying and they were in the wrong place. The bee never saw Doctor Owl's report, so he just went ahead and flew anyway. I think I know a bee or two, how about you?

The duck is the child who does well in math and poorly in English and is given tutorials by the English teacher while his classmates are doing math. He loses his edge in math, and only does passably well in English. The eagle is the child who is turned into a troublemaker because he has his "own style" of doing things. While he is not doing anything "wrong," his non-conforming is perceived as troublemaking, for which he is punished. Who does not recognize the bear? The kid who is great in camp, thrives on extra-curricular, but really just goes flat in the academics. The zebra is the heavy, thin, tall, or short, self-conscious kid whose failure in school few realize is due to a sense of social inadequacy. The kangaroo is the one who instead of persevering gives up and becomes that discouraged child whose future disappears because he was not appreciated. The fish is a child who really requires full special education and should not be in the regular classroom. (Baruch Hashem, today this child is generally identified early on and as time passes, more alternatives are becoming available. In such cases, it is wrong for parents to cover up the problem in order not to "stigmatize" the family. How unjust to deprive a child of needed help for such a reason!)

The squirrel, unlike the duck who "manages," becomes a failure. The bee, oh the bee, is the child who the school just feels it cannot deal with, yet, against all odds, with the backing of his parents, has enough self-motivation to do well even though everyone thought he couldn't. I have had the pleasure of knowing many bees!

Today there are new challenges in education that did not exist a generation ago. Parents of teenagers can easily remember that when a teacher said something harsh to us, we lowered our gaze and looked at the floor. Even if we were angry, we said nothing. Even if we were frustrated, we kept our mouths closed. Today, children answer back. Teachers hesitate to reprimand pupils even in the "good" schools. It is more challenging to be a teacher today than it was thirty and forty years ago. We must deal differently with the children of this generation. Rav Eliezer Papo claimed[3] that this change was already taking place when his epic work, *Pe'le Yoetz*, was written two hundred years ago. In reference to the statements in the Gemara that set forth the responsibility of communal leaders and teachers to "force" and "beat" their devotees into adherence, he states: "The same way that medicinal prescriptions have changed and we cannot use the old medicinal tools for our generation, so too has the nature of men changed so that we can no longer use those tools [of force]." Not every teacher is aware of this principle, and many *mechanchim*, educators, feel they should teach the way they were taught. A teacher today can use some of the tools he inherited from his own teachers, but he must take care to use only the tools that make sense and that work with the children currently under his tutelage.

One of the prime impediments in educating our children today is the intrusion of the outside world into the classroom. Our teachers are competing with superhighways of information and with ease of accessibility to all kinds of extraneous data.

I tell my students that I do not envy them because when they will be teachers, they will be competing with reasonably

---

3. *Pe'le Yoetz* vol. I, p. 290: *Kofeh.*

priced wristwatch-videos and cordless earphones (the size of a pea) in the classroom. It is already possible to watch a video on a cell phone, but at least the teacher can prohibit the use of cell phones in class. How can a teacher tell a child not to wear a wristwatch to class? How does a teacher know what kind of watch a child is wearing? This is where the world is heading. The distracting temptations already overwhelm us. Children are already hooked up to the whole world and see and know about everything. This results in a sort of mental and emotional overstimulation. And it makes new demands on a teacher to be more exciting, more charismatic, and more captivating than the competing influences. The teacher has to have phenomenal initiative if he intends to capture the children's interest and hold onto it.

We all had some teachers who were so wonderful that we bless them till today. We can all probably remember one or two, or if we were extremely lucky, three teachers in our lives whom we loved and respected, for whom we would cross a busy street to express our joy at seeing them. Most people I have spoken to feel that in all their twelve or more years of school only a few of their teachers were truly memorable and influential. Recognizing that our child rarely has more than a few "great" teachers will allow us to think about how we can compensate, how we parents can help our children do better with things as they are.

Having said that, we must once again acknowledge the fact that teachers are universally underpaid and overworked. As a result, often the financial pressures they have at home would be sufficient to make anyone edgy and irritable. Some manage to override their personal problems on the job and some do not, *but we parents are the ones who are ultimately responsible for our children.* So, if the teacher tells us that there is a problem with our child, we cannot ignore it and blame the "ineffectual" teacher, we must take it to heart and assume responsibility. Give the teacher or *rebbe* the benefit of the doubt and find out how your child is really doing.

✒ Is the Teacher Always Right?

Many of us grew up in homes where the teacher was always right, no matter what. I was lucky enough to have a different upbringing, and I think it made me a more self-aware teacher. But parents often think that the teacher has to be seen as right, because otherwise the parents are undermining the school and its approach to education, an idea that has some merit in regard to enforcing discipline. However, our children will see immediately the inconsistency and therefore the hypocrisy of this attitude. We need to find the balance between the value of supporting our child's disciplinary framework and the most essential value of honesty. When a child comes home hurt or upset about what his teacher said or did to him, he needs to feel that you are empathetic and that you care about his feelings. You need not say more than, "That must have really been painful or embarrassing." If you simply validate your child's feelings, you will not allow him to go to the next step. After validating his feeling of hurt or shame, you must help him see the full picture.

The teacher is not always right, but he usually has a valid perspective regarding his students. Although he may not have reacted to a particular provocation correctly, he probably had a reason for reacting as he did. He may not have been correct in his evaluation of the child, or perhaps he spoke to him in a manner that was not wise, but he was undoubtedly reacting to something the child did. Therefore I think we must give the teacher the benefit of the doubt, not necessarily saying that he was "right" automatically, but realizing that something happened. Then we ought to do two things. First, we should get our child back in line because we know that the teacher reacted for some reason. Something must have happened, and most likely our child had something to do with it. Second, once we put the child in his place without anger or recriminations, we have the right to explain that we may not agree with the way the teacher reacted, but we were not there, and we do not know how we would have reacted in a similar situation.

Even when the teacher is clearly *not* correct in our opinion, it is obviously detrimental to degrade him or be disrespectful or impugn him in any way, for that will certainly destroy the respect our child must have for him. We must also let our kids know that we know when they are in the wrong. If our child was hit, we have to react, because a child knows that there is almost nothing that warrants being hit by a teacher. If a teacher is berating the child, derogatorily labeling him and being totally insensitive, our child is going to be hurt. He has to know that we don't want him to be hurt, that we don't think people should hurt him. At the same time, however, he has to recognize that he had something to do with what happened. If we can keep that balance we will be standing behind our children without undermining the school or our own integrity.

Unfortunately, there are rare instances where a teacher will call a child an *"apikores"*; this is the exceptional situation in which you must stand behind your child *completely*. It is time to explain to your child that there are unfortunately some teachers (few, we hope) who, when they do not know how to answer a question, become nervous and insecure and therefore react incorrectly. Assure your child that he is in no way considered an *apikores* for asking a question. In this scenario, your standing up for the teacher would imply that, in fact, your child is an *apikores*. As far as losing respect for the teacher ... it is too late, that occurred with the unfortunate incident. We can only coach him to *act* respectfully in the classroom. Sometimes children need guidance in *how* to ask a question. We also need to teach our children to whom they can ask. But there is NO excuse for the use of that word in a classroom! There is a rare time and place when a teacher is so out of perspective that we need to ask the advice of our *rebbeim*, mentors, if we should have our child continue in the classroom of that teacher or even change schools.

Children have wonderful perception and sometimes very good judgment as to whether a teacher is doing something wrong. You will hear children say, "Oh yes, the teacher gave a quiz today because he didn't have the lesson prepared." Kids realize immediately when a teacher is not really teaching them anything; the children become a bit rowdy because they are bored, and the teacher will stand up suddenly in annoyance and announce a surprise quiz. The children in that class would tell their parents, "Sure, whenever he doesn't know what to teach he gives us a surprise test." Children see through everything — but wait a moment! Weren't they acting rowdy? Yes, there were things going on in the class that were not acceptable. We have to tell our child, "It's not your responsibility to know whether or not your teacher prepared the lesson. That's his responsibility. Your responsibility is to be a student and behave."

We are not saying that the teacher was right or wrong for giving the surprise test. We are not insisting that he did prepare, because we do not have that information, but all that is not relevant. The relevant point is that your child is the student, and you have to convey to him that in school he must behave as a student should behave. The child is going to be in many situations in life in which he will have to observe certain limitations; he may or may not be right, but he must learn to be smart, to abide by the rules, and to behave appropriately.

A clever safe-driving jingle advertised on the back of Israeli buses for many years was, "Don't be right, be smart." On the road, insisting on your lawful right of way will not save your life when an eighteen-wheeler is hurtling through the intersection regardless of a yield sign. Translating this slogan into something more applicable to guiding our children through school, the message is that we must be savvy and smart. We need to teach our children that, though their criticism may be apt, they should be smart, not right. Still, whether the school is right or wrong, it is we who are ultimately responsible because "the buck stops" with us, the parents. School is there to assist us, not replace us.

◄₂ Parental Responsibility

At this point we must highlight the fact that teachers are *shelichim*; they are our agents. Teachers are helping us by doing the things that we cannot do. Our responsibility is to take care of our children. They are our responsibility and only ours. Yes, we send them to school. Yes, we hope they will learn, but we cannot take for granted that our children will get everything they need in school; in fact, they will not.

We cannot realistically expect our children to learn *middos* and *yiras Shamayim* in school. We hope that an educator who will excite their interest and help them feel good about themselves and about Torah and mitzvos will inspire them. But we have to face the fact that this might not happen. How many children come out of our school system inspired? How many children finish school feeling wonderful about themselves and about Torah, mitzvos, and all the values that are important to us? How many children learn in school about the need to work on their *middos*, to acquire a concern for *yiras Shamayim?* While the answer is "many," *baruch Hashem*, the parental factor of those many is very high. It is sad to state that there are many who don't do as well.

But those special Torah values we just mentioned are our responsibility. We can't give our children over to the school and just assume that all this will be taken care of and that they will automatically acquire a love for learning Torah. Just because they are in school doesn't mean that they will learn exemplary *middos* there or that they will want to do mitzvos all their lives. We know that sometimes, unfortunately, they may even learn the opposite. We know that even when we send our children to a good school they might on occasion have a teacher whose *middos* leave something to be desired. Perhaps she was given her job because she was brilliant, or perhaps during her model lesson she was extremely creative, or maybe she has a relative who helps to make the decisions regarding hiring at the school. Worse than having shaky *middos*, however, is the sad fact that she really is not interested in her students. She cares more about herself and the facade she has created than about the job she is doing.

Children have actually said to me, "It's so good when the student teachers come in to observe, because on that day the teacher prepares. It is so much fun because the teacher makes the lesson exciting. I wish we could have girls coming in to observe every day so the teacher would do a great job teaching every day." Once my seminary students said when they came back from a day of observation, "Wow, what a great teacher!" I smiled sadly, because that very teacher has taught one of my daughters and I know that she's one of the most blasé teachers my daughter ever had — except for the days when teachers-in-training come to watch her teach.

It is true that the above cases are the exception rather than the rule. In the end, however, our children will acquire good *middos* only when we reinforce them. More than that — we must be positive role models for them. We cannot depend solely on the schools to do our job.

A. Be on Top of Things

We should know at all times what is going on in our children's classes. This is especially important in sixth, seventh, and eighth grades, so that when the time comes to choose a high school for them, we know what their standing in school is. *We are not acting responsibly as parents if we find out what's happening with our child only at parent-teacher conferences.* We should be in touch with the *rebbeim* and teachers more than the twice a year when we are compelled to appear in school. One parent at least should be dropping by the school on a regular basis to check up. Have you ever watched your child during recess? Do you know if he has friends? Do you know if he's the child who is sitting on the side and is not doing well either socially or scholastically?

> *I was that child. I remember what happened when I was in third and fourth grades. I clearly remember standing outside the school at recess time and watching the team leaders choose teams for punch ball. In Brooklyn we used to play punch ball with the sewer manholes as bases. The first manhole was home plate, the next one was second base, and two cars in the middle on each side were first and third base. We used to play punch ball with little, pink, pensi-pinky balls. Pensi-pinkies*

aren't around anymore. (Now they're blue and yellow.)
Anyway, I remember being that child about whom they
said, "You take him."

"No, you take him."

"No, we had him yesterday."

"I took him twice this week."

I remember the painful feeling of not being wanted
on the team. I remember telling my mother only once
when the boys did not want me on their team, though
it happened many, many times. Even though I wasn't
accepted, I kept going back because I wanted very much
to play punch ball. (HaKadosh Baruch Hu was very kind
to me, and by the time I got to eighth grade I was one of
the bigger fellows choosing sides. I hope I did better.)

But my mother knew, and supported me. I was at
least able to articulate that pain and cry on someone's
shoulder.

Do you know if this is happening to your child? You may
never know. You may know that he's making trouble. You
may know that he's getting into fights. You may know that
he's having a hard time with something. But do you know
why? He's coming home and telling you that this or that happened, but he's not telling you that he's having social problems at school. It's too embarrassing for him.

Do you know what's going on with your child in school
scholastically? You see him doing homework, but do you
know whether he is having a hard time and whether he is
the only one in his class having a hard time with it? Do you
know whether the teacher is giving assignments that no one
can complete? Have you ever spoken to the parent of another
child in the same class to find out how things are going? Is
your child the only one who seems to take six hours every
day to do homework *with* your help? When you know what is
really going on with your child, you can help him.

If your child is bored in school and needs extra challenges,
provide workshops for him, after-school activity groups, or
whatever it takes. If he needs a break, lighten his load a bit.
If he needs tutoring, get him a tutor. You have to know your

child's needs because it is your job as a parent to respond to those needs. No one else will do it.

B. Smile, Now

What do we do when a child is not and cannot be a good student in school? We've said that parents must help their children do well in school, but the goal should be to help children feel comfortable in the classroom, not necessarily to help them become high achievers. The object is for them to be satisfied with their own achievement level and to become self-motivated to go beyond. Don't forget, we are dealing with a system.

I have mentioned that I have a son who had a serious learning disability. When he was in seventh grade, I decided that it was crucial to his well-being that I speak with one of his teachers.

"Listen," I said. "Do me a favor. Please be nice to my child. As his father I absolve you of the responsibility to teach him your subject. You are my shaliach. I appreciate the fact that you're trying to help me teach my child the things that I can't teach him. That's why I send him to school. I'm asking you to change your shelichus, change the task that you are trying to accomplish for me. I am asking you to modify it slightly for my child.

"Do you know what I'd like you to do? If you can, I want you to smile at him. I want you to give him a pat on his shoulder during recess, and I want you to say that you appreciate that he's trying. I don't care if he gets a zero on every test. You're helping me, because you want to teach my child. You're my shaliach. My child is dealing right now with four other subjects that are more important. Your subject, as important as it is for every other child in the class, is not important for my child. I can take him out of your class if you insist. If he bothers you and you do not want him to come to your class, I will understand. But I'm telling you that he won't bother you if you are nice to him. Because if you are nice to him, you will become his friend.

"Children don't act up with people who are nice to them. Children annoy people who are mean to them. Leave him alone. From now on I'm assuming the respon-

sibility if he gets a zero. I am not worried about his report card, and I'm not worried about his transcript. The only thing that worries me is whether he likes school and is comfortable here. Can you help me with that?"

"All right," answered the teacher, "I can handle that. If you tell me that you don't mind if he gets a zero, there's no problem."

This was a teacher who is known as a real tiger, in the positive sense. Every child had to do well in his class. In his opinion, he taught very important subjects. Objectively, they *were* important subjects. But for my child at that point in his life, they weren't the most important subjects. As a result of parental intervention, this teacher and my son have retained a wonderful relationship until today. When they see each other they greet each other warmly.

Your child doesn't have to do objectively well; he has to do as well as he can. Your child has to be happy in school. If you can help him progress, then do so. If he needs tutoring and that is what will help, get him a tutor. If you can't arrange for a tutor and he can't understand algebra, then accept him and love him even though he can't do algebra. Not knowing algebra doesn't make him a bad person. We have to make our children feel happy and comfortable in school.

C. How Is My Child?

In one of the "best" yeshivos gedolos in Eretz Yisrael there are over fifty young men in a shiur. Hundreds of boys want to come to that yeshivah, but the yeshivah accepts only the "best of the best" of them.

"Tell me something," I once asked a rebbe. "Do you know how each boy in your shiur is doing?"

"No way. Not a chance," he said.

"What should a parent do if he wants to know how his seventeen- or eighteen-year-old son is doing, and he is not the expressive type?"

"I'll tell you," he answered. "There are a few bachurim I know. I know the bachurim who persevere, the ones

who come up to me afterward and talk to me in learning, who ask questions and speak up in shiur. I know them.

"I also know one other type of bachur. I know the student whose father calls me once in a while and says, 'Shalom aleichem. How's my son doing?' You know what happens the first time he calls? I say, 'Oh, nice boy, sure, yes. Would you mind calling me back tomorrow so we can talk more about it? I'm a little bit busy now.' Since I know the father is going to call me, I make sure to notice the boy the next day and see where he is holding. I can't know what's happening with fifty boys — it's physically impossible. But from then on I make sure that I know what's happening with that child. I know the bachurim whose parents call me. I make it my business to know what's going on with their sons because I'm going to be asked to report on it."

If you know how your child is doing and the teacher knows that you know, then you have a chance of making a good decision in the child's behalf. I don't say it's easy, but it *is* your responsibility.

D. Parents and Values

The greatest teachers will never have as much impact on a child as his parents *can* have. We hope that the values our children learn in school conform somewhat to our own, but we should never for a moment think that it is the school's responsibility to impart those values. To reiterate, values are transmitted in the home. Perhaps there will be one individual teacher whose love and commitment can teach a child some good values, but that teacher is no different from a good neighbor, an uncle, a cousin, or a friend: it's chancy. You don't rely on others to give your child the *chinuch* you want him to have. The primary responsibility of the school is to impart information, which of course should be done by teachers who are exemplary. Even in those schools where all of these good lessons do take place, it cannot be taken for granted.

Love for another Jew, self-discipline, kindness, and self-control are all things our children should learn from us. We try to send our children to a good school with other "good" children, yet unfortunately we still hear occasional horror stories from our children about how a certain child reacted to a particular situation and how detrimental it was to everyone in the class. Not everything that's important to us is as important to everyone we know, including neighbors. We are often amazed to find that a close friend teaches his children absolutely nothing about *derech eretz*, or the meaning and value of money, or respect for other people's property. Neighbors may be very nice people with whom we have many things in common; we consider them friends, but we don't really know what goes on in their homes. We know very little about how their children, who go to school with our children, are being taught to respond in different situations. Never for a moment should we fool ourselves and say, "Okay, I send my son to a good yeshivah, I send my daughter to a great Bais Yaakov, so I don't have to worry about their behavior regarding *middos, derech eretz*, or *kibud av va'em*," because this is not true. *If parents don't teach Torah values to their children, the children may never internalize those values the parents deem most important.*

E. Be Aware

We have to be aware. If we don't know what is going on in our child's life at any stage, then when a crisis occurs it may well be too late to help him. School is a very complex institution, which involves four types of people: the principal, the teachers, the children, and the parents. Each has different needs and a different perspective. When our child comes home from school, we ask him how his day went.

"Oh, I had a great day in school today."

"Are you sure? You look a little unsettled."

"No, it was a great day. We had fun."

An hour earlier, however, we had received a call from his teacher saying that our son had turned the entire class upside down. He was totally disruptive, even poured water on the *rebbe's* head, and pinched three boys. Wait a minute! The child said he had a good day. We're confused, so we call up the principal.

"Hello, is everything okay?"

The principal answers, "Yes, sure. We have had some ups and downs, but in general things are under control."

We are left with three different reports on the school day, and we don't know what to think. The strange part is that everyone is telling the truth. The child had a great day in school. It was so funny to see how the other boys jumped when he pinched them. The *rebbe* became hysterical when the boys poured water on his head and it dripped down into his beard, and the whole class was in chaos because the *rebbe* lost control and couldn't concentrate on the lesson. The child had a great day in school. He didn't lie.

The *rebbe* didn't lie either. He had a horrible day in school. This child made everyone crazy, was totally disruptive and disrespectful, and the *rebbe* doesn't know what to do about it. He is at his wit's end.

The principal has a lot of experience. He knows that children have good days and bad days. Maybe the *rebbe* was tired, so there were ups and downs. It's not so terrible. Things have been worse. (The boys could have poured glue in the *rebbe's* beard instead of water!)

If this sort of thing is confusing to us, it's because we're not in touch with our child's progress, or lack of it. Let's be practical. We have to keep in close contact not only with the teachers, but with the principal as well, because he decides policy and makes decisions in the school. Everyone needs to feel appreciated, and a principal who catches flak from students, parents, teachers, and the Board of Directors, is certainly no exception.

◄ɑ *Parent-Principal-Teacher Dynamics*

Most parents are quick to criticize and not always constructively, but few schools are all bad. Most principals welcome a few words of appreciation for their efforts. Maintenance, for example, requires a great effort on the part of the principal. On a difficult day, a little positive feedback might make a difference:

"It was such a pleasure to walk in today and see the school looking so clean."

"The boys sang so beautifully at the *Melaveh Malkah*. The *rebbeim* are obviously inspiring them to appreciate spiritual values."

"My son says that his math teacher is much more patient lately, and it's easier for him to understand the lessons. I'm sure it was your intervention that accomplished this." A pat on the back can go a long way.

How often do we go to school and offer to help in some way? We may not have money to donate, but a school has many needs: making phone calls, tutoring a weak student, chaperoning a class trip, helping to collate a mailing, organizing school functions, decorating a classroom or the halls. It gives the school staff a lift to see parents caring enough about their children's school to donate their time occasionally.

Parents who show recognition that the principal is doing his or her best despite being beset by many problems have earned the right to give constructive criticism. When such parents approach the principal with a problem, they have a much better chance of having their requests complied with than those who only criticize.

> *I once had the unfortunate experience of hearing a principal reply to a suggestion that she take a psychologist onto her staff for a few hours a week. "Why should I look under the floorboards for problems?" she answered. Any principal with eight hundred pupils who thinks that she needs to look under the floorboards to find problems that a psychologist could deal with has obviously been hiding under those same boards.*
>
> *That particular principal, who even fought against P'TACH being brought into the school (due to the foolish and backward thought that it would give the school a bad name), was very helpful when it came time to assist certain parents who had been supportive of her on other occasions.*

Any educator, whatever his qualifications, will work better with people who have worked well with him. This is to be expected, and it is particularly applicable to principals because they want their system to run smoothly. Principals whose motto might well be, "Don't rock the boat," because of the many problems inherent in administering a school, also can be worked with. If a principal who is considered somewhat less than competent faces new problems, he will be more likely to cooperate with the parents who have been supportive in the past and who he thinks are "reasonable."

A. Communicating with Teachers

Teachers need positive input and good feedback. Knowing that parents trust them will inspire them to do a better job, but how will they know that if we don't tell them?

Even in the worst-case scenario, where a less competent teacher really does not like your child and is picking on him and embarrassing him, there is a positive way to speak to that teacher.

"You know, Morah (or *Rebbe*, where applicable), I see that my child is somewhat unhappy, but I have no idea why. Can you think of any reason for it?"

She may not wish to tell you that she has long since lost patience with your daughter and has been virtually ignoring her, except for scolding her and sending her out of the room. Now that the teacher feels that you value her opinion, she'll try to think about what is making the child unhappy enough to act out. She will try to rectify the situation because it is now her job to find out why the child is unhappy.

A teacher may say, "Of course she's unhappy; do you know what happened?"

"No, please tell me. Oh, did my child do that? I'll speak to her. Do you have any suggestions about how I should bring up the subject?"

At that point even the most thoughtless teacher is forced to stop for a minute and think of an approach, because she knows that she can't just tell you to punish your daughter. She has to come up with something more intelligent than that, and she'll try.

This is one way we can become active partners in helping the teacher help our child. From personal experience I
can tell you that even incompetent teachers have helped a
child of mine who had great difficulty in a certain area to get
through the year comfortably. This method succeeded only
because there was constant contact, questioning, and discussion. In some cases, the teachers' answers were not at all
pertinent, but if *we* know our child's needs, we can help guide
even a poor teacher (unfortunately they do exist) to help our
reluctant student survive and even thrive in school.

B. Making a Difference

If there are enough parents out there asking questions and
making decisions based on a school's commitment to understanding individuals and monitoring the progress of its students, the schools will make an effort to respond to problems
and even to make changes to accommodate our needs. The
administrators and staff in our schools want to do the best
they can, but as in any market, demand creates the motivation to supply that which customers request.

Years ago, when I was running a yeshivah for young men
who previously hadn't been successful in their studies, my
oldest son had just finished elementary school. In the course
of checking out *yeshivos ketanos*, high schools, for him, I had
an experience with a *rebbe* at a school I was observing that
clearly demonstrates this process of accommodation.

> *"Tell me about your yeshivah," I said to the rebbe. He
> started telling me about the standards, the policies, the
> background, and so on.*
>
> *"Of course," he suddenly interrupted the flow, "I
> have to say that we provide individual attention to our
> bachurim." He immediately "clarified" his meaning: "Not
> that the children need it ... [as if to say, "Naturally the
> children who come here don't need individual atten-
> tion"], I just have to say that, because today if you don't
> claim that your yeshivah gives individual attention,
> you're not in the running."*

I was elated to hear that a high-achieving school in a competitive society felt the need to at least acknowledge that individual attention is important. This is the beginning of a "market change" caused by greater concern on the part of more and more parents that their child receive individual attention.

It is a mistake to think that children, even and especially the better students, don't need individual attention. Why shouldn't the child who is easy, likes to learn, gets good marks, and has fine *middos*, not receive individual attention? Why shouldn't a caring *rebbe* notice such a student? It's a special opportunity for the *rebbe* to make a significant impact on a student's life and take him to new heights that he would not have realized on his own. It is a real loss and a shame if the *rebbe* doesn't give extra time and attention to the "easy" students in his class as well.

Schools will begin to realize that they have to answer to the demands and expectations of the parents when parents go to the schools and start asking the questions that need to be asked. Little by little this is already happening. In *Eretz Yisrael*, we have a huge school system and it is growing exponentially. The number of kids in eighth grade going into secondary schools shows an overall growth rate of 200 percent over the last fifteen years. More recently, the rate has risen to something like 20 percent a year, *bli ayin hara*! It can be compared to the awesome population increase when the Jews lived in *Mitzrayim* (Egypt). That means we have to increase the number of schools and teachers in our system, and upgrade the quality of the environment to provide for all these new students. This is a great challenge, but our community, which has successfully risen to almost impossible challenges until now and maintained a high level of professionalism in its school systems, will *b'ezras Hashem* come through yet again. Yes, the system has limitations and there are problems, but overall our schools are producing a high percentage of happy, *frum*, well-adjusted children who want to do right in the eyes of Hashem. As parents, we find it hard to accept when any of our children do not fall into that percentage, but accept it we must. And we must work within the system to ameliorate the situation. The people who administer our children's schools today are doing their best against overwhelming odds. We parents have to assume our responsibility and do all we can to contribute to the continued growth and development of our children's schools.

◀ Don't Wait!

Learning to read and to write is a critical stage in your child's life.[4] If you face up to problems he or she encounters in the lower grades, you will be making a difference for a lifetime. Trying to help adolescents overcome deficiencies that should have been dealt with earlier is not only expensive and time consuming, but often in the end — after much difficulty, disappointment, and pain — help is ineffectual. Try to remember three things as your child begins his formal education:

1) observe carefully how he is developing;
2) analyze his particular needs; and
3) if necessary, get help.

Try to be aware of everything that's happening in school. Be a concerned parent, not an alarmist, and if your child is having difficulty, don't brush it off. If the *rebbe* says soothingly, "Never mind, some children have a harder time in the beginning than others — he'll probably do much better in two months," this is often true and you should give an experienced *rebbe* your confidence, but don't be complacent. Follow up on it. If the child doesn't improve in two months, don't waste any more time. You are the one who has to find out where the child's difficulty lies.

The next critical stage in a child's formal education occurs when he is introduced to abstract thinking, such as that required by Gemara study or reading comprehension. This

---

4. Important Note: In some schools, reading begins at three-and-a-half to four years old, but many children are not ready to read before the age of five or six. It is wise to hold such a child back one year before he reaches first grade.

generally takes place around the same age in both boys' and girls' schools, usually in the fourth or fifth grade. These transitions can be very challenging. Help your son understand that studying Gemara opens up a new and difficult learning process for him, and that it will take time to get used to. Monitor his work during this significant change in his studies. If you see that his grades are suddenly lower, help him as much as you can, and if he needs extra help, do not hesitate to hire a good tutor.

It is a sad fact that because of difficulties encountered when they first began to study Gemara and the sense of failure that accompanied those difficulties, some teenage boys still think of learning our most precious treasure as a foreign, noxious, and bitter memory they'd prefer to forget. Parents may be aware of the sudden deterioration of their child's marks, but they're likely to imagine it is the fault of a bad teacher.

If your child is having a hard time with his studies at the age of fifteen, and you now remember that he has been having trouble since he was ten or eleven, you have not been sufficiently in touch with his education. You have to respond immediately to the problem — get him the help he needs immediately. It may be expensive, but it's extremely inexpensive compared to the difficulties that can arise at an even later stage if the problem is not dealt with right away.

◄₰ *Rising to the Occasion*

We have made a number of suggestions to help parents assume the great responsibility of educating their children. Some readers may feel they are personally unable to implement all of them, but there are various steps that can be taken to remedy the situation. Maybe we ourselves didn't learn Gemara, or maybe we didn't have the *geshmak* and motivation in learning we'd like our children to have, so naturally we don't know how we're going to give them that pleasure, that good taste from learning Torah. Maybe we want to give our children a certain kind of *chinuch* that goes with a certain path in life that we have chosen, even though we ourselves don't have that background. Some of us grew up without any experience of a life filled with Torah and mitzvos. If so, it is extremely difficult to transmit the excitement for Torah learning that we would dearly love our children to feel.

If we can't learn with our children, what should we do? I have a friend who became observant late in life and has still not acquired some of the basics, although he's learning all the time and getting stronger and living the life of a *ben Torah*. He did something smart. He hired a yeshivah or *kollel* student for *each one* of his children to make sure that none will be as lacking in knowledge and skills as he was. "I can't learn with my children every day and I can't even ascertain how well they are doing with their schoolwork, but I want them to go to a school that reflects the kind of life I am presently living. I'm living up to the standards of the school, even though I don't have the background." This dedicated father found a way to compensate.

We must become partners in the efforts that our schools are making in order for them to succeed in their education. This does not give us the mandate to criticize and demand that teachers and principals do whatever we think should be done. It does place upon us the enormous responsibility of becoming educated consumers so that we can become realistic partners in this process. The school system as it stands today is the product of the impossible superhuman effort of thousands of wonderful people who have dedicated their lives to making it what it is today. Hashem has shone His providence on our community and has helped those dedicated individuals to achieve the standards as they are. As parents, we must do everything we can to help those principals, teachers, and community-minded laymen to continue in their, holy work, bringing Torah and *derech eretz* to our children.

By evaluating schools and schooling with that understanding, we will, with Hashem's help, achieve our goal.

Chapter Sixteen

SELECTING A HIGH SCHOOL

T he primary criterion in choosing the right high school for our child should be the learning environment that it offers and in addition, it should be one where he will succeed. (Obviously, of course, the school must have a strong Torah *hashkafah,* foster *yiras Shamayim,* and have parent and student bodies that do not contradict Torah values.) We may hope that the school will also provide inspiration and a framework in which our child will be happy, do well, and feel good about himself. These are all excellent aspirations, and we should certainly try to fulfill each of them. But first and foremost, the school must be a place of learning.

⥲ Success in School

Most people define success based on some thought of how their child is doing relative to his peers. A "successful" person in our society is one who does better than others. A successful businessman is the one who does better business than someone else; a successful singer is one who sells more CDs; and a successful teacher is the one in whose class everyone wants to be. This means that success is relative and that it applies only within the relevant subject or field.

In the field of *chinuch*, in the education of our children, the correct evaluation is that the successful child is one who does well relative only to himself. In my opinion, the child who progresses and develops into an individual who can achieve — on his own — the highest level he is capable of, that child has succeeded. Furthermore, I would call his "standing" among others irrelevant to that success. Unfortunately, we cannot accept this because we live in a success-oriented society, and a student's failure to keep pace with the rest of the class will damage his self-esteem. Our children are judged by the schools they go to, by the grades they receive, and by what they do when they finish school. They are judged by how much money they are likely to earn and by many other standards that most of us mistakenly define as success.

Today high schools have taken on the task of preparing our children to take their place in society. Our schools were originally intended to take the place of parents in teaching Torah. Today many other skills need to be taught, and many of our schools have developed into vehicles that prepare children to earn a living. Girls may start thinking about what profession to follow and, depending on the country and the school system, boys may also be encouraged to begin thinking about these things in high school. School has become a place of achievement rather than a place of learning.

There is a broader variety in the high school system for boys than for girls. Even a cursory glance at the Torah Umesorah list[1] of high schools in the United States and Canada will show that in the major cities there are many more than double the number of high schools for boys than for girls. In Yerushalayim, there are fifty-six high schools for boys and and six for girls. A greater number of schools produces a greater variety, and variety allows us a greater flexibility in choosing the most appropriate school. The smaller number of girls' schools places the parents of girls at a disadvantage. If all the girls go to the same school because there

---

1. Torah Umesorah list of day schools in North America.

is no alternative, the larger the schools, the less variety, and the fewer options reduce the likelihood that every child will find her place and gain something in it. In addition, the larger and more crowded the classes, the harder it becomes to find good teachers; the fewer good teachers, the less individual attention students receive.

◆઱ The High School that Suits You

The first component of your decision in selecting a school for your child should be to define who *you* are. You will not want to send him to a school that is going to be at odds with your persona, the way you present yourself and the way you perceive yourself. That which is important to you and that which you emphasize or de-emphasize in your life are all part of who you are. Then you have to define what you want for your child and what you want him to achieve. These are the two basic considerations on which to base your choice of school.

If you can't speak Yiddish, does it make sense to send your child to a Yiddish-speaking school just because it is stricter in observance, more *frum* than another school? If you are not going to be able to study with your child because of the language barrier, is that an intelligent decision? Is it smart to send a child to a school based on secondhand information, without finding out whether or not the school is suitable?

Sometimes it is not so simple. If you live in an area where you are different from your neighbors and the school's approach is not what you would ideally choose, but your options are limited, what can you do? Let us say you are a recent *ba'al teshuvah* still defining your place in the community and you are sending your child to a Bais Yaakov or to a Talmud Torah. Or you are an American but you are living in *Eretz Yisrael.* Or you are an Israeli and you are living in America. Or you have a yeshivah background and for any number of reasons, you live out of town where there is only one local school and it does not meet the standards of your home. What should you do?

Think about it before you make a decision. You may be required to make personal adjustments. The adjustments might have to include a compromise in your lifestyle. The adjustments might involve walking your child through a culture that is different from your own, as in the very common case with *ba'alei teshuvah*. You might have to acquire a support system to help you help your children. It is possible to live up to the higher standards of a school, even though you do not have the background for it. These are not negative adjustments, and perhaps you look forward to "fitting in" and making them. The point is that if differences do exist, you must take them into consideration. You have to look for a school that you will be comfortable with — even though the differences may be stark.

A. Evaluate the Standards

It is essential not to be at odds with your child's school. I will begin with a very strong example of this concept which actually applies to any move from community to community, as we will explain. Do you know how many American or other English-speaking children whose parents have brought them to live in *Eretz Yisrael* are in the highest risk group? I can state unequivocally that there, English-speaking children comprise the highest-risk group per capita in the *frum* community. Within that group, the children of *ba'alei teshuvah* are an even higher-risk group. Many English-speaking immigrants move to *Eretz Yisrael* for idealistic reasons. We come to *Eretz Yisrael* because we want to live up to higher ideals and standards, because we love it, because we feel closely connected to it, because we learned about it, or because we enjoyed a few years of living here. We saw that in *Eretz Yisrael* we thrived on the *ruchnius*; our spiritual life was on a higher level. The question is, are we ready to meet the standards of *Eretz Yisrael* when we relocate? There are differences in standards of *tzenius*, modesty, and there are different standards of success. There are differences in the way respect and honor are accorded, and there are differences in speech, dress, and food. The places we go and the things we do are not the same in *Eretz Yisrael* as elsewhere. It is a different culture. Many people will move from the big cities to the more "out of town" communities with the hope of achieving a more relaxed and "open" environment. You must be aware that with that openness comes different levels and forms of observance all mixed in one class. Some people want to move from "out of town" to the larger cities with the same intentions of those moving to *Eretz Yisrael*, which brings with the move myriad demands of big city schools.

B. Making Concessions

So we want to raise our children in *the new home setting*. But do we expect to raise our children as we always did in our previous home, or do we want to raise them to be like all the other children growing up in *our new community*? If we choose the latter, then we must be ready and willing to make concessions. We cannot constantly be at odds with our new society. We should not criticize the system and we should not be angry, bitter, and upset at the fact that we are not accepted because of the way we speak, dress, or act, or because of the places we go. Remember, you made a decision to move to a place that has different standards. Are you ready to meet those standards?

Know yourself. Your children do not *have* to be raised as "New Yorkers." You may have limitations that make it difficult to raise your children as such. For example, if neither parent can speak or understand Hebrew text fluently, and the school your children have always gone to had very little textual work, what type of school will be best for your children? Are you going to look for a school that will understand your child and know where he is coming from? If and when conflicts arise, will there be someone on the staff who will know how to deal with them? Is there someone in the school to whom you can speak? Are you going to look for the best-rated school, or are you going to look for the best school for your child? You must ask, "What is good for me? What is good for my child?" If you recognize your limitations and find your child a tutor who is connected to the school, this indicates that you understand your situation.

Rav Shlomo Zalman Auerbach proposed a rule that has been a beacon of light for me in understanding how to choose the right high school for a child.

> Chazal tell us[2] that "you should prefer to be the tail of a lion rather than the head of a fox." This means, Rav Auerbach said, that "when you choose a place to be, you should choose a place where you are at the bottom, where you can look up and strive, where you can look up and be inspired, where you can look up and aspire to be more."
>
> "But," Rav Auerbach added, "this Chazal is advice to adults, not to a child entering high school."

Thirteen-year-olds have to feel good about themselves. This is a point that bears repeating. They need a school where they feel comfortable and accepted, not where they are at the bottom. Do not place your child at the bottom of the barrel in order that he should strive and want to achieve more. He is not going to want to. He might just give up. Place your child in a school where he will do well and feel good about himself. Your son should be in a class where he will be able to participate, where he can speak up, where he has a place in the *beis midrash,* where he will have compatible learning partners. Your daughter should be in a class where she will have a place in the *chevrah*, in the group, and also be able to keep up with the work.

People spend a lot of time, money, and effort pushing to get their children into schools. They want them to be in the "best school," and they want their children to have the best name there, and they destroy their children in the process. The "best" school is not necessarily the best place for their child. Maybe the work is too hard. If the work is too hard and he cannot keep up, what is gained? He will be in the best high school, but he is also going to be frustrated, angry, and upset.

---

2. *Pirkei Avos* 4:20.

He will not do well. He is going to feel that he is at the bottom. What do we accomplish by getting our children into the best school? Are you satisfied that he is in a good environment? A good environment is only a good environment if a child feels at peace with it and in it. But if the child feels that he does not belong, if he feels rejected and does not have a *chavrusa*, a study partner, the good environment does nothing for him. When friends are studying together and our child is always the one who is left out, the good environment is not helpful to him. When he is at odds with his environment, he is going to fight it. We worked so hard and used all the *protektzia* in the world to get him into the best school, and the child does not do well because he does not belong in the best school. *He belongs in the school that is best for him.*

C. Who's Better?

> My father established and heads a high school in Monsey, New York. It is a school for students who did not do well in elementary school. A young girl came in with her mother for an interview. This mother looked the children over and said, "You know, many children here are not as 'good' as my daughter. I do not know if I want my daughter to study here."
>
> "I agree with you," my father said. "I understand. But in that case, every girl who's 'better' than your daughter would then leave the school."
>
> "Why? What do you mean?"
>
> "Well, if your daughter is not as 'good' as they, why should they stay in school with your daughter?"

This business of being "better" works both ways. You need to find the place where your son or daughter can do well. Children have needs, and there are children who need to be in a place where not everyone is going to be a *Rosh Yeshivah* or *Rebbetzin*. Your child can be in a school where not every child is an achiever and a star pupil, because your child is not either. What are we afraid of here? Are we afraid that it is not a good environment? Are children growing in that school? Are they doing well there? Check and see whether the school is graduating children who do well afterwards and advance to the next level successfully. Are the girls getting into seminaries? Are the boys getting into *yeshivos gedolos*? If they are, then perhaps that school can help your child. That school will understand your child and work with him. Yes, there will be children who may seem to do worse than yours. There will also be children who seem to do better. We must be honest about where our child belongs and realistic as to what is best for him or her.

I once met with the former treasurer of Israel, Dr. Moshe Mandelbaum. At one point during our meeting he said, "Do you know what I like about Israel? If you know the right people you do not need *protektzia.*" We live in a world where everything seems to work with connections. Teachers are sometimes hired with *protektzia* and even children are at times accepted with *protektzia.*

In the yeshivah I once headed, you did not really need too much *protektzia* to get in; you just needed to need to get in. We had one child who came from a very, very "c*hashuv* Israeli family" — really distinguished people. A journalist came to check out the school, knowing that our students came from many walks of life. He was curious and asked one of the boys how he came to be in this school. The student he asked happened to be the son of these distinguished people. The child blithely answered, "*Protektzia!*" He was so used to hearing how things worked in his environment that he felt this was the most prestigious answer he could give.

D. A School that Wants My Child

When my son is ready to enter *yeshivah ketanah* (secondary school), I want to find a school that wants my son. What do I want for my son? I want him to go to a secondary school. Now, there are nearly sixty high schools, or *yeshivos ketanos,* in Yerushalayim, and among them there are schools that want only the highest achievers and the most brilliant learners. There are also schools that are interested in every child, and some that take anyone they can get because they are perceived as having little to offer. There are even schools that want the children that do not do well, because they cater to them. These schools are important and often very unusual.

One child of mine does relatively well, *baruch Hashem*, and I did not want to send him to a place where I would have to force his way in because of their reluctance to accept him. If a school does not want a child, how will they treat him? If they finally accept him but do not really want him, what will they be able to do for him? I wanted a school that says, "We want this child. Give us the child. Can we have him?" That's the kind of place I wanted for my son.

Yes, I want a school that is the best school I can find to help build my child. I do not want him to go to a place that does not want him, because if he does, he almost surely will *not* succeed. But I know something about my child that no one else knows. I know that my child has a certain difficulty, but is overcoming it. I know he does not do very well in school because of that difficulty, so I have to be careful which school I choose. But I see that he is rising to the challenge, and I know that he is ready to take the next step. The school may not see this because his marks are not that great. They look at his fifth, sixth, seventh, and eighth grade report cards; they call my neighbors, uncles, and cousins. They do a case study on him before he even gets to the entrance exam. They think they know more about him than I do and may possibly decide that he is not good enough for their school. Finally, I spoke to the director of a school in which another one of my children, one who is a high achiever, did very well. The staff spent time with the younger boy and with me, and finally they said, "With this kind of motivation it is easy to overlook his report card. We want him!" *Baruch Hashem*, they did not regret it. This boy moved on to finishing *mesechtos* with real understanding and clarity.

A parent can fight for a child like that. You believe in him and know that he can do well. You know he is prepared to work hard. You can try to push him into a particular school and try it out, on the condition that they recognize the true situation. You must not pretend that there is no difficulty.

You must not pretend that everything is fine and that you are doing them a favor. Speak to them openly about the problem and see if they are *mechanchim*, educators who are interested in joining you in meeting the challenge to educate your child. If not, do not send him to that school. If you do, it will be a dismal failure. And who will be to blame? Only you, the parents, because you were looking for a school of which you would be proud to say, "My son is learning there." Be proud of your son and daughter no matter where they are learning. Your children know when you are proud of them. When you are proud of them, they have reason to be proud of themselves. When you are not proud of your child, he has no reason to be proud of himself. You must look for the school that will relate to your child as he is.

E. Shopping for a School

What do you do before you buy a car? You figure out exactly what you need, right? How much seating and trunk space you require, how expensive the insurance will be, what mileage you will get on a gallon of gas, how much upkeep and maintenance will cost, and so on. This is a big decision and a serious expense. You take your time checking the figures and then you ask for advice. Let's say you speak to several friends, but none of them can help you because they all have needs that are different from yours. One of them commutes an hour and a half every day, while you need the car more for local transportation. One of them has a family much larger than yours, and another has no financial limitations. None of you are dealing with the same issues. Finally you go to a good car mechanic and you say, "These are my needs. Tell me what will suit me best."

When you are thinking about where to send your child to school, speak to people who have children similar to yours. Speak to families that are similar to yours. Find out where their children are accepted and how they and their children feel about their *rebbeim* and about the school. Find out how the *rebbeim* feel about them. How are they and their children treated? Do you have a child that you will send to school with some trepidation? Well, before you send such a child to a particular school, find out what happens to the children who do not do so well in that school. Is it a school that immediately throws them out if they have setbacks, or does the school work with them? Find out what a school does when a child misbehaves or does not keep up. Do they come down hard on him, or do they sit down and talk to him? Do they work with the parents? Look into these questions, because they are important.

As much as you would research alternatives before investing in a car, you should do no less before investing in four years of your child's life — and they are four formative years. When your child goes off to high school, he is a cute kid. When he leaves high school, he is taller than you. In early adolescence most children are still cute; they are still small and impressionable and you can do so much with them. In late adolescence, at eighteen or nineteen, they know what they want. They have their own ideas and often they are not interested in your ideas. You want them to spend their four formative years in the school that is best for *them*. If you do not know how to do the necessary research, bring your child to a *mechanech*, to an educator, who can assess his needs and abilities.

◄₰ A Good Student Deserves a Good School

You can ask your child what he wants. Try to find him a school he wants to attend, depending, of course, on his abilities. Children usually want to go to a good school and they want to do well. If his expectations are not in sync with his abilities, you have to show him that you tried to help him get into the school of his choice, but it did not work out. Then you can find a more suitable institution. You must support him in a search for an alternative that might not be as exciting, but where he can do well. A child who wants to get into a good school will not make problems. But you must support him and try to assist him in achieving his goal. Be sure you consider more than one school with a similar orientation so that you can keep the options open until you check them out. It is sad but true that a small minority of *rebbeim* who are meant to help you make this big decision are concerned with how they will look if the boys do not get into the "best" schools, which contributes to them choosing the wrong schools for children. You must also be aware that some schools that have "sterling reputations" push children too hard. Take all this into consideration.

◄ᢒ *Fix the Bridge!*

Once your child is attending a school, communicate with his teachers. This is not the first time I have mentioned the importance of speaking with teachers and principals. I know some people who do not talk to their child's *rebbe* because they think the *rebbe* is biased. So what? Speak with his *rebbe*; hear what he has to say, bias or no bias. Meet with your child's teacher and find out what he thinks is good for the child. Maybe he/she knows something about your child that you do not. Ideally, it should not be that way, but it could happen. Hear him/her out; ask questions. Go to see the school. Watch what goes on in the school and in the classroom. Are you happy with what you see? If you are not, is there an alternative with which you would be happier? Be realistic. What is it that you really want? Our children deserve our participation in their lives. Our children will do much better if we are honest with ourselves about who we are and who they are, and if we find a school that will acknowledge them as they are.

Once, while I was the head of the yeshivah, I saw a picture that I would have loved to have hanging on the wall of my office. It was a picture of a bridge, a large bridge. In the center of one of the traffic lanes on the bridge was a hole; cars were falling through the hole. Under the bridge, on a nearby island, stood a building with a large sign reading, "This is the site of a new hospital for the victims of accidents from the bridge."

Ribbono shel Olam! Fix the bridge!

I say this with *tza'ar*, with great sorrow. I have met literally hundreds of children whom I could not help within the
dynamics of the school. It was as if someone had taken some
vases and dropped them from the eighth floor of a building,
smashing them to smithereens. The parents then came to me
with all the broken pieces and pleaded, "Rabbi Greenwald,
please, can you put them back together?"

Why put your child where he does not belong in the first
place? Why not look at what is good for your child? Why not
be realistic? Unfortunately, accidents happen even on bridges
that do not have holes. But why create the misfortune? Why
drive in the wrong lane? Why drive a hundred miles an hour
in a lane that has a gaping hole in it? Move over, there are
other lanes. There are other tracks. If I had that picture in
my office, I would tell people that I built the school to fix
the bridge, not the victims. There is another track, there is
another way. Bring the child here to begin with. Do not bring
him to me after he has been destroyed, after he is distraught
and has given up. Do not bring him here when he no longer
wants to learn and does not trust anyone anymore.

When choosing a school for your child, it is most important
that you be honest, that you know each of your children and
work with them as individuals to optimize their experiences
in the school that is best for them. This means realistically
assessing your child's level, capability, and, most important,
motivation. Then choose the school that is right for him.

◄₰ Americans Living in Israel

The issue of learning in a school with a secular program
does not arise in North America and England, because it
is a different culture and a different society from that of
Eretz Yisrael. For one thing, often a *frum* child receives a
high school diploma in the United States and Canada. In
Eretz Yisrael this is not the norm in all communities. Thus
the issue must be dealt with on an individual basis. There
are some distinguished scholars, *talmidei chachamim*, who

instruct their questioners to send a child to a school not considered the norm. You may have to deal with this issue with a specific child.

Americans living in Israel have additional concerns. Some families might feel the need to consider options other than the traditional Bais Yaakov schools or the *yeshivos ketanos* that are available in Israel, even though they may have sent their children to that type of school before they made *aliyah*. If you feel the standard school does not meet your needs, you might consider:

1) high school that is somewhat different from the one your child is used to attending;
2) yeshivah high school abroad, as a last resort.

A. A Different Type of High School

If you want to place your child in a specific learning program different from the one he was used to abroad or different from that of his friends in Israel, you will have to explain your reasoning to your son or daughter. If it is he who initiates the change to a different learning environment, you will likewise want to find out his reasoning.

Talk it over together. His reasons may not be good enough for you to agree, but they are probably good enough to hear him out. Once you hear his reasoning, you can address the weak points in it and the reservations you may have about the difficulties and challenges he may encounter in maintaining a certain level of *Yiddishkeit* in a different learning environment. You will want to emphasize that you know he himself wants to maintain his standards because you know what a great boy he is. You know that he is a special person and therefore he will not want to place himself in a situation that will test him. You know that he is a special boy, so you will ask him what he will do about friends, Shabbos, *Yamim Tovim* and other things that concern you. (The reservations we mentioned earlier in this book about a certain boy going to America were not inspired by a negative evaluation of American education, but rather by the realization that it was not the right choice for that particular boy. He had to recognize that, and he was not going to recognize it by my calling it a dumb idea.)

In addition to requiring much discussion between you and your child, the issue is significant enough to warrant getting advice from a Rav. Hopefully your Rav is somebody who knows you, who understands where you're coming from, and with whom you can speak comfortably.

In general, schools cannot be rated on a sliding scale. I believe that almost every school is good for someone and every school is *not* good for someone else. There is no such thing as a school that is good for everyone; there is only a school that is good for a certain child. Some children will thrive in the environment of a particular school, while others will not. What do you and your child want him to accomplish with the education he receives?

B. Yeshivah Abroad

Another option, when you and your child are both looking for a different type of school than any that are available in *Eretz Yisrael*, is a yeshivah abroad. This is really a last resort. Before making this decision, try to prepare yourself and the child for the differences he will encounter in the local options. You will have to try to get him excited about spending a year or two in a school that is good for him, that will teach him at his own level, whose *rebbeim* will care about him and invest in him. See if you can implant that idea in his mind, but before you make a final decision, see if there is a local program that he will be happy with. If he does not agree immediately, perhaps you can change his mind. If you are not comfortable with what is available, if sending him abroad is what you want and that's what you think is best for him, only then should you try to interest him in that option.

There are dangers in any educational setting that is not "right" for him.

You also have to consider if you have the financial ability to send him abroad, if that is what you think is best. In addition, you have to consider where he will be when he is not in yeshivah. Every child requires supervision — something he may lack overseas. You cannot assume he is out of danger just because he is out of sight. A child left with a brother-in-law's brother, or with an elderly Bubby or Zeidy, may well end up with a truly disturbing lack of supervision. I have witnessed too many youngsters living away from home who have seriously foundered because there was no one there for them in a foreign country.

On the other hand, there have been many success stories with those who really have close, smart, and caring relatives where the child feels at home. In general, the best thing to do with a boy who does not fit into the system in *Eretz Yisrael* is to work with him one year at a time. Promise him that he is never going to be forced to stay in a place he does not like, and assure him that the decisions and options are his. If the option of sending him abroad is not open to you, then you will have to seek other options at home.

Try your best to find a yeshivah where the staff will understand him, where there is a little bit more openness, where there are others with similar interests. There are yeshivos, not many perhaps, which exert a bit less pressure than others, where the boys have a little more leeway in time commitments and recreation. It is true that there may be some drawbacks that come with the lower level of motivation usually associated with such a school, but if your son needs to be in a more open yeshivah environment, you can discuss the drawbacks with him and try to prepare him to overcome them. If he is prepared, he will be able to deal with the challenges that await him.

No matter which school we select for our child, he remains our child and we need to do our best to support, help, and encourage him through these challenging years of growth and development.

Chapter Seventeen
TEACHING JUDAISM AND JEWISH VALUES

Jewish values are the essence of our lives. They give our years purpose and meaning apart from our material existence. Imbuing the next generation with these values is a great challenge. A good teacher can explain concepts and transmit information through clear, interesting discussions, but that is not enough. Many books have been written about these values, and we and our children read them, but if we do not do something to absorb and internalize them, they remain mere information that in no way impacts on our lives.

Take the idea of *tzedakah*, giving charity. We have read the sources and know how important it is. In school, our child learns that it is essential, but what does he really learn about the concept in practical terms? At what point is the information internalized? When he sees that his parents respond to a request for *tzedakah* with respect and consideration for the person requesting it, the child learns the proper way to give as well as the value and privilege of giving.

The popular dictum, "Do as I say, not as I do," is a totally self-defeating concept. In Judaism, the significance of an act becomes apparent only by experiencing it, by watching a role model. Children learn by observing their parents' conduct and reactions. They see how their parents give *tzedakah*, they observe how considerate their parents are when asked to give. On the other hand, when children see a close-fisted response, they learn to do the same.

◄ଽ *Torah with Love*

It's not enough that a rule or a value is mentioned in the Torah. The Torah is what we want to teach, but the way we teach it will define whether or not the Torah will have meaning in our children's lives. If our love for the Torah shines through our words, the Torah will be important to them. If we show them real-life examples of a Torah life, with a well-balanced, healthy sense of fear (of disobeying its strictures), then the Torah will be important to them. Sometimes when we try to teach Torah precepts and our children don't do what we want them to, it is our anger, frustration, and bitterness that come through. We must refocus and determine what we are really concerned about. We may find that we are not worried so much about *kavod haTorah*, honoring the Torah, as we are about our own *kavod*, our own honor and pride. We are worried about appearances, about what our actions will look like to others. We may be acting out of disappointment with ourselves. This negativity impacts strongly on the *chinuch* of our children.

The important thing is not how to impress our values on our children, but how we ourselves live those values. If our children are saying to us, "I hear what you're saying, but you don't mean it," then something is wrong. Why do you suppose that a child doesn't believe his parents mean what they're saying? Possibly the child has a negative association connected with the observance of a certain mitzvah. Whether it originated at home or in school, it comes from somewhere. Perhaps we ourselves have a negative image associated with one or more of the mitzvos and, although we certainly do not intend to transmit that negativity to our child, we can see by his attitude that we did.

Intellectually, we understand and profess to believe that it is a mitzvah to love every Jew, to accept everyone as having been created in the image of Hashem and therefore deserving of our respect. When we hear our children speak about other Jews with animosity or disrespect, we're surprised and upset. *Where is he getting it from? I'm an accepting person. I believe in loving every Jew.* Children pick up the finest nuances of our reactions to other people; they register what we praise and what we complain about. No matter how much they learn in principle about loving a fellow Jew and not indulging in causeless hatred, it all flies out the window the first time they hear us say, "Oh those ..."

True values are not taught in school. It is unrealistic to expect that the ideals that children learn in school are going to be real to them. Parents must be proper role models; it is our responsibility. How can we teach our children to love a mitzvah? Well, stop and think. How do we conduct ourselves when the time comes, for example, to prepare for Succos? We can learn a great deal from analyzing our own behavior at times like this.

Before *Yom Tov*, we want to buy a suit or a dress. Of course we go to a good store and try to get a fair price for the best quality. We are concerned with how it will look. Is it just right? If not, we'll go someplace else. Do I have shoes to match? Do I have socks that match my tie? How much money do I want to spend on my purchases? It's a puzzle whose pieces all have to fit and our behavior in this respect teaches our children the importance of dressing properly, of looking respectable in honor of *Yom Tov*. Then we go out to look for a *lulav* and *esrog*. Of course everybody wants a perfect *esrog*, but the children hear us complain, "Oh, the prices are so high this year. Look, there's a spot on this one here and another one there. Bring down the price and I'll consider it."

Shortly after I was married I sold *esrogim*, and that is what some of my customers said. A certain man came in, and I knew that he would want to show off his *esrog* to everyone in shul. He tried every trick he knew to show me imperfections in the *esrog* under inspection so that he could get me to lower the price.

"One second," I said. "If it's such a bad *esrog* and you want me to sell it so cheaply, why do you want to buy it at all?"

Now that was a good position to take as a salesman, but look at it from the perspective of the man's son. If I take my son with me to buy that *esrog* and he sees me haggling over the price and pointing out the imperfections, I am conveying the message that I would settle for a second-rate *esrog* if I could get a good price. But I didn't do that when I went with him to buy a suit, so what am I teaching him? I seem to be valuing the suit more than the *esrog*.

This is not factual information we are conveying. This is an experiential situation, a learning experience. He learned in school that an *esrog* should be *hadar*, magnificent, as close to perfection as possible. He knows that I will show my beautiful *esrog* to others. If he also sees me haggling over the price and saying, "See, it's not so perfect; it needs a few more bumps and the shape is not quite what it should be — so give me $10 off," what indeed have I taught him?

After thinking about this for a while, I changed my own habit. Now when I go to buy an *esrog* I take my sons with me and say to the seller, "I want a really beautiful *esrog*." He shows me one and I reject it. "No, that's not good enough." He shows me more, but they are not good enough either. In the end I pay a little more than I wanted to, even though I really would have liked to make a deal. I wanted to knock the price down, because it's part of the game and you save money. In this case, however, the best deal for me is teaching my teenagers that the mitzvah is more important than the deal, so I don't look for a good deal anymore when we go shopping for *esrogim* together.

To transmit values, we have to consider *feelings, meaning,* and *association.*

◄ₑ Feelings

Shabbos is a value. It's so important, in fact, that we leave our workplace early, get home as quickly as we can to be with our family, and try to forget about our weekday business in honor of it. We love Shabbos. Why don't our children always share this feeling?

Rav Moshe Feinstein wrote a memorable responsum in which he mentions this problem.[1]

> I mentioned a number of times how there is a man who is careful to keep the mitzvos, yet his children not only do not follow in his footsteps but he unintentionally teaches them the opposite. People gave their lives to keep Shabbos, and their children are not keeping it. What happened? Many years ago a father would come to America with nothing, and from collecting rags he built up a business that he closed on Shabbos. All the other stores were open, and everybody said to him, "Are you crazy? Everyone knows that most business is done on Saturday." Nevertheless, every Friday he closed the shop two hours before Shabbos and lost all that business. Then why don't his children keep Shabbos?

Rav Moshe writes that these parents always gave the feeling to their children that they were somehow remaining steadfast in spite of the great *nisayon*, test, sacrificing everything, for Shabbos. Had they helped their children understand that *parnasah* is determined on Rosh Hashanah and therefore they did not feel like they were giving anything up, the message would have been different. They should have said with joy, "Look, we're Jews, we have Shabbos. We have the opportunity to forget our business worries and spend time together every week. How fortunate we are!" Instead of transmitting a feeling of joy about the mitzvah, they communicated a tremendous amount of negativity without meaning to.

These parents had only said, "*Oy*, look how hard it is, it's so hard." Their children grew up thinking that Shabbos is just

---

1. *Igros Moshe, Yoreh Deah* vol. 3, Responsum 71, p. 320.

too difficult. Who needs it? Many of us grew up hearing the old Yiddish expression, *"Es iz shver tzu zein a Yid.* It's hard to be a Jew." When I hear people saying this I interject, "I'm sure it would be much harder not to be." How could we live without all of this? What purpose would there be in our lives?

◄¿ Your Children Are Watching You

Our children will accept our values only if they feel that we live by them. Everything we do reflects this. The wallpaper in our home has to be the best, but what about the *mezuzah*? Our children are watching. They know that we don't accept anything second rate. What kind of message are we sending them if we explode when we hear that a *mezuzah* costs $80?

"What! $80 for a *mezuzah*? How hard is it to write a *mezuzah* anyway? These people are taking advantage."

Contrast our attitude toward spending money on a *mezuzah* with our attitude about buying something else for our home. How do we act when we're spending money on beautiful tiles for the bathroom? Do we also complain about the cost of the tiles? Pretty bathroom tiles confer status. If we accept the prices of the tiles without batting an eye, we are teaching our children that status, reflected by special accoutrements for the house, is something important to us. What about the *mezuzah*?

"Don't you have a $30 *mezuzah* that's kosher? It doesn't have to be the best as long as it's kosher."

◄¿ Meaning

In what do we find meaning? Well, buying a home, for example, is an important investment. We compare, study, research, and ask advice from a lot of people, because we are about to make a major investment. Because money matters are important, we do a lot of preparation. We invest a tremendous amount of time in buying a home because it's important to us. Very few people walk in and say, "Okay, I'll take that apartment on the right; it doesn't matter how well the plumbing works." Our children know how important it is because they know how much time we spend on it. We talk about it during *layning,* the reading of the Torah, and during *davening,* before shul and after shul, and we ask five different people for their opinions about the street and the neighborhood.

When we want to place our most precious possessions, our children, in a school, do we conduct such an intense investigation? Do we question the philosophy of the principal, the expertise of the teachers, the size of the classes, the condition of the building? Do our children see us studying the situation with the same amount of energy and seriousness? We are teaching them the value of their education. If something happens in school and we make several phone calls to try to get to the bottom of the situation; if we listen to what our children have to say and then go to the school to find out what's really going on, they know that their education is important to us. Do we make snap judgments because we don't take the time to find out all the facts? Do we just blame them (or the school), never really taking the time to show concern? "Okay, enough, I don't have time for this!" And we don't have time. *We only find time in our lives for what is truly important to us.*

I was once speaking with a good friend of mine, Rabbi Yaakov Weisel, founder of Yad Eliezer, one of the most valuable charity organizations in Jerusalem, that provides food and other necessities to many poor families.

"Where's the borderline at which we can say, 'I can't help'?" he asked me. "Another family comes to us and says they're in need. If I knock on five more doors, I'll be able to help them. Can I say I can't knock on five more doors? Obviously, I'm going to give out as much as I can to as many people as possible. It is dangerous to say that I can't help someone in need, because if I were to find out that someone else very close to me was in need, I would somehow manage to find a way to come to his aid. So you see, I can always find a way to help someone if I am sufficiently motivated to do so. When can I not give help to a person in need? Is there any limit? Obviously there must be a limit, but at what point?"

We had a whole discussion on defining a person's limitations, but the bottom line of that conversation was that whatever is important to an individual gets done. Somehow a person is able to find the time if the matter is important to him. As I learned from my *Rebbe* Harav Wolbe, who was quoting Rav Yerucham Levovitz, if we want to know what is really important to us, we should pay attention not to what we say, but to what we actually do. We manage to get around to the things that are most important to us.

I've often had the following dialogue with students of mine.

> *"You know, Rebbe, I wanted to get up for davening, but I just couldn't."*
>
> *"What do you mean, you wanted to get up for davening? You wanted to sleep."*
>
> *"No, I wanted to get up."*
>
> *"One moment, my dear boy," I would say. "You say you wanted to come to davening; I say you wanted to sleep, but let's try to face the truth — what did you do?"*
>
> *"I slept," is the shamefaced answer.*
>
> *"Why did you sleep? Didn't you want to daven?"*
>
> *Finally the student admits, "Well, I wanted to sleep, but I wanted to daven more."*
>
> *Then I would sum up the student's dilemma. "We know you wanted to sleep, and you say you wanted to daven. I believe you. But what did you do? You slept. Now we both know that that's what you really wanted to do more, because otherwise you would have been at davening."*

We are teaching our children what is important to us when we show them where we place the most emphasis — in time, in financial investment, and/or in attention. We should consciously try to transmit to them that they, our children, are our highest priority. We want them to know that we care about them more than anything else. If they need help doing their homework and we can't provide it because we're on the phone dealing with other things, what are we telling them? They see that we place a higher value on our business, our organizations, or whatever it is that we allow to usurp our time. Yes, our jobs are time consuming and often we really are limited with time, but how do those time limits affect our other favorite pastimes? If in fact we are limited, our children will sense that we have given up even things very dear to us and will be understanding.

We cannot transmit values merely by talking about them; we have to show our children what our values are by the way we act and react to the daily occurrences of life in and around our homes.

❧ Positive Association

There's a beautiful *minhag*, a custom, which has always been a part of Yerushalayim life. More recently, Jews around the world have begun to observe it as well. When a little boy turns three, whether or not his hair is cut yet, he is wrapped in a *tallis* and taken to the school where he will study. On the table the *rebbe* has a chart of Hebrew letters smeared with honey. The child licks the honey off the letters and repeats the names of the letters after the *rebbe*, "*Alef, beis* ..." What is the underlying meaning of this *minhag*?

An associative process goes on in connection with any learning experience, and even more so in an experience that transmits Jewish values. The child experiences the sweetness of learning his letters for the first time, and it not only feels good because he's getting so much positive attention, it tastes good too. He may, of course, wind up being one of forty children in the class vying for the *rebbe's* attention, but at least that first step shows him that his father is standing by him, the *alef* is sweet, and the *beis* is sweeter. It is a happy experience.

Davening in shul is also an important learning experience. If we pull our child along by the ear and nag him during the *davening* to be quiet or to follow along in the *siddur*, "*Nu, nu, nu, nu ...*" while we're talking to our neighbor at every interval, what is he going to associate *davening* with? He will say to himself, *Coming to shul is really unpleasant for me. My father constantly tells me what to do and how to do it. But look how* he *is davening! What's the big deal? Does he want me to sit next to him so everyone can see that he has a nice-looking kid with a fancy suit? What's the point?*

I don't take my children to shul with me until they can actually take part in the service. If they are too young to participate in the *davening* they would probably annoy people around me because they'd have nothing to do. People in shul would justifiably become angry at my children, and that kind of experience in shul is clearly counterproductive for their *chinuch*. I also use the promise of going to shul with me as a privilege they have to earn.

> When a child is misbehaving at home regarding coming to shul, I say, "You can't come to davening today."
>
> The child responds, "What? I can't come to davening? Why not?"
>
> "Because davening in shul is for big boys and girls. It's not for little children. When you act like a big boy, I can take you with me."

Going to shul now has value for him. This is a different approach from taking him to shul and giving him a hard time, scolding and nagging and then saying, "Okay, I'm going to punish you today. You can't come to *davening*." His association will be entirely negative. The child might think, *Great, I'll make sure not to behave every Shabbos morning so I won't have to go to davening anymore.*

That's not the kind of *chinuch* we want to transmit. We have to teach our children from a very young age that *davening* is something important. Because they observe every nuance of our actions, they will be able to see that our prayers are important to us. Even a two- or three-year-old can understand this. When a three-year-old who has started to wear a *yarmulke* gets angry and throws his *yarmulke* on the floor and we yell at him and become upset, what are we teaching him? That he's got us by the horns? Every time he throws his *yarmulke* down on the floor we get upset, so he sees that wearing it is important to us. It's important to us, yes, but the real questions is, Why should it be important to him? We have to show him that wearing a *yarmulke* is something that gives him importance and respect as a Jew. We can teach him that only big children wear it. When he throws it off, instead of scolding we can say, "Oh, you want to be little again? That's okay." Instead of becoming angry, which means that he controls both me and the situation, we can help him to feel that *he* is losing out. We can send our child a positive message: If he doesn't wear the *yarmulke*, he is saying something about who *he* is rather than something about *me*.

The above example of the *yarmulke* speaks to the capabilities of a three-year-old. By the time our child is an adolescent, he's already been psychoanalyzing us for a while, watching our every action and reaction. The values we transmit to our children are the values we are living by. They know exactly where we really stand despite everything we say, because they can see what we actually do.

◄֎ Natural Tendencies

A child's own nature can make it harder or easier for him to absorb certain things. Some children tend to be introverted while others are more extroverted. Some people, children and adults alike, are not very spiritual by nature, so *davening* for them is not an easy and natural process. Others turn naturally to prayer as a source of comfort, dialogue, and cleansing. Those who just don't feel a natural connection with Hashem often connect more easily to other people. There are children of three or four who say things that boggle our minds with their sensitivity toward others. There is the class bully and there is the child who actually stands up for the underdog.

> *When one of my children was five, he came home very upset. "Moishy's mother died," he said, "and some kids*

were teasing him, because he doesn't have an imma. He was crying, and I was crying too, and I said, 'Stop it, stop it, he has an abba, he has an abba!'" Sensitivity like that, at such a young age, is inborn.

Every person is born with a tendency toward a certain type of personality. We can see this with our children almost from birth. This is why certain things are naturally going to be easier for some children and harder for others. The Torah does not accept contemporary sociological norms in regard to personality: *This is my personality; this is who I am and everyone else has to live with it.* The Torah demands that we be good to our fellow man and that we also observe those mitzvos that are between G-d and man. The Torah requires wholesomeness in fulfilling every part of our personality. Some mitzvos come easily and naturally while others seem to work against our natural inclinations.

Some children can sit and concentrate on one occupation for a long time. Most cannot. If we have a child who has a hard time sitting in one place (and anyone who has two children knows at least one like that!), at what point do we insist that he sit still at the table, or in shul, as we want him to? We can make this into an extremely confrontational issue — because after all, we want our child to behave properly — or we can adjust our expectations to the child's ability.

Don't take your child to shul before he's ready. If he is likely to fidget and he isn't up to sitting still for two and a half hours, bring him for fifteen minutes, but make those fifteen minutes worthwhile and pleasant. At the dinner table, have him sit still for a short time, and then let him go play. If he is forced to sit longer, he'll leave the table without permission, then we'll tell him how bad he is and he'll come back, frustrated, to try to do something that is too difficult for him.

If we want to teach our children to value things, we can't go against their nature; if we do, the objective will become associated in their minds with failure. *It's too difficult, it's impossible, I can't do it.* Instead of building appreciation and love for what we're trying to instill, it builds resentment. They will fight us every step of the way, and we won't understand why. Why are they fighting about things that are so important to us? Well, they are very important to us, but maybe over the years we expected things of them that they were incapable of living up to at the time.

A. Age-Appropriate

In the halachos of the *Shulchan Aruch*, there is a specific age mentioned for teaching a child specific mitzvos. Teaching the mitzvah of *lulav* should be when a child can hold it properly, and staying in the *succah* should begin when he can remain away from his mother for an extended period without becoming upset. There's an appropriate age to learn Torah, a different age to begin wearing *tzitzis*, and *davening* and *berachos* each have their proper times as well. The particular mitzvos I've mentioned all can be taught within a four- or five-year span, but the halachah provides specific details to work out the approximate age at which a child becomes capable of performing each of the mitzvos. The underlying concept here is that only when the child is capable of performing the mitzvah do we teach it to him; if he is not ready, we do not overwhelm him with it.

B. Sharing

Small children are not capable of understanding everything. Sharing is a difficult idea for them. Parents, of course, want to teach the important values of sharing, cooperating, and working together. Sure, but how much of this value do children see their parents putting into practice? This is another instance when one can see that children learn from the example set by their parents. But the main factor in learning to share is whether the child is of an age when he is ready to share. Can we force a baby to share something when he doesn't yet understand the concept? Of course not. Sharing, however, is something that we can gradually cajole a young child into accepting. We can say to our children, "Oh, how nicely you're sharing with your brother." You may be teaching by association — he receives a compliment, even though he's not sure what he did, but it sounds and feels good. That process can develop.

Forcing him to share, however, is always going to teach him the opposite. If I compel my child to give his possession to someone else when he doesn't understand why, I'm teaching him that his ownership has no value. If this is true, then someone else's ownership has no value either. He will not learn from this kind of "sharing" that he has the ability, merit, and opportunity to do a good deed. He is only learning that he has something that he thought was his because it was given to him, but now he is being forced to give it to someone else. Property has no intrinsic value to a young child and if his belongings can be taken, it means that his friend's belongings are free for him to take also. *He took mine and I want his.* This is not teaching him to share, but it *is* teaching the opposite. By forcing the issue, I'm teaching him that whoever is bigger can get what he wants. It is only through showing him the value of ownership that I can teach the privilege of sharing.

"The ball is yours; no one can take it from you. If you want to make your little brother happy, you can allow him to play with it for a while. As soon as you want it back, he will give it back to you, because it belongs to you." With this statement I've taught my child the *value* of ownership and the *privilege* of sharing.

C. Participating in the Mitzvos

This principle holds true for whatever we want our children to internalize. Listening quietly to *Kiddush* on Shabbos is a good example. We want our kids to become interested in doing the mitzvos because they love them. It doesn't always work out that way, though. Sometimes the way we introduce them to the mitzvos is negative. When they don't want to do something, we don't always react in a way that makes them feel inspired and want to be involved in the mitzvah. In addition to being an inspiring role model, we have to learn to talk to our children about the things they do or don't want to do. This goes back to what we have said about helping them learn to make decisions. We have to be able to talk to them about the decisions they're going to make so that they can come to an understanding and an appreciation of Torah and mitzvos. The worst thing we can do is respond the wrong way to a child's lack of interest in the Torah way. I know this is true because I make the same mistakes, and believe me, it's a horrifying experience to catch myself doing some things I've told people they shouldn't do.

Okay. It's Shabbos and you are making *Kiddush*, and your child is talking. By the time you have finished, you probably feel like walloping him. You know that at six he is big enough to love *Kiddush*. Well, occasionally children do the wrong thing. We pray that our children will view Shabbos as we do. We want them to feel that it's elevating; Shabbos should be the mitzvah that crowns our week with the whole family involved, happy and appreciating the gift Hashem has given us. It can be a beautiful experience if you don't allow your child's lack of appreciation for the mitzvah to throw you off track.

When a child tends to talk during *Kiddush*, you tell him beforehand, quietly, "I'm going to say *Kiddush* now. This is special. Please try to be very quiet while Abba says it." If you just get angry when he talks, you will turn *Kiddush* into something hateful, and his association with the mitzvah will be a negative one. He's not at all inspired by *Kiddush* because *Kiddush* on Shabbos is a time when you get angry. How can it be a time of inspiration for him? How can *Kiddush* be meaningful to him? As the child gets older and *Kiddush* has always been a time when people are angry and upset with him, it's wrong to expect that he should like this mitzvah.

When we enter some homes, we feel welcome immediately; the hosts just naturally make us feel good. In other homes, we're uncomfortable from the moment we walk in and can't wait for the ordeal to be over. We teach our children the value of having guests by the way we make our guests feel when they enter our home. We can't pretend we're happy if we're really upset that guests are coming. Our children will sense the truth. They know who we enjoy having in our home and who we do not want to come. Even the guests can sense our feelings. The example we set for our children is significant.

We have to be realistic about teaching Jewish values to our children. Education by negative pressure is one of the most destructive forces in the world. Yes, our children do need to be pushed a little bit. Just because we want our children to feel good about everything, we're not supposed to be totally laid back and say, "Okay, if he doesn't want to do it, he doesn't have to." At the same time, however, when a child feels so much pressure that he constantly feels like saying, "Leave me alone already!" we are doing something wrong. Far from teaching him values, we're affecting him the wrong way about what we feel is most important. We sometimes go overboard, demanding more than we really should at a time and in a way that he's not capable of accepting.

D. Pressure, Yes – but Make it Positive

The idea of positive association is what the first-grade *rebbe* had in mind when he orchestrated the enthusiastic *davening* of his pupils even while he was out of the room. A different *rebbe* might have scolded the children. "What's going on here? Just because I walk out of the room everybody has to stop *davening*?"

That they slowed down their *davening* while he was out of the room is normal, age-appropriate behavior on the part of his pupils. You walk out, they lose steam; you walk in and scold, they get a negative message. Instead, the *rebbe* told them they were great. Any kid's normal response will be: *I'm great? That's wonderful. I want to be great!* We all want to be great.

If a child is not sitting properly at the table and we want to teach her *derech eretz*, we say, "Wow, look how beautifully Esther is sitting; look at her, you can see she's growing up." Suddenly Esther knows everyone is looking at her. She straightens her shoulders and sits straight because she doesn't want everyone to see that she's not behaving nicely. If we say carpingly, "How many times do I have to tell you that when we sit at the table, etc., etc." we get the opposite reaction. *Leave me alone. I'm worthless anyway.*

Positive pressure is the only way to instill long-term values. In this way the child knows we really respect him and we feel good about him. Sure, it's difficult to do this consistently, because our children know that we know their faults, but there is one thing that we all like to be fooled about: how good we are.

> *Harav Chaim Shmulevitz, Rosh Yeshivah of the Mir, once said that his Rebbe, Rav Yerucham, once said, "We all live from Reb Chaim." Now everyone in the room, including Reb Chaim Shmulevitz, knew that Rav Yerucham was referring to Harav Chaim of Volozhin, who began the yeshivah movement in Europe two hundred years earlier. Nevertheless, Rav Chaim Shmulevitz said, "You know, that three-second instinctive mistake kept me going for a week!"*

We like to fool ourselves. If someone gives us a compliment that is not 100 percent honest, we're ready to accept it anyway, and children are no different. This is the one area in which they are happy to be "fooled." It won't be effective if we try to tell them they are something they're not. But when we tell them how great they are and how good we feel about them, *they want to live up to our view of them.* When we reinforce our children's good behavior by telling them how much *nachas*, pleasure, they give us, and how wonderfully they do certain things (which we'd probably like them to do a little bit better), they will accept that positive pressure to live up to that standard.

If we say it sarcastically, they will hear the sarcasm in our voice and it won't work. If we compliment the child when he really bungled something, he's going to look at us as if we're crazy. But when he tries to do something and does it pretty well, and we give not a backhanded compliment but a full, warm one, he is going to feel good about it and will try to do it again and better.

That's acceptable pressure. When the child knows that his parents respect him for doing something well, he wants to continue doing it well. He doesn't want to lose the respect we show him or the positive feedback he's getting. In this way, ideals become associatively important, or as *Chazal* teach us, *"Mitoch shelo lishmah, ba lishma,"* [2] — a person can eventually reach a desirable level even if his initial impetus comes from ulterior motives. The Rambam ordains in *Mishneh Torah* [3] that we must initially teach children using ulterior motives, in order that they can eventually develop the purest motives.

Unfortunately, sometimes we want to relive our lives through our children, expecting them to be what we never became. If this is the case, we can never value the child for who he is, because we are preoccupied with what we want him to be. Although the child may succeed in hiding his resentment, he will either explode at some point or just begin to build his own agenda. We have to be realists, and that means knowing that we clearly project to our children who we are and how we want to live. We need to know that we're raising our children with our values and that they accept what we're actually teaching them. They may not be doing as we say, but they are doing as we do. If we are not satisfied with what they do, there is a good chance that we have devalued our standards by the negative associations we have implanted in them. We may even have rendered living with our values painful for them.

E. If Your Child Wants "More"

Sometimes a child is inclined not only to accept our values but to take them a step further. We have to be secure enough in our beliefs not to limit him, not to fear that he will be "more" than we are. We don't feel threatened, nor should we, when our son beats us on the basketball court; we're actually proud of him. Why should we feel threatened if he develops his religious values and morals above and beyond ours? I

---

2. *Pesachim* 50.
3. *Hilchos Teshuvah, Perek* 10.

would hope we do not. We should be proud of him. We have to let him grow according to what is right for him. Limiting our children's growth in Jewish values, Torah, and mitzvos only shows our own insecurity.

As a Jew who has been inspired by my *rebbeim* and who strives to inspire others (my children and my students), I would hope that every parent wants his or her children to aspire to the highest level in *ruchnius* (spirituality), *Yiddishkeit,* and Torah that they possibly can. If you believe that a particular school is good for your child and it's what you want for him, that's fine. But some people find that their child wants something "more." It is a decided challenge for a parent in this situation to refrain from saying, "No, this is who I am and I don't want my child to pass me by." As parents, we need to rise to the occasion and thank Hashem for the gift of a child who has taken our values and decided to accept even more responsibility. It is up to us to decide whether or not we will hold this child back in his progress in *Yiddishkeit.*

Parents tend to fear rejection. In a situation like this they fear that a child who wants "more" will become so *"frum"* that he will no longer accept his parents. Let me offer a word of advice: In the vast majority of cases, fighting a child who wishes to achieve more usually results in precisely the outcome the parents are trying so hard to avoid. Rejection of a child's exploratory initiative causes the child to reject the parent. On the other hand, parents who guide their children as far as they can and "let them" advance further in the direction they wish to go earn the respect and appreciation of the children to a greater degree than before.

◄? All the Answers?

We live in an overly permissive society that is totally non-authoritarian. A close friend of mine who is a *rebbe* in the Mir Yeshivah shared this bit of wisdom with me.

> *I recently told my students: I'm not that much older than you, but you have to understand that when I grew up*

a slice of pizza cost 25 cents. I had to ask my mother for the 25 cents, and she said no. Today a slice of pizza costs a dollar and a quarter or more. Children generally have more money than their parents do. Which mom is going to say no today to a slice of pizza? She's not allowed to say no! Parents think they have to say yes. We live in a decadent society. We have to try to make our homes a higher place. We have to make our homes a better place. It's a very big challenge to us all.

The challenge lies in the way we in the religious community act and react to our surroundings, the way we live, the way we help our children develop, and how our children feel about themselves and their heritage as they grow up. I don't have all the answers for every situation, or even some of the answers for every situation.

When it comes to clothing, I know no magic words you can tell your daughter that will ensure that she will wear a *tzenius'dik*, modest dress, instead of the one she bought when she went shopping with her friends. There are no such words. The way to meet the challenge is a long process of building trust by discussion, trial, and error. It is also a process of holding your tongue and not fighting every issue. I can tell the concerned parent not only to choose his battles, but to decide what the real issues should be in his home. This is a top priority. You can take a different approach to the problem if the school is about to dismiss your child because of something he/she is doing or wearing. That makes a difference. It also makes a difference whether you condone it or if you decide to say, "You know that I prefer you to wear something else. You know that I'm not comfortable with this. But I understand your point of view, too." Sometimes we will make certain concessions because we have chosen our battle.

A small example: It may happen that the vast majority of your daughter's friends at school wear clothing after school hours that is not exactly in accordance with the school dress code.

You have to sit with your daughter and explain, "We chose this school because we feel that it has the most to offer of what we want for you. Sometimes things are not precisely as we would wish; however, this is the system, and there are, by far, more good things about it than otherwise. This means that, in general, we should comply at all times with the school's policy."

In the long run, however, as long as *tzenius* is not compromised, it's not such a good idea to make this your battle-stand. Don't make it the one place you go to war with your daughter.

One of my students who attended a particular school in Yerushalayim told me about her former principal who is now retired. She was a principal for decades, and every day during her long career she wore the same school uniform as her students. For fifty or sixty years she did this! That is a person I can respect. That's a principal who thinks, *These are the standards, this is what's expected in this school, so this is how I, too, will dress.* As parents, we have to do something similar. Don't criticize your child's way of dressing if you don't dress the way you want them to. Don't pick at your children's *davening* when you don't *daven* that way. Don't criticize at all unless you are a true role model and example. And then, even after you've become a true example, don't criticize, educate!

❧ In Summary

We have been speaking throughout this book of the wisdom we need to raise our children successfully. We have mentioned certain rules to follow; we have tried to present a pathway to guide our thinking and a way to communicate with our children. We have recognized that we need to learn to prioritize. And first and foremost, we must establish the goals toward which we want to direct the education of our children. We have attempted to show the necessity to think and to rethink before we speak. Each of us, however, has to find our own way to talk to our children. We have to define what we are willing to battle over and what things in our homes are not so crucial, and then we can make demands because we have established priorities. Everyone has different children, different rules, different homes, and sends their children to different schools. There is no one sure way of doing any specific thing that is guaranteed to succeed.

One thing I can guarantee, however: *The better parents we are, the more we understand, communicate, and deal realistically with our children and accept them for who they are — the more influence we will have on their lives and, in the long run, the more success they will have.* This approach works, and we all know that it works. It is just that we need a bit of support and good advice to show us how to better implement our knowledge and understanding to help our children.

We should not push our children to fit our image of what we wish them to be, or what we ourselves should have been. We must start by letting them flourish in their own ways. We must help our children grow, each with his individual personality, interests, and natural tendencies. We must give them the opportunity to develop in the areas that are right for them — by good example, with love and respect. We have the special privilege of being the children who are the recipients of Hashem's Torah. It is that absolute *Emes* that gives us the confidence to raise our children to the greatness for which the Torah prepares us. If we make the *Emes* of the Torah the basis for our lives and honestly transmit the *Mesorah* of that *Emes*, with Hashem's help we will then be successful in transmitting what is most important to us — the *Derech Hashem*, the Path of Hashem, to our dearest treasures, our children.

This volume is part of
THE ARTSCROLL SERIES®
an ongoing project of
translations, commentaries and expositions
on Scripture, Mishnah, Talmud, Halachah,
liturgy, history, the classic Rabbinic writings,
biographies and thought.

For a brochure of current publications
visit your local Hebrew bookseller
or contact the publisher:

Mesorah Publications, ltd.

4401 Second Avenue
Brooklyn, New York 11232
(718) 921-9000
www.artscroll.com